A Woman On Purpose

Become Spiritually Full, Financially Free & Confidently Unstoppable

Alexandra Gold

Piotopia Publishing

First Published in the UK in 2014 with Amazon

Hardback 10 Year Anniversary Edition
Piotopia Publishing
Imprint of Being Gold Limited
London

Copyright © Alexandra Gold 2024

All rights reserved. No part of this publication may be reproduced, stored, or transmitted in any form by any means, electronic, mechanical, photocopying or otherwise, without the prior written permission of the publisher.

The right of Alexandra Gold to be identified as Author of this work has been asserted by her in accordance with the Copyright, Designs and Patents Act, 1988.

Cover and interior illustrations copyright © Phoebe Marie Jones.
www.phoebemariejones.com

A CIP catalogue record for this book is available from the British Library.

ISBN: 978-1-916976-09-2

www.beinggold.com

Dedication

To My Sisters in the World

Yesterday, Today & Tomorrow

Especially My Mother & My Sister

Together we can make the world a better place!

I would like to thank all of the A Woman On Purpose women from all over the world who have encouraged me to put my work into books over the almost ten years I have been writing.

Sharing how I integrated my spiritual and personal transformation with you has been THE most breathtaking and awe-inspiring periods of my life.

Some of those women are no longer walking this earthly path but I think of them often.

They never gave up on me – I will do my bit for you.

#SheIsOurFuture

Contents

Author's Note	XII
Stage 1	
Foundation	
Chapter 1	2
The Principles For Foundation	
The New Paradigm	4
Feminine Leadership	8
Where Are You Now?	12
Where Do You Want To Be?	14
Join The Rev/solution - Your World Needs You	19
The Golden Compass	23
The Six Directions Of The Dragonfly	30
The Two Infinite Principles	38
Deeply Desired Destination	40
Balancing Act	52
Solid Foundations	56

The Art Of Step-By-Step Manifestation	58
Steps As Masterpieces	61
Getting Into Reality - The Art Of Mending	63
The Past	68
The Present	73
The Potential	77
Destination Divining	81
Letting Go Of Angst	84
Awareness	91
Circle Of Safety	94
Letting Go Of Guilt	96
Letting Go Of Anger & Using It As Fuel	100
Letting Go Of Negativity & The Art Of Positive Living	104
The Gifts Of Life - Choice, Chance, Change	109
Hope	111
Trust	113
Faith & Belief	116
Love	118
Forgiveness & Permission	120
The Tools Of Life	122
Money	124

Education	128
Skills	132
Experience	134
Time	137
Talent	140
Six Senses - Vision	142
Six Senses - Sound	146
Six Senses - Touch	149
Six Senses - Taste	152
Six Senses - Smell	155
Six Senses - Intuition	157
The Rhythm Of Infinite Energy - Ebb	161
The Rhythm Of Infinite Energy - Flow	165
Energy	169
Riding The Tide Of Meandering Change	173
A Grain Of Sand	175
Integrating Business & Life For The Holistic Entrepreneur	177

Stage Two
The Practice

Chapter 2	182
Infinite Principle - Self	

Self Observation, Awareness, Control & Commitment	184
Self Love & Self Motivation	190
Transformation Renaissance - Who & How You Choose To Be	194
Your Story	200
Self Confidence & Self Esteem	204
Self Respect, Responsibility & Reliance	210
Self Worth & Self Empowerment	215
LifeStyle Business - Mission Statement & Core Values	218
Chapter 3 Law & Community	222
Expanding Awareness	224
Expanding Joy	232
Empathy, Non-Judgment & Acceptance	236
Realizing Our Purpose – Golden Centre	240
Global Responsibility	254
Contribution	257
LifeStyle Business – Legal & Human Resources	261
Chapter 4 Work & Wealth	263
Personal Survival Spiral	265

Lottery Living	269
Destination Divining & Divine Destination	273
Visualization & Expansion Timeline	276
Working Your Purpose	280
Find Your Confidence For Centre Stage	286
Living Your Brand – Branding Your Life	291
StoryBoard, Craft & Creation - Integrated LifeStyle Planning	294
Lights, Camera, Action - Integrated LifeStyle Action	301
LifeStyle Business - Product & Service	304
Chapter 5 Love & Relationships	306
Love	308
The Tea Ceremony	314
Modern Love	316
Intimate Love	322
Finding A Soul Flame	327
Loving Your Family & Friends	331
Love, Guilt & Letting Go	334
Loving Your Warrior Sisters	338
LifeStyle Business – Public Relations & Networking	342

Chapter 6 Health & Wellbeing	344
Mind – Challenge, Educate, Choose	346
Body - Exercise, Food, Health	351
Soul - Discover, Nourish, Nurture	358
Handling Your Empathic Growth	363
Find Your Personal Rhythm	366
Primal Self-Love & Instinct	369
LifeStyle Business – Business Processes & Systems	373
Chapter 7 Spiritual Practice & Personal Philosophy	377
Innate Wisdom	379
Ritual & Ceremony	383
Opening Your Channel & Finding Your Guide	393
Sacred Space, Sensuality & Senses	400
Serendipity	406
Symbols	409
Meditation & Prayer	412
Call & Response & Chanting	417
LifeStyle Business – Sales & Marketing	421

Stage 3

The Embodiment

Chapter 8 Infinite Principle - Unknown	424
Zen In The Art of Gold - Your 'Aah & Aha' Moments	426
Mantras, Magic, Money, Manifesting & Miracles	428
Beauty & Feminine Wiles & Mystique	430
Self Realization & Actualization & Enlightenment	433
Golden Rhythm & Energy - Mastering Meandering Change	436
Sacred Self & Sensitivity	439
The Embodiment Of Responsible Happiness	443
Embracing Consciousness	446
LifeStyle Business – Vision & Growth	451
Golden Compass Mantra	453
Legend	454
ABOUT THE AUTHOR	455
More from A Woman On Purpose with Alexandra Gold	457

Author's Note

Use this book as you will, as a tool, as affirmation, for empathy and encouragement or simply to allow yourself the time to reflect. Read it all the way through or take one page a day seeing which title speaks to you. It takes repetition to learn, practice and embody a new belief or to let something go. All the "She is…" Anthology are intertwined enabling you to transform your life one golden nugget at a time – at your own pace, in your own way.

I have been crafting and sharing these words daily within my Facebook group, 'A Woman On Purpose with Alexandra Gold,' for the past decade. They have emerged from my deeply woven personal and spiritual journey, as I explored various facets from diverse perspectives. It is truly an honor to now share these insights with you.

Stage 1
Foundation

Chapter 1
The Principles For Foundation

Magnificent Equilibrium

1ST DIRECTION

Foundation/Balance

Powerful, Peaceful, Potential

A WOMAN ON PURPOSE

The New Paradigm & Feminine Leadership
Introduction to The Golden Compass
The Six Directions of The Dragonfly & Two Infinite Principles
Balancing Act & Solid Foundations
Getting Into Reality Letting Go of Angst, Guilt, Anger & Negativism
Gifts of Life
Tools of Life
Six Senses
Ebb & Flow - The Rhythm of Infinite Energy
LifeStyle Business - Integrating Life & Business for The Holistic Entrepreneur

The New Paradigm

Miraculous! That is what I have come to believe life is. There is something bubbling on earth right now. As you read this, as I was writing this, I categorically know that I am not the only one to feel this way. I also know that unless we harness these miracles and give them structure and direction, they will lose their magic and be easily overwhelmed by the equally huge surge of anger, greed, hatred, and discontent that is being seen all over the world. You see, anger has been given voice, greed has been fed, hatred has been grown and discontent is constantly brewing in all areas of the world. Discontent in the richer and more apathetic first world and discontent in the unenviable poverty and strife torn areas of the third world.

This is the start of a new paradigm, the beginning of a new era. A piece of history is about to be written. A story we all need to write.

Do you feel the urge to help wherever possible? Are you feeling a longing that aches in your heart and feels like a physical pain for which you have no prescription? Are you wanting to help where you cannot? Do you feel an overwhelming desire to be useful, to be of substance, to leave a legacy, to do good?

This is a feeling that a lot of women are experiencing, everyday, along with the usual feelings of inadequacy, guilt, invisibility, and inaction.

Can we keep this up and expect the world to change in our favor? No. Can we keep this up and expect the world to change in favor of our daughters, certainly not.

Why? Because we are all slightly jaded by the state of the world as it is. We hazily recall the salad days. We remember with clarity the days when the world was in plenty for the western world. We are hastily trying to forget how the hardships the past few years of austerity, turbulent uprising and environmental disasters have impacted us all and left us with the remnants of the past barely visible and yet no clear vision for the future.

The strange thing is, though, that our survival is now paramount. Whether that is personal survival or the survival of our family, we still have an overwhelming lack of security. Most of us are striving to get richer, thinner, happier, more successful and, my personal favorite, more famous!

I don't mean more famous in the most obvious way. Although 'Celebrity' has never featured higher in society than it does today. I do mean visible, though. We are all earnest in our quest to be visible for something. Visible in service. Visible in character. Visible in strength. Whatever visibility is for you.

I know that some of you will be recoiling at this. I know that it will be a hard pill to swallow so I would like to sugar coat this straight away.

We all strive for recognition. Whether this is on an hourly or daily basis or whether it is a lifetime ambition. We all love to be recognized. In this I hold my hand up. When I was singing as a young woman my best friend asked me why I didn't try to be more successful. 'Because I don't want to be recognized and lose my freedom' was my answer.

I had enough recognition playing in my hometown for that part of my life. This was my visibility shield and I was content.

I became a slave to my visibility over the next ten to fifteen years until one of my lovely business advisors, advised me that all of my good intentions and well-placed plans to start a Global Responsible Community would come to nothing unless I was willing to step out and be visible, be well-known. This would be the only way I would be able to do what I really wanted to do in the world. To achieve what I wanted to achieve in life and to give freely of my gifts, to be recognized and feel useful.

So, my first offering to you is that you need to get used to being visible. I will make it easier as we go along and I shall hold your hand.

This is where the powerful stuff begins and why visibility plays such an important part in moving into the new paradigm.

I also need you to hold my hand! Really? You call that leadership?

Yes. I know that we have to do things a little differently and that unless we get over our fears and our faults we will never be able to gently steer the world into the paradigm that will benefit our future generations.

We need to work together and we need to be brave. If we can be authentic in our fears and faults we can only be unbreakable in the face of adverse action and reactions. I am still finding it hard to be completely truthful in all of the mistakes I have made in life. If I am to be honest, I lived a shadow of my personal, dreaming, warrioress, explorer, performing, singing, traveling personality for a very long time. But I never stopped learning and I know that neither did you.

But I want it all now. I know you want it all, too.

I have made some of the biggest mistakes in life. Mistakes that will make yours look tiny. I have had the most extreme personal hardships in life and the only explanation I have for having them is that I am meant to share my stories so that others can learn without having to experience them.

I am so fortunate that I have had the gifts of time, money and universal education to help me put this system together for a reason.

I am willing to put myself in the line of fire, with my invisible (but highly decorated and beautiful) spear by my side. My heart of courage borrowed from the memory of Emmeline Pankhurst, my poise borrowed from Aung San Su Kyi, my determination from our future children and my love stoked by the fire of us all, working together, for our future, for the planets future, for the women of the world, wherever they may be - to forge a New Paradigm of Oneness that can only be created by the emergence of Feminine Leaders united in doing what is right for our planet and our people.

Feminine Leadership

What do I mean by feminine leadership? Am I being sexist? No. Am I dismissing all of the wonderful women leaders that are around now and that have led the way? No. All I mean is that things are changing. We are changing. The world is changing and we can help lead it gently into a world that we want to be a part of. We have been spoilt rotten as far as generations go and, if you are anything like me, you will want things to grow in a way that we continue to have all of our creature comforts, fill our hearts desire AND make the world better for those far less fortunate than we are and for future generations.

As I mention frequently 'I want it all'. Not in a completely selfish way but I really want to build a bridge into the future. A big, shiny, glittery bridge covered in sparkly women with their star-spangled, crystal encrusted spears, swords or shields right by their sides. With us singing into the future and for our 'famous' and far more importantly, recognized contribution to leadership lighting up the billboards.

Whatever you decided to do in life you will normally have had a leadership role at some point in your life. Whether you are a mother, a sister, a friend, a colleague, a peer or a wife or indeed a business or political figure you will use leadership skills.

What we do not necessarily have are the 'balls' to go with it. We have been led by a primarily masculine energy that has snowballed into dismissing generations of elder and gentle wisdom as it has gained momentum, power and wealth. Almost losing sight of the primary reason for happiness in life - 'love'.

I mean no one would think twice if one of the male business magnates in the world turned around and declared that he had made a decision based on a ' gut feeling', right? We just need to stand together, as women, in our power and own our feminine intuition, our sixth sense and our way of doing things. Everything is easier if we do things together, this is just a way of making the 'weaker' sex, evolve into a powerful presence for the good of all mankind and to be respected for our decisions, our thoughts, our actions and our way of doing things without having to explain or defend ourselves.

The general stirring, uncomfortable feeling that lots of women are having around our planet at the moment has created a wonderful momentum of female entrepreneurs and women who are really stepping up to leadership in a huge way, which is a huge cause for celebration.

What we have become aware of and noticing more often though is that some methods and ways of 'dealing' with situations are just not 'sitting' right with us anymore.

This is a feeling of discontent that is being channeled into wealth creation, material possession and charitable causes. Although these in themselves are fabulous ways to entrench confidence, independence and contribution into our lives we know, as women, if we were to be in charge that the world would be a very different place.

We all know how important it is to be financially, emotionally and physically independent. Let us ensure that our children can be free, healthy and happy. Let us ensure that the women (and men) who have fought so hard for our freedom have not done so in vain.

A call to arms this book is not. A call to action this book is. It is time for the women of the world to unite in gentle, compassionate leadership. It is time for us to honor our ways in leading the world back into financial and evolutionary prosperity. It is time for us to make our feminine ways visible and for us to stop thinking that we should hide our faults and failings. We all have them, every single human.

One of the first things and one of the easiest things for us to do is to join together and move forward together. As women, it is what we do best. It makes it easier to be visible, to be passionate, to be sexy, to be powerful when we have each others back. When we are in a safe environment, in community, in comfort.

This book is just the beginning of laying down those qualities that we are so good at, that make Love the main drive in evolving leader qualities. That make Peace the foundation of human behavior and that make the simple meaning of life bearable, indeed, pleasurable for every single child of our future.

This book is the culmination of years of personal struggle and born from that 'Knowledge'. I do not mean to be above any one on this planet. What I do know that this is my life's work. To be the vessel in which you can pour all of your self-doubt, inhibitions, insecurities and sadness. I am writing a guide for those who wish to have peace within, to display grace outwardly and yet feel inadequate to fill their own personal potential. I will hold your hand for no one can be more broken than I. I need you. Your future self needs you. Our children need you. Our world needs you.

Where Are You Now?

Where are you right this minute? Are you as happy as you expected to be? Do you have the security you need? What about independence? Have you got enough food? Do you indulge in too much of something you shouldn't? Are you ashamed of something you have done in the past or continue to do? Do you live in fear or angst? Are you sometimes overwhelmed with life as it is?

There are a couple of statements that you can start to employ right away to help you if you are not living your ultimate life.

Number one - There is always a way. Whether it means planning, patience, thinking differently, applying, action or just simply survival, there is always a way to get what you want if you really want it enough.

Number two - There is always change. Nothing stays the same. Whether the change is for the good or for the worse is up to you in your personal situation, or up to us all in the global sphere.

I will show you how to adopt definitive choice and change in section 2 but if you can possibly accept the above two statements you will be taking a powerful step for your life and leadership.

Even if you are the happiest you have ever been or could ever wish to be I will make the assumption that you would either want to maintain the equilibrium or increase your happiness. If you don't, I am sorry but you are reading the wrong book.

Start by visually drawing a line in the sand. That is it. Your past is your past. Your present is the here and now. Your future is yours to create.

Too simple? I didn't say that it would be easy but I do know that it is possible and that even if you are so desperately unhappy, that you only have hope left in the world, you can still choose to draw that line in the sand.

No matter how hard your life may seem at present. I know that if we join hands and work together, share together, care together that we will move together into the life that is just waiting for us to take our place.

And to make it easier, to light a fire in your belly to ignite the flame of passion that is being covered by the uncertainty at the moment, just remember that there is ALWAYS someone far worse off than you are right now. And, if nothing else, they need your help.

Where Do You Want To Be?

We all have dreams over the course of our lifetimes but at times these dreams become weaker and overshadowed by the banality of life.

Do you remember what you used to dream about as a child? Whether these were fantasy or more realistic, such as dreaming about what you wanted to be when you grew up, these dreams formed such a strategic part of our growth and ability to wonder, when we were little, that it is quite hard to recall how important these dreams were.

Depending on where you are now and your personal circumstances I bet your current dreams are far more watered down and practical. Indeed, I suspect they are just answers to or residuals of our current problems and not even the slightest bit wild or wistful.

So take a moment to think about what you really want in your wildest dreams. I say really want because some of us have a habit of covering the achievable and 'truthful desire' with whimsical stories that are reflections of other peoples dream destination and not in line with our own highly achievable wants and desires. This makes the dreams unattainable, as the passion needed to achieve them is someone else's and not born from a core spark of desire that could light your own fire.

To give you an example, we all know someone who wants to be famous. We even have celebrity reality stars that are seemingly famous for no reason. For some this seems unfair and yet seemingly desirable. What we fail to fully grasp is that these people, although known for nothing in particular, have most probably worked really hard in their chosen area of nothing in particular.

Perhaps that would be plastic surgery, hair extensions, body sculpture, endless hours at the gym and weight training in the form of a make-up bag the size of a small animal (which probably holds a small animal too!).

In order to see if your dreams are real and on purpose to you the best way is to engage in a spot of daydreaming the like of which you used to do as a child.

Sit or lie down quietly and think about what your current wants and dreams are. These may be new or they may just be stagnant but easily attainable thoughts that slightly blur the mundane and everyday monotony of life.

Now, think about this dream as if it were your reality. As if you were at home after a day of living this dream and your tomorrow would consist of the same.

Think about what time you would have to get up. Be truthful. For a lot of highly desirable dreams this is incredibly early in the morning (models, actors, dancers, yoga instructors, doctors, lawyers)! Think of the schedule for the day past and the day ahead. Factor in home life, lunch and trips to the gym or even meetings with your personal assistant.

How do you feel about the day you have just had? Make sure

that you include rejection and plain old apathy if you are at all visible in your dream position. Are you really the type of person that would be able to hold your tongue, be disciplined, smile graciously, say the right thing, do the work or simply enjoy your chosen dream way of life?

Even if you are a lady (or gent) of leisure you will have to figure out a sustainable plan of action to acquire and maintain the lifestyle you want. Is it true to you? Is it authentic? Does it fill that place in your soul that can only be filled when you are fully living on purpose and in potential.

If you have decided that your daily dreams are congruent with your desired destination then you will either need a plan, have a plan or be living that plan. If not, it is time to shake off that dream and do some real soul searching as to what would enable you to fill your wildest, scariest, hairiest dreams and completely instill passion into planning your Deeply Desired Destination.

There are a couple of questions that you can ask yourself when you are ready and if you do indeed need a little encouragement in Destination Divining!

What do you truly, deeply, and passionately CARE about?

What problems do you see people, animals, or Mother Earth having that you are truly, deeply, and passionately Angry about?

What makes you cry? On TV, Film, in the news or just in general.

What skills and opportunities have you mastered or become an expert on? Include things that may not be at the forefront of your mind such as things you do so automatically you don't even think about them.

What gives you hope in the world and on the other side of the coin what scares the living daylights out of you?

As a child, what did you want to be when you grew up. It doesn't matter if it is way off base, just remember all of your ideas and write them down. There will either be a running theme or a mixture of your early cares, problem solving and desired skill set.

What change would you like to see in the world? There is usually one thing that would really make you light up. Less poverty, less pollution, less waste, less disease, less corruption etc.

If you had all the time and money in the world, what would you do? I call this lottery living and it is one of the main dummy dreams that people use to cover up their monotonous and less than perfect lives. Run the same exercise as before but instead of the using your dream of who you would like to be. Give yourself the bank balance of freedom and run your day, week, year and lifetime in a vision through your head, not forgetting the monotony of being bombarded with wealth advisors, people trying to sell you things and having everything you have ever wanted.

Now be a bit expansive and over the top for a question and make a list of all the things that would truly blow your mind. Bigger than a bucket list. Wilder than an adventure. Go on make it!

The last question on the list is the most serious and as such I wondered if it should be the first. If you knew that you were dying what would be most important to you. There are lots of questions just in this section alone such as who would you like to see, to be with? What legacy would you like to leave? What would your epitaph say, how would you sum up your life for a headstone? What haven't you done yet that you really must do?

What would make you really sad if you didn't have the energy to do it?

Join The Rev/solution - Your World Needs You

One of the many issues we have as women and one of the most debilitating is that of feeling that we are not enough. A feeling that cripples us before we have even started anything. After we realize that we are not enough, our dreams become absolutely unattainable and unrealistic, as they are simply not in alignment with our thoughts or our actions.

How on earth are we going to save the world with that type of collective attitude? So I am going to put an end to it straight away.

The world needs YOU! Not another dictator, not another warmonger, not another shipping magnate or oil drilling masochist - the world needs nurturing, kindness, cosseting, gentleness and flow.

Just look at Mother Nature if you don't believe me. She is the leader of feminine leadership. She doesn't shout, she doesn't scream, she doesn't use force to do what she needs to do, although she does give us a kick up the butt every now and again with a storm of note or an earthquake or two, to show us that she is in charge.

I know that you are probably thinking about what you could possibly contribute to the world on your own. And I will ensure that by the end of this book you know that you are enough and needed but if you even consider your importance is not enough, with us all working together, then there are no other ways for it - I shall simply have to give you a virtual slap. So, enough with any negative thoughts about your beautiful self, You are enough and You are needed.

It is so easy for groups of 'baddies' to do harm because they are organized. The only reason we are not collectively doing good is because we are not collectively doing good. Get it?

It is all about personal opinion and choices and learning. I will explain.

When we had no choice, we collectively did as we were told, shown, asked or expected to do. As society has 'moved on' we have pushed those boundaries to the extreme. Although this has been fabulous and expansive on the whole (although spare a thought to those in modern day slavery, war or natural disaster situations which still occur all over the world) we have lost the meaning and awareness of contentment of the good that comes out of working together.

So although we are very good at making personal choices and decisions based on what we want personally and for instant gratification we have sort of lost the non-judgmental part of being non-judgmental.

There are so many choices and shiny objects that we get attracted to, that claim to make things right immediately, we are obviously drawn to them. We live in a fast-paced, stressful and unapologetic world.

We are bombarded with negativity. "You can't do this." "You

shouldn't do that." "You must try this and you certainly shouldn't let this opportunity pass you by, otherwise you will look older, be less important, get fatter, lose money, have less value and the obvious one - keep on being 'not enough'."

Well, I am no stranger to any of this but I have had the luxury of time (even if it was packaged as a debilitating and life-threatening illness) to reflect.

So, having this time and the full on determination to have a fabulous, fulfilling and drop-dead gorgeous life, I thought of all the things that should be on the top of my to-do list to make the world better and my life absolutely awesome.

This took some weighing up.

It wasn't as easy as I had thought. So I had to come up with a plan. I did. It is called the Golden Compass and I will explain more about that in the next chapter. To give you an idea of how I got my passion back and the fuel to start resolving the world's and my own problems AND to not feel guilty AND to feel 'ENOUGH' here is a list of some of the things that I felt needed to be dealt with in the world.

Poverty
Hunger
Health
Shelter
Water
Oppression
Slavery
Dominant Rich Corporations
Dominant Rich People
Ecology

Judgment
Fear

This list will probably resonate with most of you. The fact that you picked up this book tells me that. So to become 'enough' you only have to delve into those world issues that resonate with you, they don't have to come from that list. You may already feel strongly about something else but I just wanted to re-instill those feelings that give us strength as they really are the fuel that can light our individual fires but can also unite us in organized good.

What we will have to do is document all of this moving forward so that these things never happen to our future generations. For the time being we have to remember and re-instigate our gang or community spirit all in the name of saving the world.

I will help you more about limiting beliefs and the 'not enough' syndrome as we move forward and give you all the equipment and uniform you need. But for now just rest assured that you have been drafted to be A Woman On Purpose, from this moment forward. Even on your darkest, loneliest and most downtrodden day - Your world needs You, Simple.

The Golden Compass

Have you ever lost direction? I don't mean just in where you are physically going, but direction in life. Yes? Me too. Sometimes the destination has been changed or the route diverted but most of the time the road just gets literally blocked. You end up at a red light with no sign of it even changing to amber let alone green.

That happened to me. I have always had my life semi-planned. I don't mean that I monitor everything in my life but I am pretty naive and optimistic so have followed my passions and dreams, I had some outline of what I was going to do with my life, what it would look like and what dreams I would like to fulfill. I was open to the possibility of expanding those desires and dreams but never entertained any thought that these wouldn't happen, so when I discovered a lump on my forehead, which I 'knew' to be sinister, my whole life came to a halt.

The plans that I had made had almost entirely been fulfilled and although I wasn't rich, I had achieved most of my dreams including being in a folk/rock band, running a branch of a record company in South Africa, being on stage in dramatic and musical theatre, moving to London and managing a commercial music studio (pretty successfully) and giving birth to my son, Eden after having an ectopic pregnancy and being told I would never have children naturally.

I hadn't made any other plans, though, except for one, my pension plan. It consisted of Gold Lamé and Big Hair and having a multi-purpose venue where I could grow my own fruit and vegetables and sing cabaret on a Friday night.

Obviously, any thoughts of those dreams were halted. I had achieved my dreams, completely. But I had never included any monetary or health desires to my manifestation, as it had just been so good, that I had never even become aware of the necessity.

All change then. I went to the doctors and was told I was vain. What had started as a small lump was growing in size daily. I kept returning to my GP and kept getting sent away. It is a cyst. "I feel it is sinister" I told him. "I feel poisoned" I declared. "Go away and don't come back for at least a month" was the response I received.

By the time I returned two weeks later, the lump was the size of an egg and out of sheer annoyance I was directed to A&E to get it drained.

Even then my own feelings were ignored and the 'cyst' was drained and I was left to my own devices for month where the tumor just kept growing. Because of the hole in my forehead and an infection that had formed in the bone, it discharged down my face and I was wearing a bandage to stop the seepage get into my eyes.

Another month passed and I was still trying to get back to work as a single mother trying to get off benefits who had just been diagnosed with post-natal depression (the diagnosis for the pressure I felt in my head and the morbid thoughts I was having).

I was on my way to my job as a commercial property negotiator when I blew my nose and whistled through my head!

As I was working in Soho, London that day, I decided to drop into the walk-in clinic and from there on in, I was finally taken seriously.

My world had already hit rock bottom and I had been trying desperately to get myself back on track. I had been homeless after losing my home when the music studio I had managed was sold two weeks before I gave birth. The decision to help run a pub with my in-laws just hadn't worked out, when my son was only five months old. I had just been awarded a flat in the South East of London right next to a pub and a flyover. It was far from ideal but was so much better than the temporary accommodation I had been living in for around seven months where I was robbed; the first room I was given was covered in cockroaches, filthy and had no running water until I had to beg, in tears, at the homeless persons unit, that it just wasn't suitable for a baby.

All of the money I had saved to put down on a deposit for a shared-ownership home had been used up after paying forty percent tax on all of the commission I had earned, my pay and my maternity pay when the studio had been sold. My eligibility for the shared-ownership home changed as soon as I had Eden (my son) too, so that route was immediately scuppered.

But, I had my beautiful little boy, who was, indeed, a miracle baby.

I had missed an appointment (very rare for me - I completely forgot it!) to have exploratory surgery to find out my ability to have children naturally and would have lost him in the procedure if I had been more on the ball. I had been on a list for IVF too but I was trying to prepare for all of this and to do things 'properly'.

The world had other plans.

The best time in my life was also my worst time.

My direction had stopped. My future (and that of my baby's) was looking bleak. My health very uncertain. My career on hold.

I had lost all direction.

I needed to focus.

I needed to escape.

I needed to grab life by the balls, shake it up, let it fall and find some direction, pronto.

I had nothing. No health. No wealth. Not even any idea of what I would like in life as I was in such a sad place. I had already cut myself from most people due to the shame of my situation.

But I did have purpose. I had my boy. I had determination. I had hope. I had to dream again.

I had to use what I had, where I was and start immediately.

I had given no thought to my final dream (the Gold Lamé and Big Hair) for ages and it still wasn't on my radar. Life was far too real to have dreams.

But here is where life, God, mysticism, brain power, positivity and the universe (in hindsight) become wonderful, awesome, fabulous, intriguing, adventurous and astounding.

Although I had been working as a commercial property negotiator in Soho and it was ok, I had really wanted to start giving back to the world through my work in the Arts field. I had been applying for positions all over the country and had just been awarded the position of Facilities and Training Coordinator of an Arts Project at one of the largest social housing estates in Europe, which happened to be situated just across the road from where I lived.

My start date was the end of July.

It was the 25th May when I was rushed from one hospital to the next. My mother had come over from South Africa and resigned from her job when she saw that I wasn't well. She had literally just started work at Guys Hospital in London, so thought that I had just come to visit when I landed at the front entrance at around five p.m., with instructions to be taken for an immediate CT scan.

Her smile of happiness at my arrival swiftly turned into devastation. She had to collect my son from his child-minder so I had to go upstairs on my own.

We were led to a ward and then the CT scanning department was re-opened to speed me through the process. I was visited by a rush of (what seemed like) every consultant, registrar and nurse in the building, who took photos of the phenomenon that was my head, and then I was left.

An hour or so later a consultant came and sat on the side of the bed and told me what they had found.

"You have a very large mass behind your forehead, the size of my fist" he divulged, showing me his hand, which was a large masculine mound the size of an orange. "We don't know what it is but we will remove it tomorrow morning". "Will I live? I asked. "I am not sure" was his honest, kindly and sympathetic answer.

My heartbeat was pounding. My head was exploding physically and literally and my knees just gave way.

I was hooked up to antibiotics, a monitor and had blood taken for testing and I was left alone in the world that had just turned into a blur of fear.

I sat on the ward in contemplation until I heard the buzzer sound, closely followed by the pitter-patter of tiny footsteps.

I got down from my bed and opened my arms to hold my son for what I wasn't sure would be the last time. I squeezed him so hard I was scared that I might hurt him. I smelt his hair and his baby soft skin and over his shoulder told my mum the news.

After they had left I sat on the windowsill of the yellow walled ward and looked up at the stars.

I made a promise to God, to the Universe, to myself, and anyone who would listen. "If I survive this" I promised "I will do everything I can to make this world a better place".

Now, as what happens in life, it wasn't quite as simple as that. I was too ill to have the operation that morning as the infection had permeated the bone, although the tumor was benign and was removed in its entirety after a few operations, I was left with an infection of that bone that I was going to have to live with for almost ten years. However, on that day I was given a gift. Not immediately seen, that is for sure. Not immediately fulfilled, unfortunately. But a gift it was. I had been given a purpose in life, *the will to live*. The determination to give and a reason that I knew deep within my soul I would deliver.

I had direction again. It was time for me to start learning how to create my compass.

The Six Directions Of The Dragonfly

Now with every new journey you need to start at the beginning. There I was with a tumor the size of an orange, an 18-month-old baby, a new job and no idea of whether or not I would live or die.

The first thing I had to do and I did there and then in my hospital bed was to write my son a letter.

I still have that letter. I wrote to tell him how much I loved him. How I wanted him to be the best person he could be and how that is the most important thing he can do whatever his circumstance.

I told him that if he were kind, it would only serve him. I wanted him to know that I would be with him wherever I was in the universe and that he would always have a part of me with him.

I must say when I found this scrunched up piece of writing there was nothing beautiful about it. Written on a piece of scrap paper with my hand shaking from shock I found it really difficult to read and so I skimmed through it and put it back in the drawer with other not so nice memorabilia from that horrible time.

But the reason I have started with this story is the fact that it was a solid foundation from which to start filling my purpose. I was writing it at what I had to presume was the end of my life.

It was the most important thing to me. It was my legacy. My truth and my gift to my son.

Starting at the end.

It was clarity of what was important. It put everything in perspective. In that little piece of writing, and it was only one page long as I was very ill, life as I wanted it to be was written.

Now, I haven't told you any of these stories to be self-indulgent or to scare you or to make you sad but they are my truth. As scary and horrible as they were, the clarity I was gifted then I would love to gift to you.

Without you having to go through any of the pain!

So let me explain the Six Directions of the Dragonfly.

I am a great believer of being educated by the universe. I think I have mentioned that I am a greedy girl so I now live my life as if there is a God *and* as if there isn't! I take the good from everything and want it all. And after spending the last ten years working on my promise to make the world a better place and coming up with a plan to make a Global Responsible community I confidently took said plan to a business advisor.

Now, I will tell you all about my ideas for a *Global Responsible Community* when I can but for now just know that apart from being ill, I worked tirelessly on my promise, looking at what works in the world, how we can all be personally fulfilled and make the world better at the same time. By that I mean growing ourselves and maintaining our first world level of comfort, improving on these (I did mention I am a greedy girl, didn't I?) and at the same time tackle the horrendous situations that the world has to deal with so that we can all benefit from the best that life has to offer.

So when I went with said business plan to 'save the world' I obviously was incredibly confident in what I had on paper. I was clear, I was practical and I had looked at all the areas of life that need to be addressed to make us happy and to give back. When the business advisor turned around and said to me "Yes, Alex - great plan and I really think it is a fabulous business model that will be imitated immediately but my first question to you is - who are YOU? How will people know who you are and how they can trust you so that they feel confident enough to see that you do want to make the world a better place? You need to become visible. You need to show the world who you are. You have to get out there and show people your kindness, happiness, patience and non-judgmental attitude is real. You need to write a book and package all you have learnt in it. I know that the world needs it and the world needs it now. I know that there is a market for it and I know that you can do it. So go away and write that book and get used to the fact that people will want to know you."

"But I am an angry bird" I said, "just like in my sons computer game. I get angry at the injustice in the world. I get angry at unkindness. I get really angry and am not sure that I am ready to be seen or that anyone would want to hear what I have to say or teach when I am so not good, naughty and basically full of shit."

"Ah" She said "But you have just sat here, waiting for me for far longer than expected and you have been interrupted how many times and never once stopped smiling". "You want to do good. You have seen the worst of what life has to offer. You have been through some of the toughest times and you are still one of the happiest, most patient people I have ever had to deal with and that is what the world needs right now. You are the gap in the market. You need to give that back. Go and write that book, put your personal website and mentoring program together and show people how they can be happy too."

So I left the office of that business advisor a year and a half ago and had to re-think everything. I wasn't upset or perturbed but I had to re-evaluate everything that I had been working on over the past ten years.

Everything that had given my life purpose and direction I had to put into writing, into a package and I really had no idea where to start.

I fell in love with the dragonfly a few years ago now. I loved what they looked like, the transformation they represented along with the metamorphosis they went through which is how they became my muse. I had dragonfly this and then I got hold of a dragonfly that. It wasn't a quick thing. It was a gradual process where I became more aware of them as they flew my way, stuck out in artwork and generally became a part of my life. People started to buy me things with dragonflies on them or jewelry or knick-knacks (not really my thing but hey ho!).

Anyway, whilst out contemplating, meditating and walking the dog (I take multi-tasking really seriously) I was considering how to structure my package of happiness and manifestation when I was literally dive-bombed by a bright red dragonfly. At first I just looked at its beauty and carried on my walk but it kept following me. It dive-bombed me time and time again with no let up. I started to laugh but also thought that I would look up the symbolism and meaning for a dragonfly upon my return home.

This was when I found out that the dragonfly moves in all six directions! Up, down, left, right, forward and backwards. It can also hover and obviously has the ability to move anywhere it wants. Simple Direction! Of course it was the perfect way to package and explain my signature system to help anyone get passion, purpose, power, peace, presence, prosperity, patience, positivity, potential and possibility. It also leant to being a guide to direct us and so snuggly fit into being the points of the Golden Compass.

I had to then think of how this system would work in practice. I had to go back to my own journey and start at the beginning. By this time I had started integrating with real people again and started working on my visibility, my market research and the business opportunities, models and structures that had changed whilst I had been out of action. I took the advise of a couple of mentors which was really important as they were able to show me how to structure my gifts so that they were clear and understandable. Neither of which were easy feats seeing as my head still hurt after speaking passionately for more than five minutes and getting what was in my head into words that were easily absorbed and understood, either in writing or in speech, was still very difficult.

I gave myself the gift of time and money. You see, during my illness, I had to do whatever it took to survive, both from a health perspective but also from financial survival point of view. I had a purpose and a son to provide for. I worked when I could. I took any job I could get. I stepped back and became an observer and although it was very difficult to take roles in work that were not fulfilling in any way, I managed to keep my head above water whilst I fought for my life and I also fought a legal battle and I learnt an inordinate amount about many organizations and people in the process!

It took seven years. It certainly wasn't easy. I had to use ALL of my leftover brain-power to keep on top of the situation and I had to take complete RESPONSIBILITY for my case, including pointing out mistakes to my own lawyers, who on one occasion had missed something very important and were looking to drop my case, but eventually I won. This gave me the financial security I needed to get through all I had to get through.

It was 2008. I put it in the bank. I trusted myself. I did not put it in trust as I had been advised. Then the whole world banking system collapsed.

Phew, big pat on the back for listening to that gut feeling! Although I had managed to achieve everything and every dream I had ever wanted, this was the first time I had used my ability to manifest into a financial stream of revenue. It worked.

Another thing that I did take control of was my sons future. I made a will. I am very practical, too, and find that the balance of trust in the unknown, hard to explain (intuition, universal energy, God or however you would like to name it) and all that we have control of (practical, responsible and real) is essential in the manifestation process.

My finances were in order. My will was in order. My health was still in a dire situation. It did get better! Let's get back to the Six Directions of the Dragonfly.

So I had the time. I had the money. I had started giving myself scary challenges and started mixing with real, live people again.

I looked at what I had learnt, I thought of the directions and researched and corroborated all that I learnt with ancient laws, spiritual beliefs and academic teachings.

It all just worked!

Everything aligned. I could read Zen, The Tao and Native American Laws as though it was a child's fairytale and philosophical papers and academic notes such as Maslow's Hierarchy of Needs as if they were the daily tabloids. I checked out the main teachings of all the major and minor religions of the world and it all made perfect sense to me. Essentially, they were all saying the same things, through different ways, practices and stories but there were underlying truths to them all.

I had the structure I needed to form the Golden Compass with the Six Directions of the Dragonfly!

Don't you just love it when the universe comes together?

So the Six Directions of the Dragonfly were easy to define, as these were THE most important things that we as Humankind need to live full, purposeful and happy lives and I split them into the following directions.

The Foundation

Wealth & Work

Love & Relationships

Health & Wellbeing

Law & Community

Spiritual Practice &/or Personal Philosophy

The Two Infinite Principles

There were, however, two extra and very important principles that I needed to include in the overall system and they needed to bridge everyone's judgment and appeal to all for the system to make sense and work. I call these the Two Infinite Principles and they are the resin to glue this system into being.

The First Infinite Principle is the Principle of Self - all that we know and can control. Basically the central point to everyone and the part that is our authentic, abundant, true and radiant self. The Self is the one thing that you DO have control of. Our thoughts, our actions and essentially our core. Where you make things happen and take responsibility for creating and pleasing yourself and your reality.

The Second Infinite Principle is the Principle of Possibility - all that we do not know or have control over. This is where I put all the spiritual and scientific possibilities and let them hold their own. For them to dance with one another and us and change form, expose their truth and wonder as only they can, in their time and in their own unique way. This is the magical universe of opportunity that, if we can accept, could be the door to the world becoming the better place we all want it to be.

These Infinite Principles are simple, as are the directions but it has taken me years to get the 'Aha moments' to see that this is the case. And, as such, I believe it is my life's work, my life's purpose to pass on this simple system to whomever it resonates with, or whomever it will help.

I would like to make one thing clear though. I do not wish to replace anyone's beliefs. I do not wish to create a cult. I do not wish to take over the world. In fact, my ultimate Pension Plan dream is to get old wearing Gold Lamé and Big Hair in a multipurpose venue with a gin & tonic, a lemon from my lemon tree, fresh vegetables from the garden and karaoke or cabaret on a Friday.

I wish for health and enough money to live comfortably. I wish to contribute to helping to solve peoples' personal hardships and world issues as much as I can, in a gentle but consistent way. I wish for my children and my children's children to have a world where they are proud of their ancestors, where they share one another's ancestors rituals, ceremonies, stories and history. Where we have created new integrated rituals, ceremonies, stories and history, so that they can live happy, social and responsible, whole lives and can have learnt from us that they must never forget: The horrors that we have subjected our fellow humans to.

My biggest wish is that with this book, this system and with my life's work, I can help to bridge the worlds problems and be at the beginning of a new Golden Era where the world starts to work together, to help one another and to get the benefit of all its gifts in a kind, purposeful and fulfilling way.

Deeply Desired Destination

What are your deepest desires? Yes, those material things that you want right now which are important but, simultaneously, what are the things that your soul yearns for? Material wants are necessary but they are subject to change as fashions change, society changes and as we grow and change ourselves. So the most excruciating desires that we consistently feel deep inside our core are the ones we start to excavate in this section.

As a woman, I am sure you will be familiar with these feelings. They are like a deep pain that runs through our body and that nothing except an acceptance of them and fulfilling of them can begin to heal. For me, they leave me with the same sensation as when I have been sobbing for hours and wake up with bleary eyes and my throat feels as if I have swallowed a boiled sweet.

You know, when you writhe with indecision, with a desperate longing and have absolutely no idea what it is? It feels like you want to curl up into a ball and hibernate and come alive again when everything has worked out and that magic wand has done its work.

This is where I had to use every ounce of my imagination and at first I had to remember how to use that too!

I had that feeling. I had tried to fill it by eating, losing weight, becoming a slob, doing my hair and make-up (covering up the dents in my head took a lot of time!), drinking alcohol, not drinking alcohol, going out, staying in, reading self-help books and reading romances, sad autobiographies and crime fiction books and watching hospital TV programs (I know, strange and very peculiar obsession considering my position, right?) and walking in nature. Researching politics, social issues, human rights issues, healthcare reforms, child rights issues, women's rights, legal issues, local and international problems, policies and propaganda and I was still lost.

After years of this (and at this point I know you will have understood some of the above!) I just crumbled. I was no closer than when I started. I was spent and I still had that grumbling, incessant yearning inside. I was much better informed but I wasn't helping myself or anyone else from where I had got to.

I had to stop.

I had to start.

Again. From the beginning. And so I did. I went on an excavating journey of Self, of my core. I had to wipe my slate clean. Shake myself off. Get over myself to let my true self remember, reawaken and rediscover who I was.

I had tried to give back but was unhappy. I had tried to live a life that wasn't fulfilling, so was unhappy. I had tried to be a good person when I was unhappy but this just hurt, physically as well as mentally. There were times when my brain was so fuzzy and my head hurt so much I thought that I would go mad whilst walking down the road. Where my eyes couldn't even see because my head was so full of 'stuff' that just didn't make any sense and there were times when I could just not see the way out.

I felt crazy. I felt overwhelmed. I felt desperate. I felt unworthy. I felt hopeless, useless and at my lowest, lowest times questioned my own existence and wondered what the hell I had done to feel this way and be in this position.

I was too sad to cry. I was too scared to see. I was too vulnerable to ask for help. I was too over my healthy weight and (in my eyes) too ugly to be seen. I was too unsure to speak. I was not enough to even begin. I had too many secrets to be visible. I had too many imperfections to be pretty. I had too many naughty facets to expose the real me. I was too ashamed to be authentic.

I was nobody. I was useless. I was just.... well, who knew, I certainly didn't.

I remember sitting with my son, him in his light blue, fleecy all-in-one, snuggled with me on the couch that served as a sofa-bed in our flat where the mice were our only friends, using my son's toy garage as a playground and staring at us defiantly as if to say "You can't catch me". We were watching Thomas The Tank Engine, a children's program that tells the tale of a train engine who wants to be noticed, to be good, to be of service. We watched him go around and around the Island of Sodor where he lived, me half watching and just so engrossed in my emotional devastation and appreciating the cuddle, when Thomas said one of the most profound sentences I have ever heard and it went on to change my life.

"I want to be a useful engine." Said Thomas.

And that was it. I knew. I had my beginning. I wanted to be

useful. I needed to be useful.

Bloody hell. God damn it. I would be useful. No matter my circumstances. No matter my health. No matter anything. I had what I had at that moment and at that moment was where I was going to begin.

The one thing I had learnt after going through all that I had recently been through and from the jobs that I had done was that in order for me to be useful I had to come from a platform of happiness.

Not hugely famous nor hugely wealthy but most definitely hugely happy.

Over the next few weeks I thought about my happiest times in life. Where I had been, at what age and what I could assimilate into my life as it was now.

It took me years to really get this right and ask myself the right questions and to get the right answers: I hope that I can make this process easier for you if you need to use it yourself.

Where did your passion story begin? What did that magic feel like? What were the first things that stirred you in any way and why? Are there other things that were enjoyed by you as a child that you have pushed aside as frivolous, painting, singing, sport, travel, writing, illustration, music? What was your best way of learning i.e. what did you automatically rehearse, do, want to get better at? I know you are passionate; it is just finding a way to ensure that you are full up and allowing yourself that gift. No matter how trivial something seems. When a cup is full it will spill over. What we need to achieve is that when we are full it is with goodness and happiness so that when we give back it is automatically laced with that goodness and happiness.

For me, when I sat down it took time and memories, not all of which were pleasant.

Don't rush, try to muster the feelings that come with childhood - i.e. awe, wonder, breathless magic, skipping, smiling - where did you get those feelings? For me, those feelings were reading Bunty Annual, going to the theatre and seeing the magic of a ballerina on pointe, or the enjoyment of the boo-hiss at the villain in a pantomime.

Dressing up, dancing, music, reading, fairy stories, wanting to be a rock singer and a high soprano were all mixed into making my passion, my joy and action to become good at what I was doing and the dream end result!!!

Remember this is your cup. You can fill it up with anything. The more you fill it, the more it overflows and the more you can give back. You really are passionate. It is just remembering what those passions are and how you can find new ones and how they work together. If you put that with all the other areas you will be on fire. It took me ages to incorporate my love for theatre and music into my love of business. I had pushed that part of me aside when I became fearful, embarrassed and self-conscious. You will get there.

Especially listen to your intuition.

Don't get the feeling of fear mixed up with the feeling of 'absolutely not', they are two completely different things. I had to let acting, singing back in after realizing I still loved them. I was petrified of what that would mean and that I was not saying no from a rational and sound viewpoint! Surround yourself with loveliness - smells, sounds (old music, movies to remind you of stories), textures, wool, cotton, hot, cold. Flavors are great reminders. Putting just the same sort of thing in a story pot brings about completely different memories i.e. for me butter, dripping and margarine are essentially used for the same thing, but I can associate butter with a freshly carved ham sandwich made with gorgeous bread and butter at my grandparents house, either at Christmas or in summer time. Then dripping from a roast beef Sunday lunch was fought over between my brother and myself and margarine meant we were baking, a Victoria sponge with warm from the oven and slathered with strawberry jam. Most importantly - feelings - be aware of what touches you the most. Be mindful of a lump in your throat, a tingle of excitement and the memories of joy and euphoria.

I know we grow up and change with our experiences but for this practice just let go of any attachment of judgment that you have learnt over the years and allow yourself to remember the happiness. This isn't about changing your beliefs now and reverting but it is about allowing yourself to have joy in your memories and incorporate that absolute wonder into the future you are designing for your own, unique Divine Destination.

In the exercise I have devised to help others step Centre Stage in their lives, I use a few more questions that can help to get some memories back. Below you will find the questions I use for this process.

Go back to when you were born and slowly move through the years of your childhood. Noting any significant times when you were learning or interested in something. Becoming aware of any extra-curricular activities you were involved in or any particular lesson that you enjoyed.

Ask yourself a few questions as you go through the ages. What did I used to like to do, to eat, to smell? Where did I like to go?

As you move through your youth, what were the things that took over your life? What films? What feelings? What music? What people? What places?

And then start to think about your chosen education? What did you enjoy the most? What were you good at? Where did you dream of ending up? What was your chosen profession?

After this we start to think about our first jobs. What did you do well? What did you learn? What did you tolerate but do anyway? What did you excel at?

Think about your hobbies. Think about your creativity. Think about activity. Think about your feelings.

Start to think about major life events. What are the main stages of your life? What are the best bits? When were you the happiest? What were you doing? What did your life look like and consist of on a regular basis?

Eventually try to get into and really feel the feelings of the happiest moments of your life. If there are areas of your life that are not so pleasant, acknowledge them and thank them and kindly and deliberately let them go. Imagine an area of your brain that you can use as a safety deposit box, as some memories are always going to be painful. Giving them a secure place in your life to acknowledge them but put them away gives you back control. And just like any piece of unloved but valuable jewelry, acknowledge and gently put it away.

Again, access those feelings of joy that you associated with the best times of your life, and hold on to them whilst you gently come back to the present day. Slowly become aware of your surroundings.

Feel the beating of your heart. Note the rise and fall of your chest. Deliberately smile and thank yourself for the time. Now slowly open your eyes.

The first time you use this process try to go over your whole life as if you were living it as a film.

As you fill in the questions relating to the areas of your life you might like to come back to this process and focus on one area of the best times of your life at a time for the following questions?

When were you most happy?

When were you most proud?

When did you enjoy teamwork the most? In what role?

What places did you love the most?

What age group did you feel the most at home with or affiliation to now?

What were your signature themes that you used through the course of your life?

For example fashion, music, food, art, sport, games, social interests and obsessions.

These are just a few of the things that can help you find those periods in your life that filled you up.

Also be aware of any feelings that were aroused that you haven't felt for a while, such as excitement, joy, skipping, love, laughter.

So you may be wondering why I have so much time going back into the past if this section is about our Divine Destination.

The reason is simple. We have to remember who we wanted to be when we gave ourselves permission to dream. We have to remember how to do it and we have to remember what the feelings attached to anticipation, action and achievement are like when we were free enough to just Be and expect and dream and be wistful.

So now, I want you to think about those questions again, but as a dreamer, as a doer, as an action taker and as if the world depended on it. I want you to give yourself permission to DREAM. This isn't the end result. It is just learning to expand your desires in order to Divine your Destination. It is a process. A gentle process, a magical process and one in which your mind lounges on a chaise and eats grapes whilst being fanned. This is a sacred divination. This is a secret divination. This could be the nurturing your soul has been yearning for.

What would you like to be when you grow up? Here I want you to push your own boundaries. I want you to edge over your comfort zone to see what comes up for you.

What things would really make you happy? What excites you now? What could you be happiest doing now if you let yourself or if society, education, work experience allowed?

What would a dream day look like? Be honest here, if you are going to be running a B&B you will be up early and go to bed late, does that really feel like a dream life to you? A yoga teacher would have to take a few lessons a day, is that really what you would like to do? An actor will be up at all hours and in rehearsal for months before being in front of an audience and a model will be up at the crack of dawn with people messing with her/his hair and make-up - could you cope?

When do you wake up? What do you have for breakfast? What can you see, hear and smell?

In my home in London, I love the news and a cup of coffee before writing, and listen to the planes on the flight path to Heathrow. Then I take my golden retriever for a walk and to meditate/contemplate in the cemeteries ("London's parks") near where I live.

Whilst, when I am in Spain I get up, put fresh coffee on the stove, go out on the terrace and look over the pool and the neighbor's hacienda style house to the mountain, whilst listening to the birds singing.

I did mention that I am a greedy girl, right? Well if you have more than one dream day you are absolutely allowed.

Where would you like to live? Remember if it is a big house and you can't afford a cleaner with your yoga teacher salary that you get when working only two months of a year in a remote part of the Himalayas, you will have to clean it yourself BUT you could easily afford a cleaner with a yogi business so ensure that your dreams start to align with one another. There is no reason not to dream completely at the maximum, you can always tone it down if your true energy isn't quite ready for a high-octane version of yourself.

What does your house look like? This dream can morph and morph if you haven't decided so look at pictures, watch programs and sit and think about them. Go through each room, decorate them, smell them, make them real in your mind, so that you can go and have a look around any time you wish in a daydream.

What do your family and friends look like? Ensure that you use good vibes for this and compassion. Think of the ultimate relationships and what you want and need from them. Some relationships need to come to an end to make room for divine destinies to be realized, but even then they should be blessed and thanked for their part in your journey, so that they don't tarnish your next stepping stone or indeed your whole life path.

What do you want more of in your life? Socializing, dancing, eating out, rock climbing, playing tennis, learning a musical instrument or language or just sitting smelling the roses?

What excites you in this dream life? The thought of getting up early to get the red eye to a business meeting the other side of the country, or getting up to paint the hills and the horizon, or would it be a mixture of both.

There is no outside influence in this dream of yours. You have complete permission to dream the biggest dreams, to create the biggest vision in order to live your fullest life, to your best potential and be the happiest version of yourself you could be.

At this point I want you to remember all the things that mean the most to you that you have been thinking about over this journey.

I want you to start thinking about your legacy here and all the things that mean a lot to you. Things that you want to have achieved on a bigger scale, but personal to you. I.e. would you have liked to have been able to build a school in a needy area, to have all of your children's children go to a particular school, to have re-homed ten thousand dogs or to have contributed to the ecology? This is so that you have somewhere to work towards, always. These will be the things that will be your everlasting fuel and will never go away. Your Personal Bigger Picture.

I want you to start thinking about those things that you would need time, energy, health and money for so that they could get ticked off your bucket list, which are just those things that you will do once in a lifetime and not your everyday? You need to ensure that you do these whilst you are young enough or when you are old enough and factor in these things as a kind of life To-Do list that need to go on your life timeline.

Your Divine Destination I am afraid, is the same for everyone. No matter your circumstances, no matter how you live we all end up as a grain of sand and return to the earth. I give you a beautiful metaphor in this book. The main thing we can do and that we have control of is how we get there. How we live our best lives. How we make the most of everything we can and how we can contribute.

The beauty of becoming accepting of this outcome is that it takes the fear of living half a life away. We are all going to end up in the same boat. So why not live your biggest, loudest, proudest dream - no matter what?

Your gift to yourself is to start Divining your Desired Destiny today.

Balancing Act

We have all heard of work/life balance but I have come to a slightly different way of looking at things, which is easier for me to digest, more exciting in practice and easier to achieve.

And it begins with a general eighty-twenty principle. I believe that if you do your best, try your hardest, make time for as much as you can and spend the time understanding your natural rhythm, you have a very good chance of keeping your balance on the seesaw of existence because, without you even trying to muck it up, shit happens all by itself. So to explain it better if you try to do your best, be positive and live the life you desire when you can that ultimately will make up the 80 % and give you a stronger foundation to deal with challenges that present themselves!

This principle, when employed in YOUR natural rhythm, then absorbs into your work or career, your health and your lifestyle, your social habits and your family life. So without putting the emphasis on the separation of each aspect of your life you try to include them all so there is absolute flow.

In order to maintain the balance of life and to bring us right back down to earth there will always be a crisis to deal with, an illness to be borne or a hazard to be avoided, but these tend to happen all by themselves so why put anything on that side of the see-saw?

We have all heard of the term "shit happens", so I know you know what I mean when I say that it happens when we least expect it, least need it and are least able to deal with it so why give it a helping hand by separating all of your good bits and leaving them to fend for themselves if (and more likely, but I will not let it in by choice), the shit does happen!

If you have your life in flow you will have the balance to be able to deal with anything from a calm and more capable place, leaving the good bits to be perhaps hindered but not completely thrown out of so-called apple cart and all over the floor.

As we get further into this book, I will show you some simple ways to get your life 'in flow' and to find your own Personal Rhythm. If you feel that this is something that you need, I will share with you all of those little stories that helped me surrender to my own natural flow.

The way I see this in my mind is like trying to stand on a seesaw and keep it horizontal. At first, when I separated all the different aspects of my life, it was nigh on impossible to juggle all of them, keep my bearings and be grounded enough to keep the balance. When I would be waiting for an appointment for a hospital consultation and all geared up for an operation. When I had everything in order. Childcare, finances, time-off work, care in place. It would be then that I would get a call from my consultants' secretary to say that my appointment had been cancelled and would have to be re-scheduled.

When you have been ill for a long time, you have no choice

but to get used to these things happening. At first I found it incredibly difficult, frustrating and downright exhausting to be on this roller coaster of ups-but-more-often-than-not-downs.

I then made a conscious decision to embrace them as part of what is meant to be. I allowed the changes to be made in the outside world but stopped putting all of the onus on one thing changing for my balance to be completely put out of kilter.

I then watched as the people around me became frustrated and exhausted by what was happening to me but it was not affecting my own equilibrium. It was 'outside' of me and my balance was fine.

I still had everything in my life in order and the hiccup was absolved.

Life was not perfect but it was easier to manage. I was able to be calm and to use that calmness to ensure that my folks were okay with the downs as much as I was.

Life was restored to balance quicker, easier and happiness was regained without the work involved before.

And, more often than not, something better was waiting just around the corner.

As I gain momentum and trust this process, the more I FEEL the balance working. I don't fall off as much. I still go up and down but generally speaking I maintain a pose of calm, composure both outside and in.

Everything is perfect. It may not look like it but I choose to see every obstacle as just that, an obstacle and I, in true Woman On Purpose fashion, will overcome and enjoy the adventure, learning, discovering and embracing any challenges as part of my journey and as my crosses to bear.

I am becoming an acrobat of Zen in the modern world. Trying to hold my balancing pose on the seesaw of life without losing all of the apples in the apple cart!

I hope that this is the beginning of your balancing act - let's turn this show into a Circus of Purpose!

Solid Foundations

No self-respecting architect of seesaws would even consider erecting his balancing act equipment without the correct foundation for the project!

So establishing and being clear with your own personal foundation is so very important.

For every person this foundation will be different. There is one thing we all have in common though. A foundation that works as a basis for any structure or platform to be built upon, no matter where you are in life, how old you are or what your personal circumstances are and that is Rock Bottom.

I know for some of you that might be a little dramatic and I hope that the rationale for this becomes clearer as we move along, but I also know that for a lot of us that is a really good place to build from. And for some of us, and believe me I have been there; it is where we are right now.

Everyone has his or her very own Rock Bottom - It doesn't matter where you live, how you live or whether it has or hasn't ever come to that.

What does matter is that at Rock Bottom there is only one way to build, and that way is up.

Whether you have hit it in the past, are sitting on it at the moment or it is your worst nightmare, the first thing you have to do is acknowledge it, look at it, see it for what it is and become its architect. You don't have to like it but you do have to live with it. So instead of it becoming or staying a Rock Bottom block, try to turn those feelings that you associate with it into a challenge, a diversion, and start to see the foundation of the beautiful life that you want to build, the chapter that is the catalyst for change, the fuel for your existence and that it can never, ever be anything more than your foundation. Firmly under your feet, becoming the sounding board for your leap into the life you are creating.

A Woman On Purpose reaches for the stars with her feet firmly planted on the ground!

The Art Of Step-By-Step Manifestation

I have had Rock Bottom a couple of ways and in a couple of different scenarios but the one thing I have never done (although I have come close on more than one occasion) is give up.

Although I have had some really, really horrible times and fuzzy, cotton wool textured thinking without being able to see anything clearly and feeling utter despair, I have ALWAYS got through them and I have ALWAYS had the Gift of Hope and I have ALWAYS been able to see that I have got something and learnt something from these times.

I think The Art of Step By Step Manifestation was truly born whilst I was living in temporary accommodation with my then very young son. I had always been able to manifest what I wanted in my life through determined action and enjoyment but having a baby and losing my freedom from being so ill meant that I needed to give myself an escape from my reality and find ways to remember happiness, breathe and find creative ways to manifest what I wanted to achieve. I needed to think that my life and that of my son would be better and so I gave myself simple pleasures and attainable goals.

I went to second hand shops, especially bookshops, to look

around and get inspiration. I bought old magazines of homes and gardens, took them back with me and went through them to give my reality a break and my future some beauty.

Because I didn't have a home, that was my main focus. It consumed me and the feminine ache that I felt at that time was about finding a nest to bring a child up in.

It was an initial goal and something I needed in the first instance to even begin to think what the step after that would be.

I daydreamed, I prayed, I ensured that I followed up every avenue I could, I wrote letters and I made qualified complaints. The simple truth of the matter is that I took ACTION.

Eventually, and not easily, I was offered a home. It wasn't the dream home from a magazine, YET! But it was a start and the next step along the path in my Divine Destination.

It led to the next chapter in my story, which was not going to be a happy one just yet but it would add to the overall bigger picture of learning, adventure, creation and manifestation.

Each step that I took after that, and, in hindsight I have done and continue to do in order to manifest any step is that I had to take one step at a time. I had to take Action on a specific outcome and I had to research, understand and fully come to grips with every angle of my situation in order to get an outcome that would suit my needs. I did give leeway, I did understand that from where I was that a mansion in the country was not on the cards and I accepted what I was given after fighting my corner and getting what I was entitled, by law, to receive.

I did not trust that everyone was my friend and I certainly had to trust that some were plain detrimental but I also learnt to see that some people are genuine and there to help you. I gained the discernment to see the difference and to graciously move away from anything that was not in line with what was right and good.

Steps As Masterpieces

As I look back on that specific step I have a choice.

I can either see it as the beginning of the worst time of my life or I can see it as the beginning of my creation as A Woman On Purpose.

Looking back on my path of manifestation and my life path combined, I made a conscious decision to regard each step as a masterpiece.

I didn't exactly feel that way at the time but I am very proud of what I have achieved over the past ten years, given my circumstances, and I decided over a year ago (after a gentle reminder from my beautiful sister) that I am an artist and that from now on - each of my steps would be a masterpiece.

Now, I am no Michelangelo, indeed my drawings and paintings leave very much to be desired, but I am a creator, a doer, a dreamer and a lover of life, so by masterpieces I mean that every step I take, I try to do from a place of peace, of enjoyment, of excitement and adventure.

For me, each and every step that I take I do fully consciously - unless I have a bottle of Cava, which takes the ratio down to 50%!

I try to enjoy each day and I give myself permission to do whatever I want and go with my Personal Rhythm and Flow. If I am in Action, I get up, get washed, get dressed up and put the make-up on for the archetype I want to be for that day, I meditate or contemplate, dance, sing or pray - whatever need I need to fill to empower me (did I mention I was a greedy girl?) and I get about my business with gusto. Whether that is doing personal chores, business research, traveling, shopping or networking. I put on the Alexandra Gold head that suits the purpose and enjoy every minute.

The conscious decision which makes the world of difference to me, though, and one I learnt about through no choice of my own, is when I need downtime or family time or just self-indulgent me time, I take it. I languish in it, I move with it, I see it and feel it and indulge it and nobody needs to know!

It is the permission to see every single day, every single moment no matter how that moment looks, as a masterpiece, that gives you that next boost for creativity, for thought, for consciousness, for devotion, for sacred energy, for ritual, for reconnection and ultimately peaceful, awakened happiness.

If you can embrace every step as a masterpiece, as a chapter that, without it, would devoid your story of its essence and meaning then you can embrace life fully, feel less guilty, become more alive and effervescent and truly, deeply live.

Getting Into Reality - The Art Of Mending

I wasn't always Gold! I started out my life being Alexandra Lee Jones. Not that I dislike my birth name, not at all, it was just that by following the education that the universe sent me, I was assimilated into who I am today - Alexandra Gold.

A few years ago my family discovered that our family name would have been Gold had my great, great grandfather not been adopted.

You see, one of my father's cousins was investigating our family tree and shared this little nugget (do you like that?) of information. He was born within the sound of the Bow Bells, in the City of London but was adopted at birth and was from then on a Jones.

Great little story, heh? And it was then that the seed was planted in my head. As I was exploring the idea, I decided to ask around and see how people felt about the authenticity of someone who changes their names. It wasn't the positive, excited reception I had thought it would be. In fact, I was positively shot down. I succumbed to the negative responses I had been given and rapidly bought the web domain for my birth name.

I waited for inspiration. I waited for the creative energy to come. I waited for the universe to slap me around the face with a job or direction. I waited for the intention to flow and the words to write themselves. I waited for a year!

Of course, I filled my time by putting structures in place and strategies were magically manifesting during this time but I was never once drawn to BE that website. The energy I needed for its creation never changed from an uncomfortable ache and never got written.

And then, by the light of the silvery moon, (ok, it was actually a Facebook post, but that just didn't sound as romantic!) I stumbled across the Japanese Art of Mending and everything slotted into place. My energy, my alignment, my intention, my branding, my purpose and my truth just rolled into one. My Unique Expression of Essence was born.

In the ancient Japanese tradition of The Art of Mending, the attitude towards a broken object is not to just throw it away. It is not to deem the object useless, unworthy or of no value. The way of those employing this art is to take all the broken pieces, put them back together by joining them with resin and then paint the cracks with Gold. This, in turn, turns the object into a piece of individual art, a form of unique expression that can be admired and be useful. It becomes more beautiful, more valuable and ultimately a work of art that is of incredible and outstanding individuality, increasing its aesthetic and commercial value, tremendously.

In fact, this art form, which was used in the Japanese Tea Ceremony, became so popular that people started to deliberately break pots in order to mend them, in the tradition.

It was when I had seen this that my whole being took a huge sigh of relief. My body relaxed, my mind was still and my soul

KNEW.

I stepped into Alexandra Gold. I became one with everything I had been, everything I was, all that I wanted to represent and a way in which to deliver my unique gifts to the world.

It spoke to me, it spoke through me and broke through my heart in such a beautiful and powerful way that it became HOW I lived. It accepted my brokenness, my flaws, my mistakes and my humanity and SET ME FREE!

Free to truly BE. Free to give everything I had to give in a way that meant that I need not hide. I need not be ashamed. I was free enough that I could still make mistakes, still learn, still grow, still be broken in places and free enough to break again. If bad things, mistakes, improper behavior, shame, guilt and unworthiness popped up - I could still move forward. I could get up, brush myself down and fill my own flaws with Gold.

I could be proud of my imperfections. I could share my story. I could be fully present, knowing that no matter what happened, I could be authentically me.

I came ALIVE!

It gave me a humble and powerful presence. It gave me courage. It gave me a way to share my gifts in an inclusive way and a way that could positively and beautifully encompass all that I could share with the world.

You see, anybody can be Gold. A perfect solution to the ancient quest of Alchemists. There is a vein of Gold that connects the earth, the essence of all that we search for, have searched for over time and all that we continue to search for. It opens the floodgate for us to BE who we are, to KNOW that the magic in world essentially is IN us, Each and every one of us.

We can be comforted by the fact that we do not KNOW everything and that ALL will be revealed as long as we, going forward, do the best we can. As long as we keep learning, keep understanding more, keep growing together and keep becoming more accepting that all of our world is ONE. That there is enough, that we can work together as long as we continue to work on our judgment and open ourselves to the magical POSSIBILITIES that are in front of us.

We can fall into the arms of TRUST in the UNIVERSE and just start to live without worry but with understanding that we can learn. In that learning there is a magic that the alchemists searched for but that we fail to see as we get caught up in the worries of the world. A magic that can only be felt if we adopt the awe and wonder and innocent pleasure that most of us held as a child.

It is a choice.

We can choose to excavate those feelings again. Some of us have to dig deep, deep into blood that runs through the veins of Gold before we find our treasure but that I, from personal experience and from intention and from absolute determination have managed to achieve.

I can now be in tune with my deepest emotions, I allow myself to be guided by serendipity, by coincidence, by listening and by being aware of what is being shown to me.

When I hear a song, I feel it in my soul if I should be listening more intently. When I see a sign, I see it again and again until I really see it for what it is. When I feel an emotion, I do not question or jump to conclusions, I respect that emotion and try to really feel what it is teaching me.

When my body talks, it shouts and it screams, I cosset it like a baby until it is soothed and until I have paid it the attention it either needs or wants.

I will never stop listening. I will never stop learning. I have the Golden Key to the Meaning of Life within me and that is to live fully, with intentional good, try my best, share my gifts and accept my flaws.

I know that I will end up as dust and to me that is as beautiful as birth, as a work of art, as a newborn, as beautiful as a Golden sunset glistening on a grain of sand. As I am traveling this path, I will responsibly do all I can to make this earth better and to help others experience my absolute JOY in life.

I AM GOLD. I am living. I am alive and the most beautiful part of this is that I can share this treasure with the world.

Anybody can be GOLD, let me show you how!

The Past

What is *Your* past? Is it a lesson, a journey or is it part of your story? For me it is all of these things and, although parts of it were incredibly hard and painful, when I look back I have trained my memory to remember all of wonderful scenes the chapters that light my day and fill my cup.

Some parts of them I will not even mention, as they are so horrible and very hard to think about that they and the perpetrators of them do not warrant my energy or my acknowledgement. I know that we all have those chapters.

I will share with you how I deal with those things that have had a huge bearing on who I am today but which I find hard to forget completely and that I have had to deal with.

I have a Secret Vault.

Just as you would put a piece of valuable jewelry, that perhaps wasn't in a style of your taste, into a bank vault.

I acknowledge them. I know they are there. I accept the place they held in my growth and understanding, even if it was learning about hatred, unkindness, suffering and pain.

It took me a long time. I felt shame, guilt, anger and frustration and this all contributed to me not sharing my goodness and my gifts with the world. They held me back and they stifled me. In some instances, they stunted my growth for a period of time and even changed me into something I was not at all proud of, but I forgive them. I cannot forget them but if I let them take the stage, I will not be able to do any goodness whatsoever, and that, was a good enough reason for me to find a way to deal with them.

This was one of my hardest and one of the longest lessons for me to learn. I ran away and ducked and dived and tried to explain and tried to come to terms with them but I still felt dirty, embarrassed and unworthy.

So if, by writing this book, I help one, single person to come to terms with the past by sharing my secret vault, then my life on earth will be worth it. I hope it does and I hope it will but lets not dwell on just the bad bits, heh?

So, you know when you are thinking about the past and examining where you came from and how you have become who you are, what are the bits that pop up in your mind?

I have had times during my illness where my memory was so bad it was barely existent, so I have had the pleasure of regained memories as I have become more confident in the fact that I will live for tomorrow. Little things trigger my memory. Somebody put a link to Zorba The Greek on my Facebook timeline the other day, which transported me back to my family home in a small South African town. I bullied my brother and sister into Greek dancing with me up and down the hallway, getting ourselves in knots and falling over with laughter. Such a small and yet poignant memory and yet it opened the floodgates of enjoyment for me. I remembered that I had bought a load of vinyl records (the things before CD's for those of you too young to know what I am talking about!) from a jumble sale when I was about 8 years old.

They consisted of a mishmash of show tunes, from Gi-Gi to collections from musicals, Neil Sedaka, Leo Sayer, Liza Minnelli and they had such an impact on me. The only other records I had at the time were Rod Stewarts Greatest Hits, Abba's Super Trouper (which Father Christmas bought me) and Disney's Soundtrack Album. My parents had a collection of 45's (singles) and the ones that stood out for me there were Brass in Pocket (which was to become my theme tune when I sang in a Folk Rock band), D.I.S.C.O. and The Boy from New York City.

When my parents finally decided that we were emigrating to South Africa I insisted that they come with us. Little did I realize what an impact they would have on me, and my life!

I taught myself to sing better. I copied each song until I could sing it in the same way, with the same feelings and emotions and in the same key. If there was a song that I liked and that I had trouble with it, I sang it again and again and again and again until I got it right.

I fell in love with the theatre, and with musicals, and with dance, and with rhythm and filled my downtime with lofty dreams of grandeur and excitement and reality and Showtime! They were all attainable. I had no questions. I had no doubts. I just did it..... AND I loved it!

I did go on to perform on stages and used my passion to regroup an Amateur Dramatic Society that had become defunct so that the first show we put on turned a profit but what I am truly saying here is that I remembered!

I remembered the good bits, the passion, the sheer determination and absolute certainty about how my love WOULD work.

I remembered that I didn't feel embarrassed. I remembered that I practiced until I was ready (almost!). I rehearsed. I learnt. I got better and better and I got what I wanted and in my naive assuredness, I was happy! I remembered how it felt to be freely, simply and utterly happy!

This little memory helped enormously in excavating my memories of good emotions. It is amazing how our minds sometimes easily remember the bad stuff and forget how good it can feel to really use the simple, free and completely delightful memories of uncluttered emotions we felt as a child.

I am now frequently to be found walking down the street, dog on lead and singing away to a song that may or may not conjure a memory but more importantly, I am able to evoke the unabashed EMOTIONS & FEELINGS I felt as a child. I weep with joy, I feel despair at sadness, I feel Christmas excitement at the sunshine and a full moon, and smile wholeheartedly at anyone I pass.

Some people don't smile back, some people looked positively scared! I don't mean to piss them off but I sure as hell am never going to lock those liberating emotions away again.

The truth is I now play games in my head, just as I did as a child, with the smiles I give away. I give them freely and see how many I get back! Most of the time I do get a smile in return, sometimes they are tiny, thin unexpected smiles on the behalf of the giver and sometimes my receiver looks away, embarrassed or wondering how to avoid the crazy woman but occasionally and, something I am working on improving, I get a full, beautiful and open smile that sings to my soul and touches my heart in a way that only open and honest love can do!

How can you excavate that childlike awe and wonder from your past?

The Present

I went to many counselors, psychiatrists, psychologists and other kinds of 'help' until I was diagnosed with Post Traumatic Stress Disorder, during my legal wrangle.

I saw neurosurgeons, neuro-psychiatrists and head doctors of every kind, too, before, during and after my physical illness. Because of the fact that my brain moved so often with the growth of the tumor, destruction of the bone, inflammation from infection and as it settled. One of the only pieces of practical advice that worked for me was 'to live in the present moment'. I was really lucky that in my area there was a trial of Gestalt therapy happening when I was really struggling to mentally, physically and emotionally cope with living with a chronically debilitating and pro-longed illness which was not immediately visible.

None of those who were supposed to help really made a difference to my mental health and none of them diagnosed me as being anything other than normal, except for the eventual diagnosis of Post Traumatic Stress Disorder. Under the circumstances, this was not unusual, but which did add to my problems. I felt guilty at being diagnosed with a disorder which I felt was only deserved by someone who had given themselves to warfare.

I was scared, I was traumatized, I was in fear for my life and that of my son, should I not survive. I had goodish days and I had horrendous days. Days when I felt determined and hopeful that I would pull through and on other occasions I felt helpless. The only thing that helped was when I went to see the Gestalt therapist and she explained that I should truly, and in an embodied fashion, learn to live in the present moment.

Over time I became a master of this! I learnt to live for the present day and then to just live in the present and, more importantly, to enjoy every single moment.

I have since become aware that many other people have been told this little piece of advice but find it difficult to actually apply. Again, I go back to the fact that you have to CHOOSE to be in the moment. In order to master anything you have to practice; I really started out having to tell myself to come back.

It was like having two people in my head. The one was the student or child and the other acted as the master or parent. If my thoughts turned maudlin I would have the parent kindly bring me back. If I got angry I had the master gently chastise my rationale and give me other, nonjudgmental ways to think about the situation in question.

I became the Teacher & the Student. I had to. There was nobody else with my condition. I was the only one in that particular situation and it taught me that we are all unique. We can all become our own teacher; we can all become the students of our questioning, our anger and frustration. Difficult situations can be dealt with in a calm and confident and kind manner. Be a kind, considerate and compassionate teacher to yourself. Take the gift of time. Do not make rash decisions that could hurt you. Understand that any situation can be dealt with, even if you are in a place of extreme anxiety, shock, grief, ill health or depression. There is ALWAYS a way!

The one thing that I would add to living in the present - the one thing that took me a long time to get to grips with once I had finally combated all of the infection and did not have to worry anymore - and that is to live with the HOPE of TOMORROW!

By saying that I don't mean saying things like 'It will get better' or 'We'll get there' but I do mean give yourself permission to dream, to create, to expand into the next chapter and to grow.

The statements 'It will get better' or 'We'll get there' are small and just whimsical with not enough oomph or exciting, happy energy - whereas by dreaming and creating with the Hope of Tomorrow (this could be day-dreaming, vision-boarding, storyboarding), you immediately expand and put ACTION energy behind your thoughts and whether there is anything in that or not it JUST MAKES YOU HAPPIER. I am not about to look at the statistics or refer to any journals or medical research, I haven't the time to do that and I am too busy enjoying life and dreaming.

Other tips for being present that I find helpful are:

- Observation - taking a minute to really take in where you are. Look at the room you are in, look at your surroundings, look at the leaves blowing in the wind and their shape and distinct veins and colors. Take a breath and really follow how it enters your body and courses into your lungs - is it warm breath or is it a cold, sharp feeling? Does it come with heightened aroma? Smell the coffee, the roses, the food and the air. Is it raining? Is the waft of jasmine blowing through the door? Look at the clouds moving. Feel a drop, just one drop of rain!

- People watch - see people and try to ascertain their personalities and what they are doing, where they are going and what you can learn from them. Appreciate their style, their gait, and their interaction. Listen to them speak and think about how their language and tone conveys who they are and the reaction they get.

- Be compassionate - with yourself, with others, with animals and plants. When you give compassionate energy you feel good.

- Listen - take a minute to really hear your surroundings. The sounds you hear tend to really bring home the present moment and what is happening around you all the time. Whether it is a peaceful or frantic surrounding, it is your present surrounding and reminds you of life and all that is happening in the world.

The Potential

Oooooh! The possibilities! Where do we start? There are so many ways that the future can present itself in our minds. For some of us, at difficult periods in our lives, this can fill us with dread and I completely understand this feeling.

For those who feel that they fall into this category I completely recommend living in the moment until you get to a point where you feel ready to look into your future without fear, so that you are really able to enjoy it. Nobody likes an unhappy ending so make sure you are ready to create the future of your ultimate dreams, then to start the next chapter too!

For those of you ready to take a beautiful step into your potential, this is where the magic begins.

The possibilities for our potential are so unbelievable and so expansive if you are able to see them. By seeing your potential I mean using your thoughts and imagination and crystallizing all that could be, all that you want and solidifying them with your step by step manifestation.

I am lucky in that I can visualize the future and what I want and get the excitement from the creation of the path to get there.

Nothing, and I mean nothing within my personal control, is out of reach.

I will cover personal control in the Infinite Principle of Self but just want to quantify what I am saying by explaining that I don't dream of riding down the King's Road on a unicorn and parking next to the Queen of Sheba! Although I do quite fancy that idea.

What I mean is seeing ALL that could be in your life, in the life of your children and in the future of the world. Feel sparks that light you up and ways in which to achieve them.

For me I CHOOSE to see a world where we learn to be tolerant of one another and where we start to really work together rather than fragment and re-group and disintegrate. I don't just mean as individuals but as collectives. For example, there is such discord in the western world at the moment in the form of corporations, medical thought and political alignment, that we are completely obsessed with being in the RIGHT department, whether that is politically, socially, environmentally or even in what we eat! Just imagine if we were able to all work together to find a kind, just and compatible answer to all of the issues that we are facing.

Most of us know that the world is abundant. Most of us believe that there is enough for everyone but there are so many things that we are not dealing with collectively, because we are being manipulated by fear, by the media, by celebrity, by materialism and my personal favorite, the one NEVER discussed in first world discussion - PRIMAL SURVIVAL!

We all have it! Sometimes it is repressed, sometimes it is not even acknowledged but most of the time it is wrapped up in a package disguised as first world ambition and one-up-man-ship.

Unfortunately this usually manifests in power and anger but contained in packages made to look like they are the best answer!

If we, as 'first world citizens', really, truly embodied the knowledge that there is enough for everyone, we would initially be able to acknowledge that together. Then we would be working together to ensure that not only do our immediate compatriots have their basic needs met, but that we are helping ALL of mankind. No excuses, no wool over our eyes and no unlearning of all those safety measures that our ancestors put in place for us, in order to segregate ourselves further!

By this I mean we try to please sections of society rather than working together to ensure that there is balance in one country in the political arena.

By this I mean that corporations see the financial bottom line as more important than what they are providing.

By this I mean that personally we see media manipulation competing with one another and increasing want in extreme measures.

By this I mean that we all have a particular standard of living that we expect to maintain and will do ANYTHING we can in order to at least maintain that standard but, from the examples above this, usually means outdoing and outperforming that standard of living, of buying power, of political stance or career path.

I do believe that you can break through the glass ceilings. I just think that we should be more mindful of humankind and our planet and break those ceilings together.

The funny thing is, one of the best feelings in the world is contribution, I just think we have lost sight of that in the way we portray it.

For example there are so many charities, different governmental departments and philanthropic arms of corporations BUT they separate issues and only half-fill our cup of contribution by giving us all an excuse to alleviate our guilt. If we were to start encompassing the problems that these charities and organizations support, life would be easier for all of us. Happiness would be more achievable and Peace easier to maintain.

As it is, the separation and segregation of issues that should be dealt with by us all are fought by angry sections working individually. While they all have their place in society right now, I like to see a point in the future where we ALL contribute to solving ANY problem. First locally, then nationally and finally, Globally - I will deal with that when I get to the point where I am ready and able and there are enough compassionate leaders in the world to implement the Global Responsible Community I was talking to my business advisor about.

I am not idealistic about this - I have devised a way, which with correct direction, by using ancient wisdom, modern knowledge, respecting our elders and their wisdom and respecting each other, we could really make a difference in the way we do things together, as community, we could encompass all of the personal needs that we have as individuals, how we can grow, be in business for ourselves, responsibly and how we can impact the world and become a united voice for GOOD.

Wanna be in my gang??? That is down the road - let's make this step a masterpiece first!

Destination Divining

We started excavating your deeply desired destination in the Introduction and, if you are able to be comfortable with the fact, we acknowledged that we ALL end up at the same destination and become dust. But that isn't really the most motivational motivations is it?

So to begin the Destination Divining process, I like to use my Pension Plan as an example, to explain what I mean!

You see "to start with the end in mind" as Steven Covey says is a wonderful thing and I totally believe it works, but when we are thinking about our own lives I don't think it helps to go right to the end. It is definitely not as much fun as planning how you are going to enjoy your misspent dotage!

It is so much easier to put a plan in place if you know what you want to achieve and for some people it is easy to do this for short periods of time or a specific reason or goal. For clarity in this particular situation, I want you to think about something most of us fail to even acknowledge, let alone think about.

I have seen quite a few people reach retirement age and then not have a clue what to do with themselves once they have achieved this stage of life.

I am lucky in the fact that I half-jokingly included my dream of Gold Lamé and Big Hair in my overall plan from when I was very young but, over time, this has given me great comfort and also a huge amount of drive. Over the past few years as I really embodied this last of my BIG dreams and put it at the top of my pile of things to achieve. It gained status in my life and rather than being just a joke, I knew that it really had become more than a rash, whimsical idea and had gained solid foundation in my life plan.

So start thinking about your Pension Plan. Where would you like to live when you retire? Will you retire at all? Do you have hobbies that will take over from your everyday working life that can be as much of a draw card then to you? Make sure that there is real honesty behind what you are doing. Although I love to think of myself growing tomatoes and runner beans, I am more of a preserver of already grown things than a giver of life. Interpret this as I kill plants and yet I am quite a good cook! I may get better at growing things and my patience may increase exponentially in the meantime, but for now, I would rather be able to afford to buy local, organic produce and have enough energy and inclination to turn that into something sublime!

So my dream of having a multi-purpose venue began when I was still a teenager.

Over the years my sense of style has changed along with fashions and my perception and expansion of what I know has meant that my visual process has been through a lot of renovation and change.

Give yourself permission for your dreams to become shape-shifters. Allow them to morph into what you become aware of, of what you learn and what life has to offer.

A WOMAN ON PURPOSE

For me, what started as a room with black and white tiles on the floor, red velvet booths with dark wood and plenty of palms scattered around a small stage now includes my love of the Mediterranean white washed walls and a slightly less harlequin take on flooring.

I flow with the process and expand with my dreams. I know that one day I may create one and that further down the line that may change, as does style, fashion, tradition and need.

There is only one rule with this type of Pension Plan - and that is that it is Positive. We are all aware that our bodies and minds change as we get older but I would like to see us all taking responsibility for at least our happiness as we travel that particular journey. I find that every adventure is enjoyed more when you create an itinerary. When you learn a little more about your destination and create a plan that is uniquely suited to you.

What does you Personal Positive Pension Plan itinerary have on its beautiful pages?

Letting Go Of Angst

I have just had five days off!

I have just had a downer, unproductive, unhelpful and unhappy! No reason. No excuse. No anything.

No matter how happy you can be. No matter how full your life is and no matter who you are, we are all susceptible to a bout of 'The Blues'.

I don't know, as has been the way since I have lived my life acknowledging the energy of life, in flow, whether it is a bit serendipitous or just per chance that this has happened at the exact point in writing where I have to talk about Letting Go but I do feel particularly qualified to write about this subject now.

As I write, now, there is a knot of uncertainty in my stomach and as I was in the shower, just after writing the last paragraph, I forced myself to remember as many of the emotions and feelings that I have had due to trauma, circumstance and things that just happen.

The thing is, although I have learnt to deal with and live with these not so wonderful times, I still go through them.

I understand that even though you are reading this that sometimes what anybody says just does not do anything to alleviate these emotions.

I qualify them as times of despair, of hopelessness, of uselessness, of no point, of fear, of anxiety, of stress, of trauma, of sadness, of grief and sometimes, and these times seem to be the lowest, of nothingness and numbness.

Now, I am no physician or psychiatrist, and so of course if you are prone to feeling this low my immediate piece of advice is to ask for help. I will immediately follow this piece of advice with the fact that if the person you ask for help is not helpful or understanding or you just don't feel comfortable with, then ask someone else. It is your right. It is your life. It is your mental and physical health. It is your body and most importantly it is YOUR HAPPINESS.

I have had to ask for help plenty of times and it took me a long time to realize and, even longer to act on these issues.

To me FEAR is very real. I have lived with the fear of danger, the fear of unknowing and the fear of uselessness for many different reasons, not just my physical health. It is a primal emotion just as any other. It is there to keep us safe. It is part of our intuition. It is yet to be fully understood. It is still to be respected for its part that it plays in our lives and I will not underplay it.

Mental health is so important and yet still not talked about easily. It is so fundamental to our overall happiness and well-being and far more important than any GDP (Gross Domestic Product) in any country, in any language, in any society or community, whether young or old. To underplay how it manifests is fine, if on a personal level it is helpful to you, singularly. Do not expect it to work for everybody and do not blame yourself if it does not work for you. Also, do not hold judgment for those who have issues with any form of mental health illness. Some of those people are happier than you are. Some of them have been given medication that covers their anguish and some have medication that causes even more problems. I just wish that we could hurry up and find some more practical solutions to our western, first world mental health issues so that we could turn this vicious cycle around so that we could do more to help overcome the manmade issues that stem from mans' overall unhappiness.

I know that there is a saying that fear is not real. Unfortunately, I don't buy that. When I feel fear it is all consuming.

It forms a pit in my stomach and gets caught in my throat. My eyes go blurry and my head feels as if every neuron is electrified. I have no sensation in my hands and if I get a shock I physically feel immediate pins and needles in my head, my hands and my feet. I want to scream. I want to throw my head back. I want to run and my body is separate from my head which is on fire and held together with a piercing rod running through my neck and pounding the blood supply that links my brain and my heart, enabling the world to hear my veins clanging and banging so loudly that even the roar of London traffic is unable to quell them.

I don't know when fear will strike. Angst comes in many forms and for many reasons. I can only speak about my personal encounters with all forms of angst.

As I grow older, all of the different emotions and forms of Angst have formed a terrorist movement so great that, although they do not get through the border of my mind as often as they did singularly, they strike hard and they strike fast taking me out bodily and mentally and disabling me completely and destructively. Crippling!

As I have HAD no choice but to form a defense strategy and system to put into action, I can share the things that I do in order to minimize infiltration (to stop it happening in the first place), nip the feeling in the bud (recognize the initial signs and therefore try a line of first defense) or succumb to the onslaught (accept that I have been overpowered and that I need to surrender).

The first thing I do and one of the places that I live my life from now is to give myself the role of The Warrior.

I know, not the most graceful, ladylike or gentle start, but needs must and to be honest, when I put this archetype into place she takes on the world on her own.

So the way I like to think of it is twofold. I am responsible for my survival and myself; the world needs me to make it a better place, hence the need for the first.

The first one, responsibility of self, I think most people can relate too although sometimes it is really not as easy as it sounds. This requires all of your strength to muster the energy to even employ this first thought.

The second one, the world needing me to make it better, I know you probably think is a bit lofty. I don't care. There are so many bad things in the world that I know, by even doing the most menial of jobs well, I will be doing my bit. There are many cogs in the wheel of life; this is where I completely understand that NONE of them are less important than the other.

So, right now, no matter who you are or what you do, become

aware of the fact that you are enough.

I don't care what anyone else has to say, what we are led to believe or how you feel at any given time. YOU ARE ENOUGH.

We are all needed to make the world go around and the wonderful thing that we all have in common, if you are able to read or to listen to this book, is that we have so much more than many people on this planet. We have a duty to help make this world a better place for them, even if our own lives are not particularly happy or full or fruitful.

I do not use the word 'duty' lightly. It is a word that I choose to use that, when times are tough, helps me, and if I can help one of you by using my strategies then it is a useful word. If you feel angered by it, I am sorry, but you can at least use the strategy to find words that suit your purpose and personality. I am only sharing my coping mechanisms here and I can not take the place of any physician or specialist or your chosen help but my own Warrior needs this 'duty' to get off her butt when her butt is stuck!!!

This doesn't mean that the Warrior gets stuck into action straight away and all of the time! Oh no, sometimes this warrior climbs into bed for a few days, wallows in self pity and eats copious amounts of Maltesers!!!

The one thing the Warrior does do though is KNOW that this feeling WILL PASS!

It is not permanent, a temporary setback in putting the world to rights. Every warrior needs a little R&R and this warrior is no exception!

So if you are feeling down, don't beat yourself up. One of the most wonderful things that I have learnt whilst trusting this process is that almost always something wonderful comes out of the down time. Because I have such a determined commitment to duty, I tend to try not to indulge the negative (we will cover this in the negative section) but I do try not to think at all. Hence my indulging the feeling and not the negativity tends to lead to a brighter outcome.

I do this by covering any harboring negativity with other things.

For example, if I am at a very low ebb I get into bed and watch a movie, listen to an inspirational talk or if I need to really clear my messy mind, I put on a hypnosis track. (Only do this if you know that you are physically well enough, if you are in doubt or suffer from epilepsy please ensure that you check this with your doctor!). This has helped when I have been in a really bad place. In some instances when I was gravely ill I had to listen to hypnosis every day for months on end!

I have also had to take anti-depressants at one time but even they left me numb after a year and a half and took at least five weeks to work but I have had to have them and if you need them, be aware that they may change the way you think, you can't come off them cold turkey and you need to discuss any matter of concern with a physician who you like and trust.

If I was not so bad, I found meditation, going for a walk with music that contra-indicated my mood and felt right was all I needed.

Sometimes, if I am warding off the enemy I can make do with a good picture, a deep breath of air, a look at the sunshine or a good cup of coffee.

Do what YOU need to do when you need to do it. Everyone is fighting his or her own battles. What some find easy, others find insurmountable. What some find clear, others find unmanageable. What to some seems trivial, others fear cripplingly.

A couple of the other things that I find helpful when dealing with Angst in any of its forms are the Awareness of an episode of angst forming, its level of power and also the importance of having a Circle of Safety you can turn to when you know that it is happening.

Awareness

Awareness comes in many forms. For me it was a gradual increase in circumstantial shit that happened, culminating in a physical shock that wracked my body, one night, sending me into spasms that I could not control. I was lucky and I had to, at the tender age of 30, climb into bed with my mummy and she just held me for hours on end (tears are forming in my eyes just thinking about this time, which occurred just after I found out that I had a tumor).

Thinking I was going mad, losing the plot, speaking a different language or just plain stupid are all of the things that have crossed my mind either all at once or one at a time.

No matter, when they happen, they happen! I know that, so I understand that. If you are lucky enough to have never experienced any of this you are either sincerely very lucky or blessed with a neuron or substance that a lot of us are lacking. Please share quickly!

If they do not happen very often, then they may come as a bit of a shock to you. If you, like me, have had life throw you a couple of curve balls or grenades then you may have had quite a few of them, some of them for protracted amounts of time. YOU ARE NOT ALONE!

But in that moment, you will feel like it! Just become aware of what is happening and why they are happening or what has happened to induce it. The more you become aware about how and when these downturns occur, the more you can control them (loosely put here - there are always loose cannons!) You can also get your own artillery and logistics in place for deployment and early intervention!

Some of the things to put in your personal kit bag:

- An awareness of what you may have eaten or something your body needs - I always (forget initially and then remember to) take a whopping, industrial strength multivitamin after eating. In winter a lack of vitamin D or just being a woman a lack of iron or vitamin B is a usual culprit.

- Detox - I am not in the market for a crash diet here I just mean the elimination of things that may be contributing such as alcohol, medication (always check with your physician if you are taking prescriptions), time of the month, moon and mood swings and just really toxic people.

- Look up - especially if it is a blue sky.

- Go for a walk, especially in nature but at least walk a route where you can find beauty. I had to take my son to school down a really depressing street, so I found all kinds of alternative routes. I really found my mood lifted once he had changed schools and every route became a joy, filled with beauty. This is so important and I live as much as I can in a way that I experience my own kind of beauty as much as possible.

- Smile - even for yourself! Force it - go on, now!!

- Exercise - sometimes I have had to go to the gym for two hours a day, five days a week just to get rid of the anger my body was holding on to. Even when I was ill I used to watch fitness DVD's and when I got well enough my first goal was to become a Zumba instructor. I did that in six months.

- Think nice thoughts - send the horrors away. Get your positive voice to overpower the negative one, just throw the shit away. Easier said than done when your really in it up to your ears and that is why I have to employ outside influences such as hypnosis or romantic comedies to get the weeping detox process underway.

- Let yourself cry. I am a real hoarder of tears. I usually find it easier to cry in anger than I do when I am upset. Watch a heart-pulling animal or baby video. Don't watch upsetting stuff, just heart tugging, emotional triggering, cry like a baby stuff.

- Indulge yourself. Go shopping. You can go to the shops with a budget or just window shop for your future warrior outfits and dream home.

- Know that there is always a way and that what you are feeling is temporary.

- Give yourself permission. A real toughie so I will give this a section of its own. You have to be able to do this.

Circle Of Safety

No warrior is born a hero! There are not many black ops soldiers in the world or even spies who work alone and each and every one of them started out as babies. Don't think that you need to be solitary to go through anything. Even if you are alone, there will be places that you can either go to or call and that where it is their 'duty' to listen to you. Take that, claim it. You are human. Your primal instinct is to be a part of a social circle, of community or part of a collective where you feel safe.

It is only over the past few decades that we have started, in the western world, to live such intensely individual lives. I have to question whether this is due to evolution and growth or whether it is down to selfishness and material need.

What I do know is that when I only concentrate on my own intentions, which I know is necessary in the first instance to ensure my cup is full, that I still have a gaping hole in my happiness. By giving myself the 'duty' of making the world better, I feel that I am whole, but sometimes I need help. And in any case, life is usually so much better when shared.

The best help I gather around me is that of family and friends who I can trust. They don't always say the right things and when this happens I have had to take a step back in amazement but more often than not it does really help to be able to talk, or not talk to those that I feel are in my own personal Circle of Safety.

Choose your Circle of Safety wisely. When you are learning to be a warrior of the world it is only human that you will need to vent frustration and anger; you will need to be able to let those in your circle know that you need to rant. To go on a personal savage attack with someone who is going to throw your words back in your face is definitely to be avoided at all costs.

Be willing to share that you need a little respite from being nice and share your woes, your fears, your guilt, your shame, your fears and anxieties with those who know your true personality. If you are on your own be sure your words and feelings need to come out. Use a journal or a piece of paper that you can burn and release or find an organization that can help those in need, such as the Samaritans or even a local church or community organization. If need be, visit another town, or get help online. We all have pieces of ourselves that we try to hide. Me too. I have them all. The nice parts and the naughty parts. The good bits and the bad bits. The pleasantries and the expletives. Sometimes they need to come out. Let them!

Letting Go Of Guilt

I know you have some! We all do, it's a bitch. Shame, guilt and that feeling of wanting to hide yourself under the duvet and be swallowed up whole, are so very me!

You see, although I have come through a lot, I have also done a lot. And, having done a lot, quite a bit went wrong!

I am definitely one of those people who has two sides to my personality. In fact, I feel split down the middle in many aspects of my person, so when I first started hearing about the 'authenticity' buzz word going around, I thought that I would just have to pick one!

Not a good idea. You see as much as my angelic side does her best to be the best she can, she is also a pious and petulant and condescending bitch and as much as Roxy (my alter ego) is a naughty, attention seeking, over-the-top exhibitionist, she is also braver, less judgmental, and completely visible compassionate soul.

I tried to kill Roxy for years. I tried to stay at home, stayed single, I did not go dancing, not drink alcohol, not smoke, not eat anything with grain, with fat, with carbs, with e-numbers etc. and not spend any money. I stopped being brave. I stopped being outspoken. I stopped listening to music. I stopped singing. I stopped everything that was seen in the eyes of the world to be destructive. I stopped being visible and eventually I stopped being me. Essentially I was only half living.

Then I got bored with that and tried to kill the angel. I started going out again, meeting men, drinking alcohol, secretly smoking, eating anything or nothing (depending on how much alcohol I had drunk or the clothes size I wanted to be). I became braver (in some circumstances)! I became outspoken (timidly)! I started to get angry and let everyone know my opinion about anything and I sung at the top of my lungs whenever the opportunity leant itself (not, in my honest truth with any level of shame)! I let Roxy out big time. But with absolutely no guidance and my shame and guilt came crashing around me as soon as the hangover wore off!

I was self-destructing. I was not helping myself either way. Roxy didn't last long on her own. The Angel had better staying power but both were a part of me.

I was not letting myself have completely honest relationships with others or myself. I was judgmental and others were judgmental of me, only making me worse. I ostracized those who loved me the most and was not fully accepting. I was in a personal prison.

Either way - it was personal torment. Exactly the same outcome. Exactly the same guilt, shame and unhappiness.

It took a while but eventually I had to face the fact that I had created two monsters. Neither side of me was good on its own. I had to get a balance of both. Use an inordinate amount of self-control and just Let Go of the Guilt.

I minimized Roxy's outlandish behavior and maximized Angel's strengths. I let both work together to find the solution that would make myself easier to live with. Mainly for my own release of guilt and shame, but it definitely was for the greater good, too.

So occasionally you will see Roxy with a bottle of Cava singing and dancing like a mad woman, so that she gets a real night out and lets her hair down but mainly she is using her strengths for visibility and being brave enough to share her story, her pain and hopefully let others know that they are not on their own and that we all have good bits and bad bits.

To completely change your personality because it is 'seen' to be the thing to do is not really helping, either ourselves, or others.

Letting go of self-judgment is the first step in being less judgmental in the world. We all mess up.

I have a golden pedestal but I fall off it plenty. I accept that. Sometimes I say the wrong thing, words spew out of my mouth that are unintentionally hurtful or just plain stupid. I accept that this happens and that deep in my heart I only want to love and be good, compassionate, kind and gracious.

Most of the time now you will just see Alex, using all of my bits and getting the best out of all of my strengths, being less judgmental and more compassionate both to myself and more importantly, to the outside world. I am far better off losing the guilt and regaining myself.

It took a lot of work to do it. It will take a lot more. I will never be perfect. I will always be learning. That is a good thing. Life is here to be lived, if you don't make a few mistakes along the way, you cannot have lived fully.

I often wonder whether the Dalai Lama or the Queen ever let their dark side out. I hope so. I don't care anymore about what mistakes people make. We are human. I know that they don't have the day-to-day worries that most of us have but just having to be perfect is hard enough in itself, I wish them every happiness. I know how hard it is. Much respect.

So, if you feel ready to throw away your guilt, do it.

If you make mistakes, accept them. If you need to apologize, do so. If you need to forgive yourself and move on, do it.

It is a mental exercise to get rid of guilt if you are a hoarder, like me. I have to literally take those thoughts and throw them away. Discard them. Dust myself off, pick my golden pedestal and myself back up and move on.

There is no other way. My 80/10/10 principle! Try your best to do your best eighty percent of the time. Make mistakes in public and forgive yourself, make mistakes in your heart, forgive yourself.

It really has to be that simple. No matter what you have done. Try your best. It is the most any of us can do.

Letting Go Of Anger & Using It As Fuel

'I am an Angry Bird' I said to my business advisor. I get really, passionately angry. How can I show anyone how to be happy with that juxtaposition hanging over my head?

'What makes you angry?' She then asked me.

I didn't have to think about it. I get angry at injustice. I get angry at greed. I get angry at unkindness, at unfairness, at evil. I get angry at angry people. I get angry at liars. I get angry when people are supposed to do a job and they find it impossible to do so with grace. I get angry at those who are employed to help but do everything they can to minimize that help.

Oooooh! I get so bloody Angry.

But! And there is a big BUT. I get angry at the right things. I hadn't realized this until then.

I do get angry but this anger literally catapults me forward and into ACTION. I do not use my anger against anyone. I use my voice!!!

As a lowly nobody, sitting at home watching the TV and seeing all the bad things that are happening in the world, getting angry and doing nothing about it does nothing to help anything or anyone. Least of all, me!

I am also not one of those people who is able to switch off completely. My 'duty' button needs to be informed. I like to know what is going on in the world if I want to make it better. I am a bit of a Jill of all trades and master of none when it comes to world news. I just like to know what is going on. I don't necessarily understand it all but just want to be aware of what is happening, what is changing, what is being addressed and what needs to be done.

I am pretty good at surmising the bigger picture so I don't need to be right. I don't need to recite facts. I don't need to know the names of politicians or treaties or wars. I just want to be abreast of how the world is moving. Then I switch off.

I can only think of ways to solve the problems if I know about them.

I don't want them shoved in my face all the time though. I need to live from a place of happiness and beauty in order to do my bit so watching the news and daytime TV is not conducive to that!

I have learnt to use my anger to fuel my mission in life, my 'duty' and my promise to make the world a better place.

I know that directing my anger towards anyone, in any situation is absolutely futile. It serves no purpose and would just feed my guilt. By not being angry with people, I allow myself to be happier.

I am not saying that I am perfect at this either. Just that I like being happy so I use my anger wisely.

I am not saying that I don't raise my voice either. Sometimes I have to shout in order to be heard. I do not need to be angry to raise my voice but I sometimes need to be taken seriously so have to raise my voice.

Even to my son and my partner. When I raise my voice they know that I am absolutely serious. When I raise my voice I want and need to be heard. That is just me. The softer you become, the harder you need to be. Make sense?

It is more of a steadfastness and an assuredness that comes with knowing that everything I do, I do with compassion and kindness. I am not saying angelic kindness. Just from a good place that keeps the guilt away and the happiness topped up.

The main thing about having anger is the awareness of it. Awareness is yet again one of the most important and useful things about becoming more enlightened or awakened but it does take practice.

Awareness of ones anger ensures that you remain in control of how it is directed and how you can use it in a positive manner rather than pointing it to a person and getting into a negative cycle.

Once you become more aware of your anger, it becomes easier to harness and using it to fuel your passion and purpose becomes almost seamless.

Becoming more aware of what makes you angry can also help you in the discovery of your passion and purpose.

If there are certain things that really get your blood boiling then think about how you can use that in your contribution back to the world.

Once you become good at understanding the factors that contribute to your anger and then harness those emotions it almost seems too easy that life could be that simple.

Once you have mastered the anger (and I don't mean completely, we are only human remember!) you can start teaching others how to become aware of their anger and using it to not only find their contribution and purpose but to put it to good use and fuel their passion!

Letting Go Of Negativity & The Art Of Positive Living

So, we are surrounded by negative ways to solve problems. So much so that it has become common practice in this day and age to highlight everything that is wrong in the world by making commercials and charitable contributions pull at your heartstrings and, more usefully, your guilt and fear strings!

The problem with this is that we have not only become skeptical to this type of advertising but we are less likely to action our own contribution buttons as to the fact that we alleviate our guilt by giving to a cause.

Although nothing is wrong with this per se, it has gained such monumental leverage that these tactics are barraged at us all day and everyday and by every single agency trying to sell, trying to make us contribute and trying to get us to do something.

This means that most of us are so surrounded by negativity that it is more normal and more ingrained in our very beings than happiness and action. The more we hear about how not doing something will affect us, the more in fear we become. The more we feel guilty about all that is wrong in the world, the more we contribute financially to charities that perhaps could be run in a more positive manner. The more we hear about how what we eat, what we do or do not do and how and where and when we should, shouldn't or must do things, the more we close ourselves off from what and how we could be living more vibrant and happy lives.

We live in an abundant world but in order to reap this abundance, and abundance is different for everyone, we have to believe in our abilities and ourselves and not be susceptible to the abundance of negativity that we are bombarded with, day in and day out.

Yet again, the first thing to do is become aware of the negative things that surround you on a daily basis. This starts with your own thoughts. This starts as an exercise. This starts as soon as you decide to start.

I cannot make you change your thoughts but I can tell you with utmost sincerity that this one thing improves your life tenfold.

To abolish the negative thoughts that you have is like working the positive muscle and needs work, persistence and determination. There is so much negativity in the western world that to become aware of it is, at first, the most important thing as you need to make the positive muscle so strong that it can deflect the negative blows that we are thrown, day in, day out.

Once you start throwing your negative thoughts in the trashcan of your mind, you leave room for more positive choices and thoughts to take their place. This has been proven in many ways throughout existence but to be honest I don't need any statistics or research to 'make it so' for me. It just is the only way I could take all of the negativity out of my life.

It was a choice. It was a decision. I am absolutely sure that it is the right way to live and that the power of positivity could contribute so much to alleviating both personal and world problems.

How do I know? After living with 'no', with uncertainty, with risks to my health, my finances and my future I got to a point where I had so much and yet could give so little. I was well and ready to give back to the world but could not find any opportunity to share all that I learnt by giving my gifts and my energy away for free. I tried to face-paint for charities, I tried to re-open a community centre, I tried to help numerous charities and organizations and not one took up my offer! I was thwarted at every step. Not enough insurance, not enough security, not enough time, not enough support, not enough, no, NO!

I wanted to do so much but was too scared. I had so much to give and couldn't, no matter how hard I tried because of negative reactions to my ideas, offers and the help I wanted to give to many situations for free. You would not believe it. It didn't matter how positive I was. How enthusiastic I was. How keen and motivated I was to help negative situations I was hit with blank walls of negativity and disbelief and I just had to step back.

I was so sick of having this part of me that had come through so much and had so much to give being stopped and reversed by those filled with negative and patronizing energy - I just had to make the choice to get rid of ANY negativity that I had in my head to make room for ME and MY GIFTS to get into POSITIVE ACTION.

The beautiful thing about this letting go is that all of this negativity abolition is that it opened up my world. Not only to positivity but also to the creativity to do the good that I needed to do. It gave me the anger to fuel my passion and the passion to brand my purpose and ultimately gave me the freedom to help far more people and, indeed, the world.

I now choose to SEE negativity and become AWARE of how it affects the situation it has settled on but I have NO ROOM in my head for it.

I AM FUELED BY POSITIVE ENERGY and it works like a rocket fueled DREAM.

I realize the ART of POSITIVE LIVING. I am convinced that we could all do so much more for the world by harnessing this power. I aim to qualify this by experimentation once I have more traction and leverage, to make a difference. So please let me know if you would like, and have practiced POSITIVE LIVING for a long enough amount of time to embody and feel how good and happy it makes you feel.

It takes time and it takes dedication but it is so worth it - give it a go!

Interjection

At this point I want to say that I am not sure whether or not this book is being channeled by some Godly force or whether my thought process and dedication to service and 'duty' has controlled the writing of this book, but I want to make it known that at every point, so far, I have experienced the feeling that goes with the particular section of the book that I am working on.

I have no attachment to either explanation, which, in itself, lends to recapturing wonder and amazement in life.

I will explain more in the Infinite Principle of Possibility but needed to put some real emotion behind the words to impart my devotion and KNOWING that this is my path of purpose and that by applying these principles they can truly help you.

In the next section I am about to embark on we look at the more wondrous aspects of living so personally I am glad to leave this more negative chapter behind, but needed to let you know that, either way, no matter what your beliefs or knowledge, the Art of Positive or Negative Living is very, very real. You get to choose!

No matter whether it is from God or from Science. It is Life as we experience it and you can experience it positively.

The Gifts Of Life - Choice, Chance, Change

I am sure that you have heard the saying "You have to make the CHOICE and take the CHANCE if you are ever going to CHANGE".

I actually hadn't heard it or should I say really acknowledged it until I had already embraced the principle. I like to think of it a Decisive Choice, Decisive Chance and Decisive Change.

You see you have to choose to accept this next section and you have to take the chance that it might help change the situation.

I did. It was the best thing too. I have never been let down by the Gifts in Life.

Following on from the Art of Positive Living in the last section, the Gifts of Life just seem to sail along beside the same principle.

You see once you start looking on the Brighter Side of Life and you have made the CHOICE to live from the Art of Positive Living then your own personal flow starts to gain its own momentum and take on a life of its own.

You can't let down your guard though. No matter how many times the demons of negativity and laws of destruction come knocking, you need to keep believing.

That is why I call this next section the Gifts of Life. They are there, as gifts, if you CHOOSE to accept them.

So get those brain muscles into Positive Flow again.

Decide to make Positive Choices.

Decide to take Positive Chances.

Decide to make Positive Changes.

Hope

Hope is a beautiful thing. It is gentle, it is safe, it is steadfast and always there when you need it like a mother's love.

It is so soft that lots of people dismiss its very existence. I was even asked recently if I thought that there was any such thing as hope and was it really our intuition, our 'knowing'.

For me, there is a definite distinction between the two. Hope has a very real place in your life when you are desperate, when your world has spun out of your control and you have no clue, let alone resource to do anything about it. Knowing (our intuition) can only be released when we are not in fear.

When you are at a low ebb. When you are in fear. When you are cold. When you are hungry. When you have no money or home. When your health is failing. When your child is hurt or missing. When you have not found a job. When your debts far outweigh your income. When your heart has been thrown aside by a lover or a friend. When you are stuck in a world that from the outside looks perfect but from deep within your soul it is just an empty space. This is when you can call on the Gift of Hope, the Wise Old Woman who leads the Gift as an Elder would lead his tribe. Passing on wisdom, making you feel safe and holding you until you feel a little better.

I know Hope. She is kind and compassionate. She is nonjudgmental and she lives in that piece of our heart that is sacred and can be called on in emergencies. She isn't loud or obnoxious and doesn't mind if you don't even notice her, but when you need her she can always be relied upon.

When you are curled up and your heart is breaking and your head has stopped processing any helpful or useful thoughts, you can reach down into that sacred place and call her name.

She will come to your aid just as soon as you open the passage and cosset you in her bosom until you are ready and strong enough to face the world again.

She gently whispers in your ear 'Hope, my dear, have Hope - I give it freely and you need only take it' and whilst soothing you she rocks you to a better place and introduces you to her friends.

Trust

Trust is Hope's best friend. They are joined at the hip and run from the same sacred strand. Trust is the stronger of the two. Just about the same age but with a more rugged temperament. If you need help moving on from Hope, then Trust is your woman.

She presents herself with cynical humor that makes it hard to latch on to in the first instance. But once you get to know her you realize that this is just her way of testing you. Once you have gained her, she will be your stalwart and never fail you. She may run off occasionally in order to ensure that she has your attention or even turn up in a completely different guise but she is there to just be.

She knows that, but she needs you to know that too.

She needs you to trust her! She needs you to trust yourself! She needs you to trust Hope! She has you in training to lean back and Trust your journey. To ride the waves of Ebb & Flow with grace, with dignity and for those waves to be able to carry you to your highest heights and to those dreams you haven't even dared to dream.

Leaning back into Trust helps your foundation. It helps you regain your balance and ensure you find your Magnificent Equilibrium.

She knows you are meant for great things and she needs you to be ready for them. To gain her Trust is to Trust in her. To trust your knowledge, your wisdom, your divine path, your sacred destination in order to share your gifts you must be prepared and Trust knows that the waves are not always kind. She needs you to know that she is there for you every step of the journey. That you are not alone. That you are enough.

She needs you to trust that all will be revealed in the end and that, as a woman, you in your heart of hearts, know that the time has come for the divine feminine energy to become a gentle force of reckoning.

She needs you to trust your own skills, your own experience, your own passions and your gifts. She needs you to trust your own sacred journey.

She needs you to enjoy this journey and to take up gentle arms against the power of destruction, together with your sisters. She needs you to remember your ancient, wise feminine leadership. She needs you to join your sisters to lead the world and future generations in a way that nurtures, is kind and compassionate and lets peace reign. She needs you to remember that this is a truth. She needs you to Trust this truth.

She needs you to Trust that whatever you want to do is right. That feminine intuition is as real as gut instinct and deserves to be seated side by side with its masculine counterpart, to soothe any conflict and resolve worldly issues with kindness and compassion.

Her humor is derived from knowing that the path you chose to follow, or even have to follow, is yours to make the best with. Sometimes you will become angry with her but she is not afraid of your anger. She will never turn her back on you and will always be there to get you through.

Trust is the woman for you once you have let Hope into your heart. There are many other Gifts and Tools that I will remind you of as we go along, but Hope is your anchor whilst Trust is helping you ride the waves.

Faith & Belief

I believe that these two rascals are like two peas in a pod. They are like teenagers and they are always right! They have great respect for Hope and Trust but they are still finding their way. Always trying to outdo one-another when, if they really look closely, they are wanting the same things.

They are politically charged and religiously motivated and neither is ever wrong, although they are always changing their mind! Every once in a while they realize that they both want the same thing and can give each other those gifts. They realize that they are one and the same if they just use their kind and compassionate heart.

They change their style, give themselves different names and compete for one-up-woman-ship. At the end of the day, though they know their own value and, although they can feel tested and unheard at times, they always come back to a safe home when they rely upon one another, and sit at the hearth with Trust and Hope.

Faith is always being tested and one's Belief is often shunned but, like teenagers throughout the ages, they get through it and grow up, believable and faithful to their core.

When they get to this stage of their lives they look back and see that, when kindness and compassion are leading them, all Faiths and Beliefs are basically saying the same things.

They become comfortable in their own skin. Proud of who they have become and ready to share their purpose with the rest of the world.

No matter what your Belief or Faith is, as long as you are working from a kind and compassionate place, your God, your Universe, your Soul or Heart can be safe in any of your beliefs and your faith can be a savior.

Love

L ove is the newborn baby! She needs Hope and Faith and Trust and Belief to ensure her wellbeing.

She is pure, unabashed joy in a bundle. She is helpless and yet so strong as she has been born in every single one of us. She is our future. She is of our ancestors. She is the link to bind us and the light to guide our way.

She must be nurtured and fed with happiness. She cries out to be heard when she is in need.

She is the epitome of Being. She is life at its best. She is living in all of us. The child of perfection that smells so sweet and feels so soft.

She brings out the best in us. She ensures that we are grounded in mutual energy and never stops Being.

She is omnipresent. She is kindness, she is compassion, she is empathy, she is non-judgment. She is unity and individuality and must be shared with the world.

To completely take care of Love, she needs to know that she is taken care of. She needs to know that she is at the top of your list of desires and needs. She needs to be carried all day, resting at your bosom and assured.

She is the Gift that everyone wants. She is the Gift that everyone needs. She is sometimes so tiny that you only catch a glimpse of her hair peeking from below the swaddling but at other times she can hold an audience enthralled with her laughing elixir.

Don't be fooled by an impostor of Love. She is always pure. She will never need anything more than Love. She will not come in disguise although sometimes you have to look closely and not miss her.

She is buried in the heart of all of us, the Sweetest, most precious Gift of Love. She is a yearning that you cannot run from. Acceptance of our desire for Love, our need for Love and the Endless Possibilities that we can replicate from Love is what each of us are ultimately made for, and from, The Ultimate Paradox, The Universal Truth and The Golden Heart and the Earthly Core of Humankind and the World.

Forgiveness & Permission

Forgiveness is the Mother of the Universe. She is the big one, The Mother of the Unknown. She is the bridge between who we are and who we want to be. She is the only one who can offer us redemption.

She sits above us and places her hand upon our heads, releasing us from our burdens. She has a firm grip on all that we could be but knows that we are attached to our Permission, The Mother of the Earth, our primal mother, whose first instinct is to protect our survival. Both are there for us and not against us, Forgiveness, an ethereal being, light and bright. Although she is of the Unknown does not mean that she, herself is unaware. Forgiveness gives of herself freely. She knows that the most we can ever do on this plane is to accept her and so she gives her blessing to everything for which we are truly sorry. She accepts that we will continue to make mistakes and until we cross the bridge to the unknown, there will always be a place for her.

Permission is our Earthly Mother, swathed in a vein of Gold wrapped up in leaves of instinct; she is only thwarted by our evolving conscience. She has always been there but the need for her grows stronger as we grow further from her grip. The vein of Gold dissipating as we think our need for primal instinct becomes less.

We, as is always, need them both. These Mothers who give us their energy freely and never stop releasing us from what is holding us back.

You are Love.

You can trust yourself.

You can have faith in yourself.

You can believe in your dreams.

You can forgive yourself.

You can give yourself permission.

You are Enough.

The Tools Of Life

Introduction

The beauty of the Tools of Life is that they are all available for us to gather.

There are varying levels of all of them and society is very good at letting us know that we are better, because we gather more of them.

What I want to let you know at this stage is that there are ways, no matter where you are now, where you come from or where you want to get to, that enable you to increase any of these tools.

You set your own limitations. You decide when you have enough. You decide what you will use and what you will learn. You decide how and where you will gather more.

Yes, there are circumstantial elements that come into play. Things like where you live, what your expenses are, what you have been told to do and what you have been exposed to, but essentially you are the only person that can put limits on these tools.

I am not saying that any of these Tools of Life come without any sort of Action, and in this instance the word Action is a euphemism for work. Work can become something that you enjoy though that enables you to become one with who you are and how you do in life.

I have enjoyed periods of my life when I am happy utilizing and gathering only some of these Tools. There are times in my life when some of my skills have been used more prolifically than others. Where I have used my time rather than my experience or talents in necessity to gather money, in order to just survive. There are other times where I have used everything I have and not gathered much of anything, but utilized all that I have in order to live my life to the full and be extraordinarily happy.

Only you can decide what that is right now. Remember, too, that your needs and gathering ability will change with the tide of life. As long as you are using the Tools in your Kit for what you need, then you will know how much time and energy you have to gather more.

Money

Money. Some say that it is the route of all evil. Some feel it is the route to eternal happiness. It is neither. It is just a tool that is recognized throughout our world as a way to measure the value of our needs and desires.

Take the energy from Money and you are left with a knowledge that anything is possible. Take the value from Money and know also that it can buy us any possibility. It is but a Tool.

I am not saying that it isn't necessary. It is. In the western world we buy everything from water to handbags, we donate to charity and invest in property. I do not have the answer to living without it and at this stage in my life I do not feel that I would be able to achieve a calm and peaceful society by doing so. In this accord I seek to make us comfortable with money, for us to start living with it as an exchange and not as a weapon.

Only you can decide how much money you need. In order to do this you have to decide want you want from life, how you want to move forward and then link it to a plan that helps you take action on your Desired Destination.

You need to take steps to further your journey and only you know what that journey looks like. Do your Steps as Masterpieces all link up with a gradual pathway to your destination, or are they more like a ladder to climb?

Either way, you have to know the direction you want to take and also be comfortable with doing everything that needs to be done in order to travel in comfort and to enjoy the ride.

Nobody wants to be comfortable in lacking but you do have to be honest about your levels of desire. Nothing is wrong with your decision here except for your alignment with it.

Depending on your personal circumstance, your level of need will be ascertained by giving your own energy to the traveling time and speed!

You may be in a situation where you think there is no way to gather more money. There is always a way it just depends on the energy behind the intention, that determines whether your desires are always out of reach or highly attainable and decorative (for your Masterpiece Step)!

I have been without money and still gathered. I have been with money and had to make do with decoration! I now live with both in mind and intend to gather more of all of the Tools of Life as I go along.

I, you see, do not mind being a Gatherer. A Gatherer is a worker. A Gatherer takes Action. A Gatherer enjoys Gathering and A Gatherer leaves a trail of Masterpieces behind her!

It is always a lot easier to gather money if you have a Desired Destination or Goal to gather for.

No matter whether your Destination is a long way away or just around the corner it is much easier to work with something specific to work and gather for.

You must be true to yourself, though, and to the Desired Destination.

You will not get to your next stop, or step, without Action and your journey will be more tiring and lengthy if you decide to divert and go the scenic route, via an expensive handbag, holiday or deviate from the route altogether.

You must also never feel guilty about measuring your own value, either. If you have something to give (your gifts), you can use money to give it. Likewise, if you decide that you want something of value, you must be prepared to pay the value placed on it by its seller.

There is nothing complicated in the system. It is just our perception of Money that has permeated our society, to have obscene levels of value on essentials and poor value on individuality, creativity and global need.

As with all things, if you deliver value with kindness and compassion at a level that is affordable to your audience, you cannot go wrong.

Once you are in alignment and have become used to the Ebb & Flow and found your own Personal Rhythm, this will become easier.

Also, circumstance might dictate value, disabling you to reach for the step above the next. That is also OK as finding a way to envisage, implement and action the next stage of your journey will become a part of that Masterpiece.

Do not blame others. It does not help you. Do use any way you can, legally and morally to gain and gather more money in order for you to climb the steps, or retain your momentum, so that you do not lose sight of your Divine Destination and become trapped.

This is not necessarily by gaining more money but it may involve a maintenance plan. You may have to start thinking differently if your circumstances are such that you have necessary needs that need to be taken care of on a daily basis.

We are so lucky that we have such a transient, virtual community space in which to gather knowledge. Use it. If you can get a job to cover the cost for comfort, *Get* that job. It will give you the security to dream bigger and create a more Divine Step or even Destination. Even if the job is boring, *Use* it. This is time to think. If the job is a dead end - start Gathering from the other Tools of Life.

There are no limitations in the western world. If you have no water, no home, no health, no transport. These are issues. If you are able to read this and write then there is no limit to your personal travel plans. Only you can plan your journey. Make sure it suits you!

Education

F ormal education is a wonderful thing but it isn't everything.

The grades you get when you work hard do wonders when it comes to opening the doors of your chosen career or further education and if you have gone down that route I applaud you.

There are some things Education does not educate you about in the western world, though, and there are some things that I feel are sadly missing within our ever transient society.

It fails to allow you to learn the path of life. It fails to equip the masses with common sense and most of all it fails to equip anyone with the most sought after meaning of life - love.

Now I know that education plays a huge part in how we live and grow in our society but for the best part of a couple of centuries it has set to increase the class system and allow judgment and compassion to be left to politics and religion, which we all know is like trying to mix oil with water.

You must not degrade any education that you have received formally, though, as it will impact your life forever more.

The one thing that you must continue to do in order to attain happiness is to keep on learning.

Education has full stops in the world at the moment and in the formal education route. That is helpful when defining a job specification and qualifications to apply for many aspects of life, as we know it, but the value of constantly and consistently Gathering knowledge has been lost, due to the fact that once a certificate has been received, for most, it is put somewhere safe and not given another thought.

It is the Gathering of Knowledge over a lifetime, up to and including death, that is one of the true forms of magic and mystery that make life worth living.

I know there are many of you that will have read and continue to read and to educate yourself both formally and for personal development but there are so few people who actually embrace the Gathering of Knowledge as though it is as much a miracle as Gathering Money.

One of the main problems we have as a woman is that we are unable to trust a bit of knowledge enough to have the courage to put it into practice.

It is a bit like opening a recipe book and starting at the beginning and deciding to make the first dish that really catches your eye. The first time you make it, it is a flop. It is burnt or not cooked and you blame the recipe. You may try the same recipe from the same book again or you may look for the same recipe in another book. You may not even like the recipe at all but keep on trying to get the end result to look like the picture that originally sparked your taste buds.

Sometimes you have to put your knowledge into practice.

Sometimes you may serve up a dish that may not be perfect. You may keep trying. You may look elsewhere and you may give up entirely. I bet you wouldn't serve it at a dinner party though until you have made it picture and taste bud perfect so that you can put the dish on the table with pride.

Us girls are a bit like that. We never think we are knowledgeable enough. We always feel that we should read the next journal, find the next best thing, practice a little more or take more training.

I say we embrace Education always. We Gather it as we go along but don't ever let education get in the way of giving yourself an opportunity.

We have to be more willing to take a few more risks and Gather as we go along.

Take a few chances and read the synopsis or 'how to' if you need to but it will never matter how much Education you Gather unless you share your gifts. There will always be someone ahead of you but there will always be someone trying to catch up to you, too, and it is your job to share all your Gathered knowledge in your own way, from a kind and compassionate place as you walk your path.

Presently formal education does not embrace mindfulness enough to enable all children to be comfortable sitting, thinking, listening, observing, feeling and understanding their intuition. It does not encourage enough compassion. It does not encourage enough kindness and it certainly does not encourage us to conquer the world issues that we all have to face and are bombarded with as soon as we are able to acknowledge them.

It is our job, as women, to do this. No matter how far up the chain of Education you may be or how low you perceive your place in the scheme of things, we have the answers to what the world needs, now.

This is within you and I. If you have nothing else to light your flame then I hope that this may help spark something inside you.

If being educated or the lack of education holds you back from following that spark, then don't let it. All of your sparks can be brought together to light a huge fire and we need to shine light on the world. Together we can make the world a better place.

Skills

I love Skills. Sometimes they are sadly overlooked but I make a mean family dinner and have organized some rip-roaring get-togethers in my time, I enjoy it.

I learnt to cook from my mother, friends and family, especially my grandfather, who was a rambunctious chef in his day. I learnt to entertain by watching my elders when putting together shows and theatrical evenings.

I took those skills with me throughout my life and applied them to all of my jobs. I didn't pay them heed at all but I realized quite late in life that not everyone was comfortable or even thought about the skills involved to do well in either cooking a full meal or planning an event.

All of your skills are useful. Make a list of all of your skills to find out what you can do more of what you enjoy.

Some people are good with children from an early age and yet don't even acknowledge that as a skill. I am in awe of them as being a mother was not a natural skill set for me!!!!

Some people are good at keeping the house tidy or very beautiful (another thing that I am not a natural at). Some people are good at fishing or mending things or fashion or repurposing.

Some people are really good at DIY or crafting. Whatever your skills are they can become more of a player in your life if you just acknowledge them and include them, however possible. And it is always possible, in your life.

Do you make jam? Do you knit? Do you read? Do you paint? Do you dance? Do you sing? Are you a natural comedian or writer of poetry or lyrics?

We have a very big issue about including all of our skills in our daily life or acknowledging them in the first place.

The thing about *skillage* (do you like my youth talk?) is that we very rarely notice them, as they are the things that we automatically do without any fear, any self- recrimination and expect others to do them also.

That is certainly not always, and very often not at all, the case. The Skills that you have are yours to exploit easily! How cool is that?

Experience

Experience is different from Skills, as you Gather Experience with the Knowledge that you are Gathering them, if you get my drift.

Whilst Skills are Tools of Life that you very rarely notice you are acquiring, Experience you can look back and see exactly where you started the learning process and you were aware of Gathering and learning more and more about the process.

To explain this a little clearer, I know that I learnt rhythm during music and piano classes and I learnt a little more from tap and ballet. When I left the UK and went to live in South Africa, I was unable to carry on but I did keep on Gathering my experience of them and although I can not read music, I am pretty good at being in time, in rhythm and I have gathered more dancing experience through being involved in musicals and stage work, and more experience of rhythm and its importance in my life through working in the music industry and singing in a band.

I was able to transfer those experiences and let them help lead my personal Divine Direction in all that I have done throughout my life. (Except for that bit in the middle I have told you about when I exchanged happy authentic Alex for the person she thought she should be)!

What experience have you had? Another few things that I have had experience in and that have given me more awareness have been working as a cash register operator in a local supermarket, being one of two 'white' girls working for an Indian family in a right wing town during apartheid in South Africa!!! Being treated badly for that because of the color of my skin and yet feeling proud of what I was doing and learning and by earning my own money. Though I was upset at the injustice and hatred that most of the country I had learned to call my home was blanketing one another with.

I also helped to teach drama in the townships close to where I lived with my stand-in literature teacher, who was also against apartheid. We had to keep this secret as it was against the law at the time but I loved drama so much and knew its value in empowering individuals so much, I did not care.

What have you experienced in your life? What experiences have you gathered?

Just in these short stories alone I have shown that the experiences we have are not necessarily just from what we have done but also form our awareness of situations and of injustices that occur.

They are usually fueled by passion either from something we love or from something we are making a stand against, or at least help us form those opinions and become more aware of our experiences. Where and how we experienced them helps us to see if they are indeed helpful or useful, now.

I was lucky or unlucky but I chose to pick the former. I need to employ these Experiences here and now, to not only show you how I formed my ideas but to show you that the method I used was as useful and needed, then as it is now. I know that my experience from learning to listen to rhythm and by gaining confidence through drama is something that others need and would be of extreme benefit to most people. I also know that leaders will be created by empowerment and if I had not gained this experience I would not be able to pass this Experience on.

Every Experience, good or bad, can help share your story, your expertise or your gifts.

Every Experience and Gathered Experience makes you more able to pass on kindness and compassion and to show people, either in a physical gift or in a gift of knowledge, why this experience was needed for you. How it has impacted your life and how it can impact theirs.

Time

Time is a wonderful Tool and I also see it as one of the most precious Gifts of Life, so it was hard for me to categorize in this area. In modern society it is featured more as a Tool than as a Gift, so I have put it in here, for now, but hopefully, once you master your own personal rhythm, you will be able to use time as a marker for congregation and just to sync with others, rather than for personal flow.

I find Time best spent in the moment daydreaming about ways I can share my gifts and taking action to achieve this. I have integrated my life to such an extent that I do not waste a precious moment.

I had to spend a very long period of my life with Time. I spent it worrying, asking 'why me?' Waiting for appointments, looking at my watch to see when my next dose of medication was due, counting the hours until I could go home and basically not enjoying the moments that I had.

Now, I know that this enables me to understand others who have gone through or who are presently experiencing this type of anxiety, but Time did not produce anything for me until I decided to embrace the moment and really feel what I was going through, good or bad. I utilized the Time to think about how I would create, package and action all the Time that I was spending.

I have now been able to take multi-tasking to another, invisible but highly productive level.

You see, when I am doing the tasks that are historically done by a woman for example, cooking, cleaning, walking the dog or shopping, I make sure that I truly get the most from them.

The first thing I do is take a minute to see what it is that I need to think about for myself before I take on these tasks to make the best use of the time and to enjoy the whole process. I feel in my body what action I need to take and that dictates what I think about, try to soothe, create or mastermind with myself during these tasks. What I call now, Down Time. It gives me respite from my business tasks and forces me to think about the bigger picture or just life.

I then automatically and joyfully use the time that I have purposefully. Whether I meditate, contemplate, chant, dance, sing, use call and response or just strategize, I know that the time I am using is being used On Purpose.

You can never get Time back and it is wise to remember that like any other Tool it is possible to waste it quite easily!

I know that traditional Time management is always helpful in creating an overall structure but the best way to enjoy every moment and to be present is to allow that structure to be flexible.

If you are late, call. If you are early, use the time wisely. It you are running to catch a train, enjoy the beating of your heart and if you are stuck in a traffic jam, sing! Whatever your Time allows you and whatever Time you are at, both personally and from a work perspective, don't let it rule you.

In today's modern society we are so wrapped up in the management of the moment that we all too often forget to really Be in the moment.

As I learnt from having my Time dictated to me, I had to learn to Be OK with that. Sitting in a queue and waiting for the doctor or nurse to call your name meant my life depended on it, literally. I had to trust that Time would come, use that Time usefully and manage my reaction to the Time passing.

I became so adept at waiting and waiting Purposefully that it started to decrease my waiting Time.

As those whom I was waiting for realized that I was happy after waiting greater lengths of Time they either decided to see me first because I was happier or gave me better service because I was patient. As I have embraced this attitude to Time further in my life, I find that the outcomes I get seem to work perfectly.

I choose to see everything as perfect - it does seem to work better and increases everything in my life from Flow to Joy.

Talent

Talent is different from both Skills and Experience in that it is something that you are born with. You are inherently good at.

Talent can be honed and you can become more skillful at it and you can obviously gain more experience the more you devote your energy to it, but ultimately if you are good at something you should bring it into your everyday life.

No matter how old you are, what your circumstances are or where you are, when you are good at something it would be a downright shame not to use it.

These are your natural gifts.

If you can sing, you can sing. If you can't, well then, 'nuff said!

If you are a natural dancer, skater, artist, designer, creator, sportswoman, caretaker, engineer, fixer, gardener, farmer or inventor then you should nurture your gifts. Learn to be at one with them.

Bring them into your life so that they are a part of you and not something that you used to be or do.

If you think about what your talents are and they don't necessarily fit into the life you are leading or want to lead then it is time for you to think differently about them.

For me, I was a dancer before I could walk. I could wiggle my nappy next to any baby but as I grew older I forgot about it.

Yes, I would go out and have a boogie but in my way of thinking now, I want it to be something that I do everyday. Just a little wiggle, not too much but enough to do all of the things it should.

It should make me feel alive, feel good, feel vibrant and part of the world. It should make me move my body so that I don't have to go to the gym but so that it is a part of my life and my moment of Being. It should get me to connect to my core, to my known self, to the unknown and feel at peace with myself and the earth and everything.

I feel almost spiritual when I get lost in dance. I am ethereal and nobody can come between "my universe" and me.

What can you lose yourself in, *or*, if you don't anymore, What did you used to lose yourself in?

Whether you have to go back to last week or when you were a baby try to think of something that you used to do that stopped your Time. Something that was all consuming and nothing around you mattered.

Something that you excel in - even if you don't want to admit it or it scares the shit out of you!!!

Six Senses - Vision

What can you see? No, I mean really see. Is it a room, a window, a sky or Infinite Possibility? That is what I see now.

I am so grateful for my sight, especially seeing as I am a bit of a nosey girl as well as a greedy one.

I get to observe the everyday. I see things in rooms that most people take no notice of. There are some things that I miss of course but I do like a good look around!

I do choose to look more closely at things that are beautiful to me though. I turn my head away when my core being is not able to deal with what it sees. I am the director in this movie. It is my creation. Whichever streets I walk down I choose to cross the road if there is less litter or no neglected property on the other side. If I get a choice of scenic route or shortest on my internal GPS system in my heart I will always choose scenic. That helps me to live in the moment and to BE. I will look for gargoyles on buildings and stained glass windows in doors. I appreciate the beauty and imagine the history behind them.

When I look through a window I see which routes I have yet to discover or watch as the clouds form silhouettes in the sky.

When I look at a leaf at my feet I choose to see the veins and its color in all of its glory and when I look at flowers I see which way they face and look to see what they are seeing. I play games with the seasons and watch for the bulbs to graze the frozen soil and set my Time constraints with when they shall blossom so that my rhythms are in harmony with nature.

When you see the sun playing outside do you follow its' rays to see where their sparkles are leading you or when the moon beams down do you see what glitters in its path?

Do you look into the old mans eyes and see the stories he holds in his heart? Do you see the tiredness written on a young mother's face as she darts between people on the sidewalk with her baby looking straight into your soul? Do you watch the commuters storming their way through the swarms of workers all heads bowed low so as not to have to deal with another on a human level or perhaps catch the fleeting glance of someone watching you?

When I cross the road I wait until the car has stopped and thank the driver with a wave or a smile. Just this in itself has saved my life on a couple of occasions, as I find that some drivers look away and do not see a pedestrian crossing nor the pedestrian crossing!

I long for a returned smile as it lights up my soul and I give them away freely, as I have mentioned. Real, big, juicy smiles are a rarity nowadays but I get gifted them sometimes and they make my heart sing.

I love watching children play and see if I can recreate that in my step. I love watching people become other people in the theatre or on a movie screen.

I love sitting quietly and watching the candles glitter in their crystal holders in the breeze and for the candle in a Buddha statue's lotus filled hand light up his face, as I sit in gentle agreement and mimic his lazing Buddha's cheeky and yet knowing grin.

I watch the smoke come through the chimney tops in London and from the bonfires in the countryside in Spain. I see the wind playing tag with a stranger's hat as he runs and tries to catch it!

These are the wonderful things that I see AND the way in which I choose to see them but they have also helped me create and devise products and target markets and helped me with research, doing it in a way that feeds my Soul Purpose.

Just yesterday I was on the London Underground and noticed that all of the advertisements were aimed at my core Golden Compass themes. Instilling even more confidence in what I know to be true but also seeing what and how London marketeers appeal to their core audience.

At this moment I sat in my seat and felt slightly bemused as I watched the other passengers just looking at their feet. You see I want to appeal to their hearts, not just to the soles of their feet or their eyes that are looking away at the advertisements only to avoid eye contact with anyone. And as I sit and watch them I want to reach out and help but know that I am a simple, madwoman. That, as a matter of fact, is quite OK with me. Unfortunately, most people still have aversions to simple, mad women so I have to package my gifts in this visual and more societally accepting manner so that they appeal to them and this amuses me more.

You see, no matter what I feel. I have to appeal to you in order to even get your attention. It doesn't matter how much good I want to do, I have to do it in a modern manner.

What do you see? Do you see Infinite Possibilities and Potential in every moment? Are you able to experience them in your core, in your soul or in your Being?

Try to start painting, the colors, the textures and its calming influence no matter how rubbish you are at it, to begin with.

Try getting your favorite colors in whatever you feel would brighten your world.

Try looking at pictures and buildings and nature and really seeing what speaks to your inner core.

Try seeing your closest family and friends in a different way.

Try seeing interactions between people, animals and nature and machine.

Six Senses - Sound

What can you hear? No, I mean really hear. Is it the tapping of rain, the beat of a drum or a hammer or a plane or Infinite Possibility? That is what I hear, now.

I am so grateful for my hearing. I don't mind if there are bangs and crashes, whispers and chanting, rock music or happy clapping. I love all sounds. I choose to love sounds as this adds to my awareness and my learning.

I can feel the sounds in my body. I can get lost and found in music whilst I dance, chant or sing along to a call and response ditty.

Whether I object to it or not doesn't make me hear it less, so I embrace sound in whatever form it is gifted to me. It doesn't have to take away my moment of bliss, unless I choose to make it do so.

Obviously I choose what I listen to when it is in my hands but, being a mother and a partner and a colleague and a friend, this isn't always the case.

So instead of turning the TV down when my son's favorite cartoon comes on I choose to wait to hear his raucous laughter. Instead of changing the music when my partner is working, I choose to watch his head bounce up and down in time with his headphones on. Instead of insisting that the neighbors turn down the music at midnight whilst having a party, I choose to enjoy the laughter and the pool games and, ok that last one might be a bit of a fib because it is what I wish my neighbors would do when we have a party but you get my drift!!!

What do you think when you hear a plane overhead? Does it make you mad or can you try to imagine where it came from and whom it holds and what they might be doing.

When you listen to your television do you just hear what is being said or do you try to figure out who wrote it and see if how they wrote it makes the storyline more appealing?

When you listen to someone talking do you hear what comes from their lips or do you try to understand what is in their heart?

When you listen to your loved ones do you hear their words and their tone of voice, or try to fathom what is going on that you can heal?

I do enjoy a frivolous conversation now and again but I am not very good at remembering them, as I have usually been given a glass of Cava or a coffee or a chocolate and what comes out of my mouth is usually a script good enough to do stand-up with, and that in itself is therapeutic.

I listen to my own words, to my own voice and to what I say so that most of the time I am at peace with what is delivered from brain to mouth. Sometimes I get it wrong and sometimes I put my foot in it.

I listen and I talk and then I listen some more.

I listened to my body and what it told me - it scared me for a while and then, when I was calm enough to not be afraid of it, I understood it better.

I listen to the souls in the wind, the sparks in someone's anger, the pride in someone's tone. I listen to the crackle of paper, of fire and of ice.

I listen to the birds sing and wonder what they say. I listen to the raindrops and listen to the grey. I listen to the sunshine as it gently warms my face and I listen to the moonshine lighting up the way.

I listen to the agony of those who cannot say, what they really mean or in the correct way.

I listen to the call of hope that rings from tree to tree and I listen to the preacher who is ranting 'Hell for thee'.

I listen to the kind words that the people want to share only to be misheard and thwarted with a scorn.

I listen to a stranger's eyes and open up my heart and I listen to the children's breath that sings just like a harp.

I listen to the world around and want to share the awe, to all of you, my gentle friends, for you to all adore.

I gently ride the ebb and flow of life upon the way, and want to give you everything to make a better day.

What do you hear? Do you hear Infinite Possibilities and Potential in every moment? Are you able to experience them in your core, in your soul or in your Being?

Six Senses - Touch

What can you feel? No, I mean really feel. Does it feel soft or shaky or does it feel like Infinite Possibility?

This is what I feel now.

I am so grateful for my sense of Touch. The first time I was really captivated by ability to feel and my sensory nerves were heightened was not through an epiphany but on a regular workday.

I was the manager for a music studio in Soho, London when I really felt something special. I was 29 years old and I was washing my hands. The water was cool as it washed over me and I was lost in the sensation of it. I really, really felt it, its connection to me, its connection to nature, and the connection between us.

I know this isn't the most profound statement or the most elegant. The taps were old fashioned and the sink had seen better days but I was so completely devoured by the moment I shall hold it dear for the rest of my life.

No major awakening. Not a spiritual enlightenment. Just a clear and ecstatic moment of belonging to the world.

From that moment onwards I savored washing my hands, especially when I could really feel the water. I then explored with warm water in wintertime and then swishing my hands in the pool or gently allowing myself to be supported by the waves in the ocean.

Ebb and Flow was born within me. There was no going back.

For those of you who have been incapacitated and had to stay in bed a long time I know that you will understand my next stage.

I became obsessed with linen, of changing my sheets and changing the fabric conditioner with the seasons and my mood. I loved the touch of cotton and the fleecy blankets that I could envelope myself in. I lounged in luxury in my very cheap but oh, so comfortable pajamas and dressing gown. I made sure that I bought socks that made my feet bounce and recently I discovered silky underwear.

Never one for extravagance, I am the thrifty type and with no boobs to brag about, had never even considered that I might get sophisticated or worthy enough to enjoy such glamorous, frivolous garments.

I love touching the fur on my dog. I love touching sand. I love touching earth between my toes. Grass that is soft and grass that is coarse.

I love warmth underfoot and look for places where the sun has shone just to bath in this simple pleasure.

I love to cuddle. Little cuddles, Big cuddles and Huge Bear Hugs.

I love touching a loved ones skin. I love touching a strangers arm, in empathy, in joy or in jest.

I love touching bark on trees and stone on walls, connecting with the energy of both. I don't care if anyone sees, as it is what I feel that is important and I can give them my energy and they can give me theirs, we don't have to know as it is an automatic transfer.

I love making dough and kneading bread. I love the feeling I get when I meditate and I connect with above and below and I am a vessel - I am restored by feeling - by touch and by sensing which part of my body needs attention.

I am still learning to touch the inanimate and receive the energy from manmade articles. I have to remind myself that everything comes from the world and even if what we make is not good, it still has value and energy.

What do you touch? Do you touch Infinite Possibilities and Potential in every moment? Are you able to experience them in your core, in your soul or in your Being?

Six Senses - Taste

"Failure is the condiment that gives success its flavor" - Truman Capote

What can you taste? No, I mean really taste. Does it taste sweet or savory or does it taste like infinite possibility? That is what I taste now.

I am so grateful for my sense of taste. Did I mention that I am a greedy girl?

During one of the periods of my illness and just after one of the procedures of my sinuses, I lost my sense of smell and therefore my sense of taste was affected tremendously. This gave me a whole different meaning to taste once it finally returned.

I so love my food. I so love the coolness and different flavors of water. Where I grew up in Uitenhage, South Africa, we were fortunate enough to have natural spring water on tap and we were so proud and so grateful whenever we went anywhere else as we could taste the difference easily.

In Spain after a storm, the tap water becomes incredibly dirty and so you are made aware of the luxury of water and I am fully aware that even the humble drop can come in so many forms.

During my experiences in life I have enjoyed my food but my likes and dislikes have changed dramatically. The way I think affects my taste. What I see affects my taste. How my body reacts and gets older and its ability to digest all affects my sense of taste.

One of my most favorite tastes now is bread and butter. Oh my, I could live on that if it were just my sense of taste at play. Unfortunately, my body says otherwise and I find it more difficult to tolerate both from a digestive and body weight point of view so living off bread and butter is not an everyday occurrence, but every now and again I indulge.

This has not diminished my life. In fact, it has enhanced it. I now totally immerse myself in the flavor and experience and the moment when I partake of a nice slice of bread and butter.

I really appreciate each mouthful, each texture and I allow the flavor to roll around my senses feeling sensuous and pleasure filled.

I do not have the luxury of being able to eat anything anymore. Whether it is from so much medication, the fact that I am getting older or a combination of both the fact is my body needs to be heard so I train myself to live simply and look forward to treats.

I have times when I completely overlook this self-induced rule, then I get to a place where I am uncomfortable and nothing tastes good, as all of my senses are out of personal alignment.

So when I am being a little stricter with myself, I find that my senses are heightened and then my pleasure is increased.

It took me years to find this out for myself and to listen to my senses and then, when I did, I made a pact with myself to follow and to enjoy their guidance, I was given the gift of heightened awareness AND heightened joy.

When I sit down to a seafood paella and a chilled glass of rosé, all of my taste buds are aroused and in turn enhance my other senses. I do not sit down to this every night but I love the routine of making an occasion out of this taste celebration. When we sit down as a family at a restaurant on the beach overlooking the Mediterranean sea - all of my senses retain the memory of joy, love, pleasure and taste, making the memory both something to look back on and look forward to.

When I sit down to a Sunday roast with my parents, the aroma and flavor of the gravy brings back memories of childhood and the complete happiness and acknowledgement of how fortunate I am is instilled with every mouthful.

When I indulge in a fast-food chicken meal with my son, every naughty and mischievous morsel is instilled with precious love.

When I take time out and go dancing with my man and have a cocktail or a beer or a Malibu, I completely get lost in the youthfulness and summer exuberance that these tastes are associated with in my mind, bringing my playfulness out and letting me laugh with abandon and kiss life without fear.

I sometimes make mistakes in what I taste but most of the time I savor and enjoy.

What do you taste? Do you taste Infinite Possibilities and Potential in every moment? Are you able to experience them in your core, in your soul or in your Being?

Six Senses - Smell

What can you smell? No, I mean really smell. The sweet scent of success or the odor of fear or do you smell the infinite possibility? That is what I smell now.

As I mentioned before I have had the occasion to live without a sense of smell and therefore I am incredibly grateful for the ability to smell the coffee or the roses.

My memories hold the scent of my grandmothers perfume, 'Pagan', intermingled with the faint hint of cigarette smoke. She was a strong woman and when I am reminded of this it immediately invokes my own strength, vulnerability and the awareness that I should live every moment to the full and make each moment count.

When I smell the rain, it instills the awareness of new beginnings and cleaning away the cobwebs of discontent.

When I smell bacon it evokes community spirit in its ability to persuade most of the family into each other's company almost magnetically or on remote control.

When I choose a perfume of my own, and I have one for the summer and one for the winter or day and night depending on my desires, it helps to define who I am, what I want to impart and the impression I would like to make.

When I hug my man, I gain comfort, security and love with my eyes closed and my senses infused.

When I smell baby, there is a purity that is combined with talc and softness and responsibility is heightened with the not so pleasant whiff of puke and poo!

When I smell my dog, I smell commitment and contentment and all that is free.

When I smell the socks of my son and his desire for man spray, I smell the inevitability of change and the sweet sorrow of passing time and immense pride all rolled into one.

When I smell the heat and it gets stuck in my nostrils and fills my lungs, I smell excitement and sparkle.

When I smell the first orange blossom of the year, my heart leaps and I cry and make the children roll down their windows, riding through the groves with the most positive songs playing in the background, enabling us to sing along together in the spirit of renewal and revival and the epitome of happiness. Creating a new tradition and ceremony of worship to the sweet, sensual and my most adored scent.

What do you smell? Do you smell Infinite Possibilities and Potential in every moment? Are you able to experience them in your core, in your soul or in your Being?

Six Senses - Intuition

What can you Know? No, I mean really Know. Is it a feeling, a certainty, a hunch or Infinite Possibility? That is what I Know, now.

I am so grateful for my intuition. I have included it in the senses as I just accept it. If I were a wealthy billionaire, you wouldn't doubt it if 'I was just following my gut' and therefore I include it as normal.

We are all aware of the phenomenon. What gets me is that in this day and age we are so influenced by proof and science that even if we all readily accept its existence, Intuition is still almost as taboo a subject in mainstream conversation, other than in emphasis that we do not actively study or engage in proving it.

The way I like to explain it and the ability to use it more readily is that it is very much like hunger. You know when you are hungry as you generally feel a grumble in your belly and start thinking about food and what food is available.

Intuition can be used and used more experientially in the same way.

When you are hungry and only have to feed yourself you can tap into your senses to see what you fancy, you can go to the fridge or the store cupboard and see what you have that is available to you, and then you can indulge accordingly.

When you have to plan a family meal. Most of the time this is done a little in advance as you have to ensure that there is enough for a family and that it meets dietary and family requirements.

When you plan a dinner party or celebration you have to start thinking about what you would like to serve quite ahead of time.

When most people tap into their intuition, the most acceptable and spoken sense that is used in everyday conversation is that of the immediate hunger.

It is OK to say that something just doesn't feel right in the immediate sense.

What is less accepted and more likely to raise an eyebrow or two is when you tap into that feeling for something that is in the near future.

What is practically never spoken about is when your Intuition plays a genuine part in your planning for business, life and your personal purposeful potential.

I would like to make this far more acceptable not only to be spoken about but in the excavation and employment of planning.

Rather than just thinking about your future or what you would like to happen, really try to feel how your intuition-based reaction to that thinking feels.

It is not as difficult as you would imagine. The only things coming between you and your intuitively based potential are usually external everyday influences.

So when you sit down to vision board or really think about how you would like your future to be, just spend some time cultivating and taking notice of how your intuition feels.

This does not mean excitement from a purchase of a brand new high-end vehicle or designer wardrobe. This means really owning the vision, stepping into the car and seeing if it would meet your requirements for that period of your life. Stepping into the designer wardrobe and seeing if it really works for you and how you want to feel and look to yourself and portray yourself to the world.

It takes practice. I know this because on my path to visibility I ruled out ever going on stage as I 'thought' that it wasn't necessary to my ongoing vision to save the world. I later realized that I was basing that thought on fear and not intuition.

My intuition, when I finally felt it and acknowledged it and then embodied it, showed me that it would be bloody scary, that I would have fear to face, but that getting back on stage would give me my USP (unique selling point) and would be perfect for branding and the embodiment of that brand.

By facing my fear I could really empower a larger audience, create more visibility and BE what I was providing.

Women, who lead by example, become empowered and want to work together to make the world a better place.

What I discovered was that my intuition could be as much a guide and business tool in my life than standard and acceptably included modern business strategies.

What can your ESP (extra sensorial perception) tell you about your USP?

What do you intuitively know? Do you intuitively know the Infinite Possibilities and Potential in every moment? Are you able to experience them in your core, in your soul or in your Being?

The Rhythm Of Infinite Energy - Ebb

We all know that at times 'Life is Shit'. In fact, when I was out with my cousin recently she added that this could be the tagline for this book! But, as you will probably now have gathered, I do not like harping on the negative and for this reason I have chosen to get the Ebb out of the way first in this section.

I am not saying that having an Ebb is all bad. Quite the contrary, actually. I just acknowledge them and make sure that I get something good from them. Either a learning, a gentle push or a deeper understanding, which usually leads to a solution. It is just the word I use for the challenges one faces in life.

The one thing I want to observe, though, is that they are never planned. You don't see them coming. They are usually really helpful or lead you to creating or enhancing your story or gifts, but at the time that is the last thing you can think of.

I have mostly spoken about how we can deal with the negative side of things in the 'Letting Go' Chapter. This section is more about how to deal with 'Ebbs' on a greater scale and so that they become part of riding the tide instead of complete stop signals.

When you start to think of life as a journey and a journey that you should enjoy, you also have to create a junction for the Ebbs of Life to be stationed and re-attached.

By having a mental place that, although not at the forefront of your mind, can readily assimilate and divert any immediate or chronic diversions to your journey, you not only deal with them more calmly and more quickly but they readily become a positive deviation from the original map.

In order to do this you have to acknowledge that, at times, 'Life is Shit' and by doing so it almost releases that immediate feeling of incapacitation. I am not saying that feeling the moment is any easier, it is just because you have the Emergency Planning Junction always available you have the where-with-all to make the best of a bad situation and deal with the situation from a place of expanded awareness. Therefore you can usually come up with a leadership plan of action that anyone will listen to or will take as the best decision.

By taking a step back from being directly involved in the heat of the moment (and I acknowledge that at times this is an impossibility so don't beat yourself up), you can usually get what is best for you. In other words - your own way.

As long as the junction is loaded with kindness, compassion, and thoughtful intuitive ways of looking at things, you can most certainly get your desired outcome.

No matter your circumstance. No matter where you are and no matter what you have.

Try to deal with bigger problems on paper (or electronically) and always employ the above principles of kindness, compassion and thoughtful intuition. Think about and describe everyone who is involved and their thoughts and emotions. Do not criticize. Do give a solution that benefits all and gets them all off the hook, yet gives you the outcome you desire and makes them look like the hero. Always keep correspondence. Always refer back if you are given a negative response and always look for mistakes made in these responses. There are almost always mistakes that you can point out in your favor if you keep up the character of the kind and knowledgeable person you are.

Even the little Ebbs we have can floor us for an amount of time that we haven't bargained for, an unkind word, a moment of being openhearted and not getting the expected response or no response at all.

An argument with a loved one. An illness. An unexpected change in plans. All of these things happen.

The secret in dealing with the Ebbs in order for them to be ridden more smoothly is to accept them and lead them gently to the junction where they can be encapsulated into the overall journey. Your plan can be changed with as little upheaval as possible and you can carry on, albeit on a slightly more scenic route, with your travels.

The more you do this, the less the Ebbs become an issue in your life. They become a part of life and you can gain much from them through co-existence without them making your path too rugged or the tide too rough.

The more you see the Ebbs of Life as a part of the journey and merely forks in the road that everyone has, you become more in control of your destiny, of your purpose and your ultimate potential increases exponentially.

Try seeing problems as perfect. Try to see diversions as blessings.

Try to see faults as lessons and your whole world will become more alive with wonder and with awe and with infinite possibilities.

The Rhythm Of Infinite Energy - Flow

Let it Flow, Let it Flow, Let it Flow!

I love Flow. I am inspired by Flow. I am in Flow. In sync with Flow. Just as nature Knows when it needs to change, for the seasons, for the weather, for evolution, I have learnt that for me to work and for my personal potential that Flow is the only time management I need to adhere to.

I use Flow for action and for learning. I accept what happens in my life that I have no control over and I accept what happens in my life that I can control.

I think about what happens, expand my awareness and try my best to keep traveling my journey, as if I am a half inch off the ground, gathering and utilizing my tools and my gifts in order to make the steps I need to take, masterpieces.

I like to visualize my personal flow as if I am riding the tide of life on a magic carpet. Gently gliding over the ups and downs of life and incorporating all that I see, I feel and am made aware of as I go.

As A Woman On Purpose, my mission has evolved and never stops evolving. In order to really get into Flow, it is crucial that this is accepted, acknowledged and encompassed in order for my mission to be on track.

This means that I have to go against the grain in some ways. This means that I have to use self-control and not be swayed by external influences, that I must really hone into my own Intuitive Flow in order to create, produce and take action.

I will use writing this book as an example.

I initially started writing my personal journey as a means to journal my story, to use in conjunction with and to gain market exposure for the Global Responsible Community I was hoping to create at first.

This was about seven years ago.

After the cranial reconstruction, when I was gravely ill, I blogged about my experience in real time as it was all the energy I had.

This was about four years ago.

When I was planning for the Global Responsible Community, I created a business plan and website.

This was three years ago.

When I took that business plan to an advisor I was encouraged to write a book, about my life and my experiences along with what I have learnt.

This is where I am now.

None of what I have written has been wasted. It hasn't been an easy journey but I have learnt a lot along the way and I now feel ready to write my purpose in the correct manner. For my previous writings were maudlin, angry and unable to convey what I truly wanted and knew I had to share with the world.

I didn't stop. I kept going. I changed. The writing changed. The end result changed and I am sure that there will be deviations along the way but I will never give up and I have no regrets.

I can look back and really access the memories and emotions that I felt at the time in order for me to be more empathic to others and to write with authority about those areas that I have experienced first hand.

I do set myself Flow challenges but I try not to be too hard on myself as I know that I need to keep the Flow going in order to create my best work.

I realized late last year that I HAD to write this book. It was to be the catalyst for my Purpose. It was the culmination of what I had learned and it was my gift to share. It was not a self-indulgent spree. It was the WAY - My way to expand the awareness that most of us are feeling.

The only way I give in to competition is when I am in a gentle race with nature so in October I downloaded and completed the formal structure of the book. Looking at the Golden Compass for my map and following the Six Directions of the Dragonfly for direction.

I set myself the initial goal of finishing the book before the first bulbs burst their snowdrops. I lost that one. Then I thought a little race against the daffodils could be put in place. I lost that one too. The third goal was the crocuses. They beat me fair and square. This is where I am now. The beginning of February and my next gentle race is to Flow into springtime. To download the words as they form, to communicate my Purpose as I scribe, a rhythmic record of how I should fill my life and enhance the life of others.

To be in Flow is to understand and trust that everything will work out exactly as it should.

If you are asked to change a date in your diary, it will be perfectly timed. There will be something that happens that makes it so. Whether you gather further information to make the date more valuable, whether you gather knowledge to arm your cause. It may just free up your time for something that is supposed to happen, or it may just give time for a miracle to occur, as in Flow as it can be, as it has been given the energy and time needed to unfold.

Let Flow take precedence in your life and the door of wonder will be opened so don't forget to look.

Let Flow take a hold of you and you will never again be tempted to fall back into the modern concept of punctuality. You will be guided more by the precision of Infinite Possibilities.

Energy

Energy can take many forms and yet it is omnipresent. It is the creator and the form. It is the matter and it is the catalyst. It is the beginning and it is the culmination of everything and nothing. Energy is everything we know and everything we do not know. Energy is filled with Infinite Possibilities and Potential.

When you become at one with the Ebb and Flow of your own personal rhythm and you ride the gentle tide of life your expansion of awareness and consciousness grow exponentially.

As you become one with nature you start to become aware that everything has and is Energy.

It is the true paradox that starts to make everything clear and yet make you realize that you know so little.

The energy in our Universe is so all consuming and gains momentum just as a river flows down to the sea.

As you contain it, it will form. As you expand it, it will grow. Energy is just that and yet it can be likened to a shape shifter and, given the exposure, can create anything you desire.

It is up to you to take control of your Energy. It is so powerful and yet so transparent that it is often overlooked.

However you, or we as a collective, harness Energy it will change its shape to Flow with our thoughts and our will. So a word of caution here, be careful with your power.

Your personal Energy is so Powerful it is so very hard to comprehend. Just as a battery has both ends, so we have the power to convey negative or positive Energy through our thoughts and our actions and, most importantly, our intentions.

Just as the presence of a person can be electric with their Power as they control a room, so can our thoughts as they work through everyday life and challenges.

Fill your energy with positive outcomes and they shall Flow in a positive charge. Fill your energy with negativity and they will no doubt be overwhelming and oppressive.

You choose your Energy, your Energetic Field and how that is portrayed.

One of my mentors, Rachel Jayne Groover explains the ability to contain and control your energy as a light globe. With your core as the filament and your containment as the glass that encapsulates it.

She goes on to say that the filament is the spark and that you have the control over how big or small the containment can be, according to the situation and necessity. You can shine a dim light and have a tiny sphere that hardly shows any glimpse of who you are or you can fill an entire room with the flick of a switch.

If you can master this, the world is your oyster and I find it one of the easiest ways to increase my own energy levels and control the energy of any situation.

Your Energy is powerful stuff. Make no mistake.

Collective Energy is unfathomable and there is no end to the ways it can be utilized.

This is one of the reasons that not only gave me the fuel to really serve my purpose in a big way but also makes it my obligation in life.

I cannot sit still and live a small, solitary life whilst knowing that the Collective Energy on the planet is being harnessed by forces that are ultimately evil. I do not make light of the term evil but as congregations of those happy to use war, corruption and hunger as excuses to bring fear and hardship unto our world, I think it is necessary to use words that are familiar to the masses to convey the message.

As I have mentioned before I understand the power of organized crime and I see it as part of my Purpose to harness, gather and unite all of those who inherently feel goodness to come together against it.

I am not asking everyone to don hippy attire and peace keeping banners (although I do like any excuse to dress up and celebrate) but I am just trying to bridge the never ending bridges that separate all of us, leaving us unarmed against those who have a full arsenal and are not in the slightest afraid to use it to get what they want.

Funnily enough, this only lends to the paradox of Energy as most of those involved in the collective of organized evil are wanting Power, in effect, more Energy!

This leads me to use old-fashioned terms in a very modern and much energized manner. I want to see the Power of Good take over the world. I want to see the Energy of Collective Positivity encapsulate all that is wrong and put the world to rights by encompassing and including those seeking power to be absorbed in this Energy of Infinite Possibilities.

Riding The Tide Of Meandering Change

Change is inevitable and Change is what happens when Life is in Flow, or in Ebb and Flow, or even when you think that nothing is happening, when you have such a routine that you think you have complete control.

Ha, ha! Nothing stays the same. You get older. Things happen. You take action. Somebody else takes action. You learn. You are exposed. You expand. The seasons change. You grow. You grow up, and out, and shrink and transform.

Change happens whether you like it or not and therefore it is easier to accept, acknowledge and embrace it wherever you are in your cycle of life.

I know older people who have such routine that they can't function outside of it when change happens and happen it does.

You become frailer, less cognitive, less mobile and less open to change but you cannot stop it.

So why not make the best of it. From those that I have seen, it seems the best examples of growing old are from those who are in control and yet still open to change.

As you embrace the Ebb and Flow of Life, harness the energy

and accept inevitable changes, you become happier, more pliant, your ability to adapt and assimilate increases dramatically and therefore your self-confidence, demeanor and attitude become magnetic.

All because you accept that life is what it is and it changes constantly.

It is so simple to be at peace with yourself and convey that to others with these little nuggets. They are not rocket science and yet they are the true alchemy that has been sought for thousands of years and in many a place.

The changes you can make are within you. Within your attitude and within your action. They are your core, your self, your Being.

The changes outside of your control are the Infinite Possibilities. All of the wonders that behold us now and can behold us in the future and that mean that our future will never be boring and as long as we continue to harness the Collective Energy of Good, the Possibilities of what we can achieve together are mind-boggling.

A Grain Of Sand

Before we move onto the next stage I want you to become a little more comfortable with the concept of death.

As we live in the western world I find it increasingly important that we open our minds to addressing the inevitable and becoming open and honest in our conversations about and around death, so that we are not as afraid of it and more importantly, can reap the benefit of the Energy that acceptance gives us, we can explore the Freedom it can give us to live our lives to the full and to enjoy the journey even more.

After coming so close to death on a number of occasions, I decided that I needed to come up with a metaphor for death and this is how I like to think of it now.

The first time I faced death there was no doubt that I was in shock. The second time it was speaking to my partner about how I would like to be buried with bright flowers and a camper van. By the third time I was truly overcome with Peace.

When I overcame my fear of death I became unstoppable. It gave me the freedom to dream, the freedom to get out of my own way, the freedom to become the Superhero of my own destiny and the freedom to truly, deeply live and love. It gave me the courage to share my freedom with the world and to do so with a ferocious passion, because I know within my heart that my purpose in life is so magnificently greater than any fear I could possibly feel in my human form. It gave me the ability to see the INFINITE POSSIBILITIES that I know and that I do not know and the wonder and awe to keep on uncovering them. It made paradox easy to understand and the meaning of life was to live riding the tide of the freedom that gave me.

-O-

I think of a beach, with the sun coming up and glistening, at first, on the water and then as it gains momentum it starts permeating each and every grain of sand. As a whole, without each grain of sand the picture would not be as beautiful. As the sun glistens, as the moon shines down it reflects off each grain of sand and links it to the stars and the universe and the unknown, the Unknown is not feared by me anymore. I am happy to be a grain of sand. A part of that bigger picture and have no attachment to what happens when I become that grain of sand because, I know that without it, the picture would not be the same. It gives me comfort. It takes the fear away and allows me to fill my present moment working on making that picture beautiful everyday and building a bridge from the sun to the moon and back down to earth and the Infinite Possibilities that I can be a part of whilst I am here.

Integrating Business & Life For The Holistic Entrepreneur

Throughout this book I shall be talking about life & business in the same way. This is because my work is part of my life and to live fully in my purpose I must share my gifts with the world. This is my work.

I know that this is so for a lot of women, also. I know that for some that is how they wish to live; some are so happy with their lives at present that it has yet to occur to them - Aren't they lucky?

Anyway, for each section of the Golden Compass I have made provision for a small chapter to be dedicated completely to how the compass works for business, so that it may be defined in a way that will enable it to be seen for it's own merit in the system. When I teach the system further it can be segregated for those who are not entirely interested in integrating their life and business at this time or already happy in one area and need to focus on the other.

For me, it was imperative that I create my own life. I love business, so it was a natural progression for me to make what I knew was my purpose in life and turn it into a full-time profession, to empower others into kind and compassionate leadership for the New Paradigm with sustainable and thriving businesses for our future and future generations and the future of our planet.

I know that these seem very lofty ideas but I am on a mission to make the world a better place. Just seeing and trusting the method that I am setting down in this book, I am convinced, determined and unstoppable with my vision for a better future and a Globally Responsible Community.

So, by giving the LifeStyle Business its own dedicated description within the Golden Compass, I hope to make the concept easier to understand for those who are contemplating it; easier to integrate life, work and spirituality for those who are already working or in their own business and an overview for those who have yet to have heard of the concept.

To me, Life and Business are now one. I think about my purpose as my life and my life as my business. A beautiful circle of integration that completely makes sense to me, gives me the freedom to live my dreams and to contribute to the world. In essence, I have found Gold!

It all links so seamlessly and just feels so right. Because I have looked at all I need in my life to be full and to keep my vessel full to overflowing, I have all angles covered.

As I have been fortunate enough to have had the experience of running a business, and working my way up through the ranks, I am able to integrate and to give credence to the importance that the proper implementation of business strategies from this perspective and, be able to share them with you through the Golden Compass for Business.

The chapters here will be brief overviews of how this works and how easily both life and business can be seen to fall under the same umbrella.

I have not made anything up in the business section - it is completely business. It fits into the same categories of life. Each section is vitally important and I can state that since I have put this together everything just falls into place, I would love to see the implementation of the Golden Compass into the corporate, government and religious sections of the world, too, to form an umbrella for everyone to work together and have full and purposeful lives. I hope you get inspired!

Stage Two
The Practice

Piotopia Publishing

Chapter 2
Infinite Principle - Self

All that we know and can control

Personal Patience

Self Observation, Awareness, Control & Commitment
Self Love & Self Motivation
Transformation Renaissance - Who & How You Choose To Be
Your Story
Self Confidence & Self Esteem
Self Respect, Responsibility & Reliance
Self Worth & Self Empowerment
LifeStyle Business - Mission Statement & Core Values

Self Observation, Awareness, Control & Commitment

I have already introduced you to the Infinite Principle Self but here I would like to share the simple ways of acceptance that I use to take full responsibility, not only for yourself in the present, but in order for you to be able to step into your next step as a masterpiece and ultimately lead you to your divine desired destination, whatever that may be.

The biggest lesson I learnt is that you should not have too much attachment as to how these steps unfold but to do everything in your control to steer the ship.

The Infinite Principle of Self is to truly embrace all that we can control. Strangely enough, this is where we can gain true power and the mere fact that we take control gives us confidence.

The first step in this section is to observe and become aware of your personal Golden Rhythm.

Without attachment and with love, really start to become aware of your thoughts, your words, your actions, your reactions, your body, your environment and of course your true feelings and emotions.

It is almost like stepping out of yourself and looking at yourself through the eyes of your future soul. The God, so to speak, that lives inside you.

When you do this, and it takes some time to be comfortable and willing to embody this fully, it gives you ultimate freedom. When you are able to accept who you are and what you do and how you do it, you get a surge of energy likened to a power that no man made elixir could ever dream of providing.

When you start being the boss or leader of yourself, you get an innate sense of the infinite possibilities that you are capable of, the true sense of Being at one with yourself and with the Universe.

It is the time when you really grow up. I will be honest with you, there is no looking back. At first it may feel like a burden to be aware of yourself in this heightened enlightenment but I promise that you will be able to get to that sense of peace that each and every one of us seek out over the course of our lifetime. With this awakening comes an innate contentment, which evolves at the same rate as you do. Ultimately opening your eyes and teaching you at a rate that supports your internal sense of calm and adds to the beauty of your personal steps as masterpieces.

It is time to don your dark glasses, put on your hat, perfect that disguise and become your own Personal Private Investigator. We start off with ourselves, as in order to be a true Woman On Purpose we have to become observant, aware, in control and committed to our dreams and divine destination. Everything in Nature has cycles, seasons and rhythm, we are no different, becoming aware of your immediate energy flow and how your previous cycles have led you to where you are today enforces your ability to map out your future in all of its glory and the sacred power of perfection that guides us on, and within, our journey.

Once you have got the hang of being a PI (Private Investigator) your skills in the above unleash a whole host of possibilities that can help you in every step of your life. In your career, your wealth and abundance, your parenting, your goals, your friendships, your personal relationships and, my personal favorite, your business.

The first thing to observe is your energy. By this I mean where is your energy and how are you using it? It doesn't matter here whether you are running a marathon or laying in bed as I am talking about the energy that you are devoting to your thoughts or actions overall and not the levels of glucose or your physical ability.

We all have the power to direct our own energy, our Innate Power force. What some people refer to as driving force. What are your areas of focus at this time in your life? Is it your health, your job, your children, your finances, your home, your appearance? Whatever it is, own it? Wherever you are, be it? Whatever you have, observe it?

Be your own boss, like a parent to a child, or an elder to her tribe, or mistress to her house. If you can be happy with all that you are, with all that you say and how you say it, with all that you do and how you do it - you are on the right track.

To be observant with oneself takes honesty. To be observant with your actions takes tenacity. To be observant with your present takes ownership. When you have the ability to do that for as much of the time as possible, it gives you Power and ultimately, Freedom.

This is one of the best lessons I have ever learnt. This is one of the most calming effects I have ever felt. This is something that, although like looking through a cloudy, rose colored glass to begin with, ultimately gives you the ability to see everything in its own perfect beauty - starting with yourself.

It isn't the easiest thing in the world to begin. Like all things that are worth the wait, this takes time and devotion. I promise you again though that it will be worth it.

Once you become observant of yourself and gain that insight, you can slowly become aware of how you impact external situations and the people you interact with. As your awareness and observation grow, you can start to manipulate (see below) and manifest people and things to fit in with your overall plan.

I know, I mentioned manipulate! Please be aware that you are stepping into your power here. Your energy can be manipulated and as you gain more awareness you will start to see how you can manipulate and manifest practically anything you want – I mean it to be used in goodness.

This is where Self Control is so important. Your energy is exponentially Powerful and in this context and throughout my life I ONLY use my Energy for good. I have expanded my awareness so much and throw a blanket of goodness over ALL of my actions, words, deeds and THOUGHTS. To make this work and for us to embrace and embody this New Paradigm together, it is ESSENTIAL for you to do the same.

If you are in the early stages of observation and embodying your energy, please, please take heed that you are responsible for the outcomes. Ensure that this energy comes from, and is seen in, goodness at all times.

As you grow in your observation and awareness you can Commit to a desired outcome.

As you grow in Self Control, you can gain the Power to focus your Energy to a specific outcome.

To harness this power it is easiest to start with commitment to something that is personal to you.

I seem to think that this is the teaching that most religions pass on through fasting.

Although in religions it shows commitment to a specific God, I feel that fasting gives you the lessons I would like to share for you to get your Personal Power, Godly or not, whatever your beliefs.

I have fasted for many different reasons over the years, for religious reasons, for bodily reasons and for charitable reasons and so I know that, for me, I get the same satisfaction and inner peace and power that I am trying to translate to you.

If you can commit to a small goal and achieve it, being totally in control, totally committed, totally aware and in complete observation during the process you will know exactly how much Power you have over your energy and the energy you place in focus.

I do not mean giving in to addiction, I do mean restraining from. I do not mean forever, I do mean for a short amount of given and available time. I do not mean that this is the only way to move forward, I only mean this as a way for you to become aware of your self, your body, your environment and the ultimate freedom that comes with the KNOWLEDGE and not becoming obsessed with but IN TUNE with your personal rhythm.

Everything needs to be brought into balance here. There is flow in everything, there is change in everything and there is energy in everything. Balance is key.

When you have gained Balance in your observation, awareness, control and commitment you will be able to move forward. If you are fooling yourself into obsessive behavior the balance will not reveal itself. You will be out of kilter and your ability to manifest will not be given the freedom of goodness to make itself unfold.

As you gain more balance, you gain more flow, you feel more in tune and your personal rhythm reveals itself and your ability to ride the tide of life becomes calmer, more relaxed and more beautiful.

You gain time as your energy is in focus and yet in tune. You gain more momentum, as you are not fazed by challenges that arise. You gain energy as your enthusiasm increases with your awareness of your power and you gain clarity as the freedom you are given from this process clears the way.

Self Love & Self Motivation

If you are still experiencing periods of self doubt and loathing, do not think you are alone. We all experience these moments. The only way you can truly overcome these periods in your life is to love yourself a little bit more.

You want to give, you want to be of service, you want to be recognized in whatever form that is to you and most of all you want to be happy.

Happiness comes in many forms and in many ways but the most fruitful and compelling form of happiness is when you connect to your soul. When you accept yourself fully for who you are, mistakes and all and accept that, in life, you need not be perfect in every way in order to Be Perfect.

Just allowing yourself to love each wrinkle, each blemish, each scar and each hair out of place expands your ability to love and that in itself is Perfect.

To love oneself doesn't mean that you have to be vain or selfish but it does mean that by accepting oneself that you have the ability to be less judgmental and that is beautiful.

When you can see beauty in everything, life becomes happier. When you can see beauty in yourself, everyone, including you, has the freedom to see beauty in everything and everyone. Giving happiness and freedom from a place of Love is a beautiful gift to yourself and everyone you touch.

Take a minute to thank yourself for every mistake and every wrongdoing you have made and then take a minute to thank yourself for every good thing you have done. I bet that you found it hard to fill the first minute and easy to fill the second!

This is where my eighty, ten, ten (Eighty percent your best leaving twenty percent to make mistakes/deal with challenges - ten percent public/ten percent private) principle becomes visible again. Using the last exercise I suspect that you found it easy to memorize the more sociably acceptable misgivings you have made and then kept some hidden even from your own consciousness. I don't want you to linger on that. Just know that you are not alone.

I know that some people think that you need to get to the bottom of some of the terrible things that we have done to ourselves or had done to us but I don't think that is necessary. For all of us, and if you fit into this category just put the heinous memories in the secret vault, acknowledge them for the part they have played and move on.

I know that by excavating my story I have found that those moments that wounded me the most do not form part of the story that I want to share. In fact, I do not need them nor want to give them credence, in how I share my gifts. I do have the experiences to empathize with others but do not want to spend the rest of my life reliving them.

I have chosen to share the beautiful moments - I can dip into the darker moments, but can share what I need to from a place of beauty, which is where I choose to live from.

What does beauty look like to you? Paint your world with love, starting with yourself. To motivate myself I find it so much easier if I am having fun. We have gone over so much of finding out your favorite things that I am sure that you are getting a good idea of what beauty and fun look like to you.

I have found my purpose and this book is a huge part of the foundation I am putting into place in order to share my gifts. But as I have mentioned it has taken some time.

I have now had to use all of my Self Control to set aside time to be a hermit and write. This is so important to me and as I have been committed to finishing this book for a few months now, I have noticed that I have literally lost touch with the outside world. My focus is so on track that I have found myself wondering what month it is, unable to answer basic questions and finding it difficult to get my brain to function in any other, side-stepping business.

It is hard to explain this to people but I am SO motivated and SO loved up in my comfortable hermit hole. I know that I will transform at the end and enjoy the process of emerging like a dragonfly once this stage is over. I shall be exposed to the colors, aromas and desires that I need in order to move on in this particular cycle of my life and I will LOVE it.

Motivation is easier when you put yourself first. When you give yourself love and start un-raveling your purpose, following those bread crumbs, trusting the process then things seem compelling.

Even words that have negative connotations in today's world

become part of your Self Love language.

If you work from a place of Your Beauty (whatever that looks like to you and incorporating any extra loves along the way) you can start to want to pass along your obligations, duties, jobs and sense of purpose.

A bit like an excited dog, you get happier and happier so that your purpose takes over and motivation is your purpose and Self Love is overflowing.

You will get to a point where you want to show everyone that sacred core that almost feels wrong, because it feels so darn good.

This is when you know you are cracking the nut. When you are opening your heart so much that the light just has to shine. It shines in and it shines out!

Infinite possibilities, Love, Beauty - all leaving a trail of gold dust in your wake!

Transformation Renaissance - Who & How You Choose To Be

We have already established that everything changes so I just want to make it clear that this section is not about making you better, or prettier or cleverer than you are, as you are already perfect, exactly how you are. You are Enough. Period.

This is just about enjoying every part of the journey and a part of Self Love is about creating and recreating who you are and how you want to be at any given moment.

This is about becoming a child, again, and opening the dressing up chest and pulling out the 'authentic you' outfit and realizing that it is Magic!

I have always loved dressing up and BE-coming another persona. Whether that is for a whimsical moment or a practical protracted period of time.

When I lost myself at the bottom of the confidence chest and had to fight my way through the multitude of magnificence that I was surrounded by I found the best way for me to step into a role was to fully embrace the character of choice and embody her.

This was easier said than done until I remembered the way I used to get into character before heading onto stage. I recalled how much I enjoyed the process of transformation and the calm and empowering feelings that I used to get at the time.

I decided to try this out for myself in the real world. I had a couple of incidents whilst I was ill and recovering that really made me realize the importance of first impressions, peoples perceptions and how they can impact not only your life but the lives of others.

The first one was when I was really not very well. I was wearing track-suit bottoms and a hoody for comfort and going along a back street to the pharmacy, as I was avoiding crowds. Suddenly a Land Rover with a camera attached to the roof came to a sudden stop just in front of me and a couple of people jumped out and made themselves towards me in quite an aggressive manner. The man and the woman came to a halt on either side of me and then seemed to stutter.

The woman then proceeded to ask me if I had seen any teenagers causing trouble in the area as there had been reports of this happening.

I was startled at first and to be honest a little bit frightened. I then understood that they had thought that I was one of these so-called 'troublemakers'.

They had been so attacking in their approach to me I understood that it was no wonder they were having problems with teenagers, if that was their initial response to them.

The two community officers then backtracked after introducing themselves and trying to back out of their self-presumed situation and asked me to be on the lookout. It was such an eye-opener for me to realize that this was considered an acceptable introduction and that they had assumed that I was a part of the gang, simply because of what I was wearing! Although I was quite flattered by them considering my youth, I saw that they quickly realized their mistake when they got close enough to see a few grey hairs and a couple of wrinkles.

The second situation occurred a few months after the operation that saved my life. I had a vein and muscle from my thigh put into my forehead to compensate for losing the bone, failed titanium plate and veins that had been infected again. I had healed quite well and the huge lump on my head been covered by my hair.

I was gingerly taking my dog, Aura, a Golden Retriever, for a walk in the nearby cemetery when I was shouted at by a couple of men who were in charge of a Rottweiler and a few cans of lager.

The dogs barked and I moved quickly on until a man approached me whilst on a bicycle with his Jack Russell running alongside him. He asked me to be wary of the two men in question and I replied that I had already had to deal with their retorts.

He immediately got angry and, despite my protests to the contrary, decided to have words with them. This was not a good idea and what ensued can only be described as a scene from a cartoon!

Slow motion fisticuffs and hysterical masculinity being thrown from every angle.

Needless to say the police were called and I was asked to appear in court when the time came.

This time I was given the authority of being the exemplary witness. Being of neat appearance and of good voice, I was called upon and thanked and supported.

All because of the fact that since the last episode of being taken for a teenage hoodlum I had decided that, no matter how difficult it was, I was going to be the best dressed I could possibly be and regain some dignity!

So you see where and why I decided to get back to the dressing up box. I realized that I could manipulate the outcome of some situations just by my attire and so, being me, I decided that I would do this from a place of beauty too and I started to employ a mixture of dressing up from being a little girl and getting into character from my time on stage.

I loved it so much I decided to make it a part of my life and I hope that it can help you, too.

Whatever your situation or day or appointment, really enjoy becoming the person you not only want to be or project but really loving that person, both inside and out.

Decide what she looks like, what she wears, how she walks and how she talks. Give her the tools and qualities she needs to make the impression you want to give and step into her fully and enjoy every moment.

I know that with so much emphasis on authenticity nowadays that this may seem a little fraudulent, but to me, it was the freedom I needed to really fill my authentic self and gain the power to really Be who I wanted to be.

I have gone on to create the whole persona of Alexandra Gold, A Woman On Purpose and I have never felt as authentic as I do now. Well, not since I was a little girl with not a care in the world and every dream in the Universe available to me.

I urge you to try it. For you and your own authentic self to shine through.

This way you can create the person you want to be now and in the future and you eventually get to a place where you find the perfect fit.

Where you can get up in the morning and step into your true authentic self, whatever that may feel like on the day. You will find a general theme and a few ways to overcome your fears. Eventually you can settle into a style that completely suits you and what you want to project. Almost like becoming your own brand.

Be adventurous. Try new things. Try new styles. Try new hairstyles. Try new places. Try new things. Throw your net over everything that catches your eye and then settle for the things that make you feel really, really good.

It doesn't matter how much money you have. It is great to repurpose, reuse, buy second hand and create your individual style.

That is the really beautiful thing about transforming. It never has to end but you can enjoy every season.

Think ahead as well as thinking in the moment. As I sit here now I am in my dressing gown being a hermit writer. As I sit here now dreaming about the Alexandra Gold who will be visible as soon as I have finished this book, I think Gold and bronze and orange and white and sunshine and laughter. Everything is enjoyable to me now and I am in the moment. I am creating

A WOMAN ON PURPOSE

and Being at the same time. I am Being and doing. I am Being and dreaming. I am transforming and just Being here with you.

In the summer when I was the thinner, browner, blonder version of Alexandra Gold, I drank in the sunshine and the water and the beach and the warmth. I created the vision of the hermit who cuddled in pajamas and wrote, ate chocolate and comfort food, lit a roaring fire and wore comfortable clothes.

Everything is perfect. Everything changes. Everything can be created and transformed and can be kept the same. Whatever and whoever you are right now is perfect and can be manipulated and transformed only to make you happier and healthier but most of all to help you enjoy every single moment along your own personal journey of life.

Try not to get lost in the authentic present because a huge part of the paradox of Zen is that you are in joy and at peace at any given time. Enjoy your authentic self whatever that might look like but don't forget to enjoy the moment and accept your immediate self, too, because that is the beauty of you.

Enjoy it. Enjoy You. Enjoy Being. Step into the magical creation of you and whom you choose to be!

Your Story

What is your story? What story would you love to tell? What story defined you? What story lives in you? What story is trying to break free?

We all have a story. We come from a long line of storytellers. It is in our DNA as humans. Storytelling is incredibly powerful and everyone has a different one making each and every story unique and as important as the next.

Owning your story is empowering. Sharing your story is courageous. Writing the next chapter and standing Centre-Stage could be one of the best things you could ever do in your life and in the lives of others.

I use storytelling to give real life and modern examples of how I have integrated all that I love, with all that I have learnt in order to share my gifts with others.

I call this truly Responsible Empowering Altruistic Living (REAL) - accepting all the ups and downs in life to create a harmonious flow that is passionate, purposeful, practical, prosperous, philanthropic and full of potential with Infinite Possibilities.

I have been able to find a way to live that encompasses everything I want and need in life in a way that supports me financially, that enables me to give back and fill me up in harmony with the world. I work with what I have to gain, what I need and do no harm.

My story is a little different, but then so is everyone's. I use mine in a way that enables me to excavate your story to help you create a REAL life that fully supports you whatever that might look like.

It doesn't matter what your story is about. It only matters if and how you decide to use it.

Lots of people have lots of little stories that make a series. Some people have a big chunk of a story that enables them to convey an epic and others have stories that they wish to keep to themselves.

No matter what your story is, do not be afraid of it. You are not bound by it unless you choose to be. You can use it if you wish. You can forget it if that is preferable.

What you can do that is immediately empowering is to storyboard your next chapter, to put the stones in place for the next step of your masterpiece.

You can choose to pick up the pen and sketch the outline of your chosen path. Putting stakes in the scenic routes at the points of interest that take your fancy and creating the soundtrack for the rest of your life.

Of course, you can choose to use the story that you already have. It doesn't matter how insignificant it may seem to you, to somebody else it may just be the inspiration they need to hear.

As I have mentioned before, there are no jobs that are more significant than any other, no people that are more important than the other and there are certainly no stories that are greater than any other.

Whatever your story and how you choose to use it is up to you. Whether you are an artisan craftsman who uses a story to generate interest in your chosen field or the CEO of a global organization who is able to tell the story of incorporation, the only thing that will matter is how you share your story.

Be enthusiastic, be passionate, be creative, be alive and be true.

Those people who need to listen will be able to hear and those who need to see will be able to visualize all they need to by how you convey your message.

Whether your story is your gift or if it is the way of passing along your gifts - storytelling is an age-old way of sharing your experience, knowledge and personality on to others.

You can be a part of your story or just the messenger. You can embellish your story or make it more palatable. You can make your characters come alive through speech or simply display their personalities through words.

Crafting your story is important whether it is for business or for personal use. You are choosing the words to advertise yourself to potential partners, friends, lovers, peers, colleagues, bosses, in-laws or enemies!

Be careful how you portray yourself and perhaps craft a couple of different introductory stories that enable you to confidently impress and impart the qualities you need, at any given time or in any situation.

You have dramatic license to embellish the facts but do not outright lie, as this is just too much like hard work! Be truthful, it is easier. Be yourself that is easier too. Be your best you, though, because that is your job and everyone's divine destination is happiness!

If you choose to impart your story as a business, then embrace the best bits. We all have stories that enable us to sympathize, empathize and gain rapport with others, but in order for you to relate your story everyday you need to make it enjoyable for you. I have found that by really emphasizing the learning and the beauty that you gained, rather than harboring on the negative, enables you to BE the story and incorporate it into your brand and REAL life.

Whatever you decide to do with your story, remember it is yours, it is unique and it is useful. Even if you only ever share it with your children or grandchildren it is still one of the most important and freely available gifts any one of us has!

Self Confidence & Self Esteem

This whole book has been written not only to share my story but also to empower women, as I think it is my 'job' to do so.

I have been through many of life's circumstances which enable me to empathize with others, but my overall mission is to see the feminine leadership and the skills that come naturally to us, such as kindness, compassion and care become mainstream. This will allow us to step into positions of authority that have a positive influence on our lives and the futures of both our children and the planet.

Self Confidence and Self Esteem are some of the most sought after and essential ingredients for leadership that we, as women, need to embrace in order for us to share our innate wisdom with firm clarity and compassion.

The world needs you and it needs you now.

We are talking about being Women on Purpose, here, so we need to address our confidence in how we relate to sharing our gifts and also our overriding feelings about ourselves.

This first statement should be one of the most confidence giving messages you need in order to give yourself permission to be

A WOMAN ON PURPOSE

confident in your ability to lead!

No matter what, how much confidence and self esteem you give to your children, the most important and the most beneficial gift you can give them, in order that they get a chance to use their own, is to BE self confident and hold yourself in high esteem, right now.

I need you, too. I want to change the world. I want to make it better. For me. For you. For those who are suffering, dying, experiencing war, famine and health problems. For those suffering at the hands of others, for those without shelter or water or getting their basic needs met.

We need to be confident enough to take on those who are, maybe not on purpose, influencing those that are harming the planet. In order to do that we need to work together.

We need to be in a good place, ourselves, to start with. Remember that it is always best to give from a cup that is overflowing.

So in order to do that we need to be confident enough to ensure that we are in a good place ourselves.

Are you happy? Are you free? Are you housed sufficiently for your circumstance and environment? Do you have enough money to feed and clothe your family? Do you have enough to give yourself little pleasures, often, and bigger pleasures when you need them?

These are all questions to start with and to help you gain confidence where you are, with what you have.

If the above needs are met then I ask you to gain confidence to Join the Resolution!

The Resolution to make the world a better place.

Starting with being confident enough to stand up for yourself and those who rely on you. Confident enough to expand that ability to compassionately stand up for what is right and just in the bigger picture.

There are many ways to explore and develop our own self-confidence and I will help you as much as possible because I truly, honestly and fervently believe that we need to work together to make the world a better place.

The reason I have given you such a big, hairy introduction to gaining more self-confidence is that to have a big, hairy purpose instills you with confidence, automatically. It may be a little scary and daunting but if you truly step into the role of what I like to call the "Piotopian Warrior" (Pioneering a better world through compassionate action), then you can instantly imagine donning your armor and fighting against all the wrongs in the world.

Getting a sense of purpose really released my ability to be confident and the more confidence I gained in my ability to share my purpose, the more confident I became.

Everything that I write in this book is cyclical. It should be and seem to be simple. When we get to the end of the book and explore gaining your own spiritual or philosophical path along with embracing the Unknown, all of these little nuggets should start to fall into place along with your own personal sense of calm and determination.

The confidence you need to get to that point can be borrowed or embodied, whichever way works for you but on the Self Esteem side of things I only have one statement.

YOU ARE ENOUGH!

There is no difference between you or anyone else. If you are able to embrace that - become aware, observant, graceful and purposeful, everything else will fall into place.

Trust the journey and if you come up against resistance, just examine, contemplate and re-evaluate the situation. It might be you, so ask yourself if you have gained the other perspective, been kind, thoughtful and compassionate in your process. Done all you can possibly do for the situation to proceed in the direction you require.

If you have and you still do not receive your required outcome, it is time to let go.

If it is meant to be, the Universe will give you a slap in the face until you take notice. If not, there are other avenues to explore, scenic routes to uncover and another adventure to undertake.

Did I mention - YOU ARE ENOUGH?

Let's get back to self-confidence and those little boosts you may or may not need, now or forever!

Stand up tall. A little thing but have a look in the mirror at how you present yourself. If you can gain the confidence to do this in all aspects of your outer existence it will only do you good in the outer world.

Groom yourself. Ensure that you are in the right attire for the situation you find yourself. Make sure you look the part. Take the time to find out what others are wearing if you are unsure.

Get the shoes - you know you want to! This will help you stand tall!

Smile - It makes you look confident even if you don't feel it. I love smiling - it is like having a secret weapon as it makes you feel better at the same time. This will help you feel taller!

Speak clearly and use the language suited to the situation you are in. If you are good at adapting your accent then this is a great time to use those skills. It is always easier to fit in if you can speak the lingo and 'fit in' in a colloquial manner. This won't do anything to make you taller but will not leave you on the outskirts!

Be kind. If there is anything more powerful than the ability to be gracefully kind, I would like you to point it out to me. Doesn't matter about your height at all in this instance - you can be the most powerful person in the room by just employing graceful kindness.

Be prepared for the situation at hand. Try your best to be knowledgeable. This is empowering as you will be able to focus on those kind, yet graceful answers rather than what you think others are talking about!

Be positive - make sure that you are positive in actions and your body language. This will make you a magnet!!!

Be helpful. You would be surprised at how many people fail to be helpful and could just offer to make the tea. By doing this you immediately command respect and attention from the right people. Anyone who cannot see it will not be worthy anyway and you will be standing so tall you won't notice. You will be a magnet, remember!!! It is not subservient to be generous and good manners are always remembered. So too are bad manners!

Put on that dress - you know that magical one that empowers you for any situation, and instills all of the confidence you will ever need. If you can't find THE one, then have a look in the dress up chest - there will be one that suits the occasion there.

I hope that these little ways help you in your Self Confidence. They are only little steps as I am hoping that you will be gaining the backbone of confidence from the whole of this book as you go along.

Did I mention - YOU ARE ENOUGH!

Self Respect, Responsibility & Reliance

You!

You are!

You are Enough!

You need to respect this, you need to take responsibility for this and you need to rely on this!

There are no exceptions. Even when you are completely vulnerable and completely reliant, externally, for your care, this is still true.

You need to be so completely respectful, responsible and reliant on your thoughts so that this becomes part of your DNA, a part of your inner core and in your energy. It needs to be instilled in your subconscious and able to be relied on, innately.

All of your approaches to this, and regarding this, are so important to develop in order to overcome any emotional, spiritual or physical challenges, when you are not in direct control.

I know that in reality it is very easy to forget these things and that it is sometimes easier to rely on the fairy tale notion that you can be taken care of by your true love, but to adopt these

A WOMAN ON PURPOSE

principles holds a magic all of its own.

To respect yourself enough to take responsibility for your own thoughts, actions, words and dreams gives you the power to truly appreciate life in a way that no other person can do for you.

To rely on oneself is to take back the energy to steer your journey and, paradoxically, allows the people you love the freedom to meet you on theirs.

We have become a society that expects. We expect a certain standard of living. We expect to be able to get what we want and when we want it, but we have forgotten the fundamental meaning of life in the process - To enjoy the journey!

Each and every life journey is unique. You cannot expect others to want exactly the same things as you and you are very lucky if you find someone who is on a similar path.

We are living in such a transient world that we have no map for the vast experiences that we are now able to live; we have fallen into a trap of media expectations and our travel guide comes in the form of branding and luxury.

In order to be authentic to ourselves we have to respect our own desires and be true to what we want and need in a responsible fashion.

So many of us are caught up in either guilt or material drive. By this I mean you are either so focused on a certain charitable purpose that has been given media attention that you become obsessed and overwhelmed with guilt, so that you are boxed in by your supposedly 'purposeful' actions or you are driven by media materialism and envy for the yacht, the designer outfits, the way of life that you fail to tap into your core desires.

If you are reading this book you will know that I am generalizing, here, but understand the underlying course that we are following.

By becoming obsessed with either we leave the driven society to control our obsessions, enabling paradox to be used against us, rather than for us.

By taking responsibility for ourselves and respecting ourselves enough to do so not only gives you power but energetically the good energy in the world increases.

By taking action for what you believe in you are joining the collective good. By taking responsibility for yourself and your environment you take back power from others hell bent on greedy and oppressive action. I do not mean to be negative at all but I do feel that the more of us joining up in the power of good, the better.

We have lived for thousands of years in oppressive and controlled circumstances, so it would be silly of me to think that we will all gain freedom from such authority in a short amount of time. I also know that for some very brave hero's and heroine's of our past it would be amiss to disregard all that they have fought for and for us to just expect to live in a freedom that suits us now, without thinking of the future of our children and planet, rather than taking responsibility for our future.

Whatever you want in life you can get through living responsibly. We do not have to be perfect but it is in all of our interests to do our bit for the planet. A bit like war effort and patriotism for the planet. The trick about doing this collectively is that we take responsibility for what we believe in and what we can afford to do and yet do not judge others for their choices.

Everyone is at a different stage of life and at a different point in their own journey.

Just because you can afford to give to a charity that is dear to your heart does not mean that others can or that they care any less. It also does not have to lessen your resolve to do something about the problems and just alleviate your guilt by giving financially.

Just because you can afford to buy ecologically and fairly traded goods does not mean that others can or care any less. It also doesn't have to lessen your resolve to ensure that all products are ecologically friendly and fairly traded, alleviating your desire to change the production of this any less.

Just because you can afford to buy organic food and eat at restaurants that supply healthy options does not mean that others can or that they care any less. In order to fill the bellies of even first world families, choices must be made and a loaf of bread or a packet of chips is going to go much further than a bag of organically grown spinach.

Just because you can afford to buy the latest gadgets and designer clothes does not mean that others can or should or that they want to be less trendy than you. In order to be at the top of the game we should be looking at ways that make the planet work better. The factories that make these products should comply to our moral sense of responsibility, just as much as our initial moral compass directs us, i.e. the things that are material necessities seem to fall foul of our testament of being good, as we want them all far more than our care of where and how they are made.

Just because we are okay and giving, eating and living organically and responsibly does not mean that we have done all we can.

We need to work together to make the world a better place.

To rely on oneself is a must. It is sometimes a hard truth that none of us want to hear but it is a truth nevertheless. Even in the most romantic of stories there comes a time where self-reliance is a necessity. I do not want to cover the illusion or disguise the magic by making us all Amazon Warrior Women but being able to rely on ones own sense of survival has been a part of our repression as women.

I do not wish to make us all do without men. In fact I think that the ability to rely on ourselves will only release men to embrace kind and compassionate masculinity. We have lived in a society where the man is responsible and to be relied upon singularly to provide for his family.

By arming ourselves with our own kind and compassionate and uniquely feminine way of responsible reliance we give the masculine power respite. By being self- reliant we do not emasculate men but allow them to explore their own divine path. By respecting ourselves we lead them to respect us more. By being responsible for ourselves we collectively join hands in creating a better world.

Self Worth & Self Empowerment

In order to be truly happy you need to value yourself. You need to understand that you have the ability to be happy and that you have every right to be happy.

You are worthy of happiness. Deep down in your very being it is your birthright, no matter what you have done or what you have been told, you are never, ever less than enough.

In order to truly understand your worth, think of all the things you have done in your life to help others and all the things you could in order to help, further.

We all need each other and every one of us has a place in this jigsaw of life. Nobody is more important than anyone else. Nobody is irreplaceable and yet you are!

Nobody else can take your place on this earth. You may step aside or you may not even step in, but you will still take up space. The space that you fill is for you to decorate at your will and in order to decorate that in your own unique style you have to place value on that space. So even if you really believe you have no value, it is still your job alone to put a stamp on your space of existence. So take charge of your space. Put some value on it. Dream it. Create it. Do it.

Make your space sparkly and shiny. Make your space as valuable as the vein of gold that runs through the earth because ultimately that is your space too.

Try to outdo your space. The only competition you have is with yourself so exploit it. You are so worthy of that creation. You are that creation. Be creative.

This creation of worthiness, in itself, is empowering. It creates a distinct stamp that only you can deliver. Your space is given just by you being born. If you are lucky enough to live in the western world you have been born into an abundant world that can be filled with treasures along the way.

Let your worthiness shine through you, empower you. Just by working in this flow you will deliver the gifts of worthiness and empowerment to others.

We live in a beautiful world of plenty. If you choose to hide away, that is worthy to. If you choose to be a hermit and be alone by choice, then that is what you should do. If you choose to share your gift with others you are indeed blessed and a blessing, so please choose to share your worthiness when you are ready, but do not feel pressured. You will know when it is your time to break through and spread your gifts. Just because society represents that celebrity, wealth and materialism are superior; don't ever feel that you are not worthy.

Empower yourself with what you need. Do you need to be alone? Do you need the sun? Do you need sustenance? Do you need a hug? Do you need to give? Do you need to receive?

The whole meaning and understanding of empowerment has been delivered to us as something we get externally, when we have all of the answers inside us.

Listen to your heart. Listen to your body. Follow the particles that shine out at you. No matter how small. If they sparkle in your direction, follow them. Let yourself be empowered by the education the universe imparts to you.

It will not fail you if you listen to it with a heart that is cracked open and ready to receive. It will light your way and if you fail to see its glow it will shine a little brighter, so do not be afraid of missing a bit.

Empower yourself inwardly for your purposeful journey.

There is no going back now. Hold on! You are in for the ride of your life!

LifeStyle Business - Mission Statement & Core Values

Every Life and every Business needs to have values, so it goes without saying that these would be the core of your LifeStyle Business. They are tantamount to the very essence of your being and if you get this right they can be one and the same.

No matter where you are in your life or where you come from, when you become an adult you make the choice as to which values mean a great deal to you, the values you would like to project as an adult moving forward. Some will be inherent, some will be passed down through generations and some will be learnt from external influences, but you will have some core things that mean a lot to you and have inner 'house rules' that you will live by.

The same goes for business. No matter if they are a one woman show or a global corporate, it is imperative that at the core of the company there are values that are held sacred, values that lead the way forward. Not only at the beginning but also throughout time and throughout every section of the business, into the vision for the future, ultimately creating a promise for your client from inception and into the Infinite Possibilities.

Mainly expressed through a Mission Statement, your LifeStyle Business's Core Value will guide you and your business and often **be** the driving force of your creation of service, or product. It will be the driving force of your momentum as well as the end goal, Infinite with Possibilities, but keeping you on track.

The core values that we attain in life are slightly different from those in the corporate world. Within a LifeStyle Business they intertwine far more and help keep focus, drive and ultimate ambition on target.

Some of the core values of life would be:

Your beliefs in regard to religion.
Your beliefs in regard to work and home.
Your beliefs in regard to good manners
Your beliefs in regard to the future.
Your beliefs in regard to bringing up children.
Your beliefs in regard to money.
Your beliefs in regard to health and wellbeing.
Your beliefs in regard to our planet.

Whether these are for yourself or for choosing a life partner, they are the things that ultimately drive your life so it is essential that you are honest with yourself about them.

When you are considering the core values of your business, a lot of these core values will automatically become a part of your vision.

When establishing Core values for your business there are a few other things to consider as these values will be your window to clients and customers. They will be what shines out to them and make them loyal.

Some of the core values of a LifeStyle Business you could consider are:

- Sustainability (what ecological ground rules do you have now and moving forward)

- Experience (what experience would your ideal client have)

- Community (do you offer a way for your clients to interact? What do you consider as your business's social responsibility?)

- Your commitment to doing no harm (ensuring that you work within a guideline of win-win)

- A commitment to Vision (To change with the times and keep thriving)

Here are some words to help engage you in a core value exercise. Glance over them and see which ones jump out at you, which will give you the guideline of what is most important to you.

Dependable	Reliable	Loyal
Committed	Open-minded	Consistent
Honest	Efficient	Innovative
Creative	Humorous	Fun-loving
Adventurous	Motivated	Positive
Optimistic	Inspiring	Passionate
Respectful	Athletic	Fit
Courageous	Educate	Respected
Loving	Nurturing	Empathic

The next thing to consider is writing your business Mission Statement.

This goes towards encapsulating all of the values you wish to adhere to within your LifeStyle Business. Quite simply, the reason your business exists.

A short, simple statement that says what your business aims to deliver, how it aims to deliver it and in the way it wishes to deliver.

I see it as something I can really be proud of delivering in person or written down, a statement that will be sustainable in the future as well as the present.

The Mission Statement for A Woman On Purpose is.

To provide women with financial, spiritual and personal empowerment and independence under an umbrella of unity, which lends a voice to the New Paradigm through training, opportunities and inspiring initiatives. To help women become self-sustaining, respected, authoritative leaders and ambassadors for the future of an integrated, compassionate world, doing so from a place of beauty.

Chapter 3
Law & Community

2ND DIRECTION

Purpose, Perception, Philanthropy

Expanding Awareness
Expanding Joy
Empathy, Non-Judgment & Acceptance
Realizing Your Purpose - Golden Centre
Global Responsibility
Contribution
LifeStyle Business - Legal & Human Resources

Expanding Awareness

A Woman On Purpose has a role to play in her community and the Global community, as well.

I know that putting Law & Community at the forefront of the directions may seem a little strange, but in fact it is so much a part of us that we fail to see its' relevance.

When you are a woman on a mission, and by reading this book I suspect you are, your purpose will almost certainly be to help others!

So, in all aspects, this is where you will find your ultimate purpose. In order to really embrace whatever it is that is your specific and unique gift, it is really important to Love It!

Expanding your awareness is a treat. It gives you the ability to be happier, more creative and to reach a greater audience.

Expanding your awareness is something that everyone experiences, whilst awakening to that greater power that has such a pull for us Women On Purpose.

Expanding your awareness allows you to really become non-judgmental in a way that is tangible and easy. Expanding your awareness allows you to start experiencing wonder and enjoyment in everyday moments that were once out of your radar and unavailable to you.

Expanding your awareness allows your life to be filled with grace and contentment that transcends all levels of stress and competes with the elusive happiness that could only be found in religious texts or ancient teachings.

This is where your choice to be fulfilled takes on a will of it's own. It can be dedicated to a plentiful life that is full of riches and abundance, whilst giving back to the universe/world and, in so doing, enables you to live a balanced life of pure, unadulterated joy.

The wonderful thing about Expanding your Awareness, though, is its simplicity. You just have to choose to start.

The ability to expand your awareness comes from thinking about the bigger picture. There are no rules as to how much or how fast you expand, as it is personal to yourself.

The more you expand your own personal awareness only goes to exponentially increase, organically, once you have made the decision.

Essentially it is choosing to awaken your soul or become enlightened and if you are reading this then I am sure that you have already begun this process.

Wherever you are and whatever your circumstance, the secret to expansion of your personal awareness comes from your situation in the moment.

As moments are forever changing, it doesn't matter where you begin and, as you are here, there is no turning back from the path you are on.

The wondrous thing about this is that it seems to be a global awakening, so feel secure in the knowledge that you are not alone on your journey.

Everybody's journey is different so you will never be able to judge your expansion against another. The only thing you will have control of is acknowledgment of another's journey.

So although your path is your own you are in it together. No competition. Just waving at your compatriots and smiling in the knowledge of your expansion.

The easiest way to describe the process of expanding your awareness is to throw your net and catch a little more.

As we are growing we are exposed to the views of others, constantly. The expansion of awareness in the first instance just means to take control of ones thoughts and actions in relation to these thoughts.

When we are young we seem to be happy in ourselves. The more exposed we are to negativity and opinions of what is right ensures that we start to lose our personal freedom.

By expanding our personal awareness we are taking back our control over our freedom to think and to take action in a way that is suitable for our personal happiness and ability to live peaceful, passionate lives.

You will have felt uncomfortable in circumstances during your life. The expansion process gives you permission to question the rules of others and initiate contemplative thoughts.

As long as you are open to the innate feelings you hold and ensure that your actions are right and just, you will not fail in your questioning or rationale.

But you really have to think things through. You will make mistakes but as long as you put kindness and compassion as the Queen of your thoughts and actions you will undoubtedly get back on track.

Start small. Expand your awareness of your surroundings and the way the 'rules' work in relation to a specific area of your life that needs to be addressed.

As patience is a key factor in enlightenment, you may have to accept the 'rules' as given for the time being. You do not have to stop there though. You can think of ways that utilize the 'rules' or change the rules to benefit the area in question.

Patience, kindness, compassion, wisdom, humility and responsibility are the key components for enlightenment, so these principles are to be consulted as members of your personal counsel in every circumstance.

As you expand your awareness you will become more confident in your ability to manipulate any given situation, as long as you employ this counsel!

You will be able to throw your net further and to understand how you can not only manipulate certain circumstances to benefit yourself and your immediate circle, but you start to see how you can rectify situations outside of this circle, in order to benefit others.

I am not saying that you will not get hindered in your quest for a better awareness, only that you will be able to see them as problems that need to be solved.

Even with all the best will in the world you will come up against seemingly stupid 'rules'. 'Rules' that are supposed to be in place to protect and help others. See these challenges as part of your expansion of your awareness and try to figure out ways that could rectify and improve the situation.

These challenges get greater as your expansion increases.

I will not lie to you. These will not go away. I will tell you though, that they can be the most enlightening factors in your personal awakening.

In order to see a way out of a situation that is unkind, potentially hazardous, restricting and disempowering is, from this moment forward, part of Your Personal Purpose.

It is in my experience that if the challenge is presented to you. No way will you be able to ignore it.

It will become a bane in your life if you do. Rather think of throwing your net of kindness over the situation or challenge and deal with it with your newfound awareness.

The Art of Expanding Awareness is not an easy option. You will become more aware of the inequalities in life and you will feel the urge to help in many a given situation.

To truly be of service and remain on purpose and in flow you will have to maintain a full personal cup. You cannot help everyone and everything.

To expand your awareness in practice, think of the effects of your actions and words. Can you be kinder? Can you be craftier? I mean it. There are lots of people in power who do their job as easily as possible and you will need to think outside the arena in order to get the results you require.

Do not feel guilty about working around systems for the greater good. Always be in line with the law but do not give up because there is a system in place to try to stop you.

Just because a 'rule' has been put in place does not make it right in the new paradigm. You have to fight your own corner in order to be of greater service. Do this with kindness, compassion, within the law and the Universe will work with you. I do not mean to flog a dead horse but only to improve the situation at hand in order that it is of greater benefit for you and others. Do not do things just to get up a rung of a ladder of self-service. It just won't work for long or it will lead to more trouble for yourself.

You must truly listen to your call to be of ultimate service. No matter how small that call may feel to you be sure to observe it.

If you have to look after your children, then do so. If you have to work in a factory line, then do so. If you have to compete in the Olympics then do so. Whatever you calling you must honor that. The more you honor your particular and unique call or mission, the more you can concentrate on expanding your awareness and do what is right and just in that arena.

By honoring this system you will automatically be guided to the next area of expansion.

A word of caution, though. Do not think that you can save the world all by yourself. I would never have had the time or money to write this book for you if I had given my time and money to everything that pulled on my heartstrings.

It is like becoming the ruler of your own country. You must lead from your heart but be rational in thought. The more you have, the more you can give. If that is only time for your child then that is all you have to worry about. That, in itself, will give you enough to think about in order to make the world a better place.

If you only have enough money to barely make the rent, then you must ensure that you keep that going and build on it. There will be opportunities to put rational thought and better systems in place wherever you work or even on the journey.

If you are at the top of your game, then continue to rise and observe the way that game is played to make it fairer to all.

You need to give yourself considerable boundaries in action to ensure that there is enough of you to fulfill your own personal journey.

Do not worry about the world hunger situation unless you can positively influence the situation or it is your direct calling?

Do not worry about war unless you can put an end to it through immediate action or fit it in around your personal responsibilities and duties.

It is imperative that we all work together and grow as leaders in order to lead by example and rise through the storm. It will be difficult but it will be worth it.

As your awareness grows so does your compassion. You will feel more sensitive and your emotions will be raw. You are not alone and we need to stick together in this Resolution Revolution.

There is no going back. You are now A Woman On Purpose.

Expanding Joy

It is not all solemn news! As much as you can't go back to being free in an oppressed world, you can choose to expand your joy, just as exponentially as you expand your awareness.

You can choose to be happy and increase that joy to be as expansive as your imagination allows you to be.

Just as you have become aware of the issues that you face, you can become aware of the joy that you are able to experience at any given moment.

It isn't easy to do in this media obsessed world. We are constantly barraged with unpleasant and sometimes atrocious scenarios day in and day out. What we can do though is to limit our responsibility for every little thing.

Start feeling the pull of joy whenever you can. Start thinking about things as if they are there for your joy and not for your immediate involvement.

No matter what your heart leads you to in a responsible manner and that call of your heart that leads you to your particular purpose, you must be full with joy as much as you can.

To start the process of Expanding your Joy, think of something that gets your goat (annoys or irritates) you, something that you have an inordinate dislike for.

For me, it was the new windmills. I didn't like the look of them. I chose to enjoy them and I now love them so much my heart bursts when I see them in action wherever they are. I am not naive enough to think that they will not come without their own negative aspects as we become aware of them, only that they are a better and cleaner alternative now.

Try to understand a different type of music. Listen to the lyrics of a song to truly hear what the singer is projecting. Read a different newspaper. Watch a different type of film or TV show.

Start to think about the other side of an argument. This helps if you have someone to banter with who understands what you are trying to do. It also helps to expand your awareness as you take a side of thought that would not normally be your usual perspective.

Start to wear a different color. See how it looks and how it feels.

Try something different on the menu. Ask for a taste and really try to enjoy it. It doesn't matter if you don't like it as you can have fun not liking something, too!

All of these things lend to you being happier and being better informed, to make better choices and better decisions.

The more you know and understand the greater your awareness and so the cycle continues. You become more at peace with where you are as you are throwing your net and catching the jewels as well as the lobsters!

You can have so much fun by increasing your joy. Let go of some of your inhibitions.

Try to dance. If you are rubbish, then laugh! Try to sing. If you are rubbish, then laugh! Try to cook something different. If it is rubbish, then laugh!

Don't take life or being A Woman On Purpose too seriously. There is no race as there is no competition except with yourself to see how much joy you can fit in.

Do not be a slave to old school judgments of what is acceptable and the right thing to do. As long as you approach things with a good and gentle heart, you are allowed to eat cake with your fingers and lick the spoon.

We have grown up with so many things that we are told are bad mannered, so we have to find out and think about what is kind again.

Make your own decisions. Make your own rules. Make space for laughter and self-expression in whatever form you choose.

Make space for creativity. Draw, even if it is badly. Paint, even if it makes a mess. Bake, even if your cake turns out like a biscuit.

Enjoy the aromas, the colors, the feel and the sights.

Splash in a puddle. Wear odd socks (OK, this is where my OCD finds it a bit weird but I even try that as long as they feel the same!).

There is so much I can say about expanding your joy but as long as you take the time to stop and smell the roses, the coffee and laugh at the smelly drains, you are on the right track.

You can expand your joy in secret or in the open. If you want to listen to Bon Jovi because you didn't quite get it when you were younger (nobody needs to know) - although in hindsight I now know why my mates fancied Jon!!!!

You choose your joy so why not expand it to as much joy as possible. I know that I do and then, funnily enough, some of the things that are portrayed to us as unworthy or not acceptable seem so much better, too.

I see an advert of a girl writing a letter outside on a bench in the sunshine under a tree. It is advertising charity funding for girls and although it is heart warming and I do feel the pull, I also feel a sense of guilt for not providing my son with the simple life and joy of nature as much, especially when he is cooped up in a London secondary school where they have a 'no touch' policy so can't even play 'tag'.

Expanding your Joy expands your awareness. I am not saying that the money for girls to go to school isn't important. It is. Just that we need to increase everyone's joy and circumstances and give them freedom to choose that joy for themselves.

Empathy, Non-Judgment & Acceptance

To gain enlightenment is to be kind and compassionate. The easiest route to this is to empathize, be nonjudgmental and accepting of everyone.

To Empathize is to truly put yourself in the position of someone else and to feel the honest feeling, thoughts, predicaments and constraints of the other person before you even think of yourself and react. It is to put aside your immediate judgment and accept that person for who and where they are, treating them with compassion and kindness, as if you were them.

To be enlightened all the time is bloody difficult. I doubt that I will ever get there, but I strive to be as humanly enlightened as I can be at any time. Part of the journey is to accept that I will never gain complete enlightenment and that keeps me striving to be a better person.

To be enlightened is to accept that we are all forever on the journey that is filled with lessons and to become aware of all the areas in our self that we can work on.

When you accept that this is the case, you are half way there. When you try your best and employ these particular ways of being as much as you possibly can, you are nearly there (enlightened). When you accept that here and now is there (Being in the moment, our present state), then you will be aware that there is a place that we will never ever get to as we are always, always there (present) now!

Make sense? Ha ha! Probably not but I am sure that lots of you will get the gist of what I mean. All I hope to impart in this section is that to look at our mannerisms and ways of dealing with situations from the outside in and from a calm and aware place, gives us all we need to know that we are doing all we can.

To empathize with someone is to try to see things from their side. From where they are standing and within their shoes.

I try to do this from a very simple and primal place. Seeing as we are all born with a sense of survival, what would I do if I were in a certain situation, or had certain habits or needed to get out of a bad situation?

I find that in most circumstances I cannot be sure of my actions and therefore it is easier for me to empathize.

If I were in a war, I would do everything I could to protect my family. If I had been in a war, I would do everything I could to ensure that I would never be in that situation again. If I had remembered the war, I would ensure that I would make my world and that of my family a better place, starting at home.

Everyone has faced a war of some form or another. I try my best to see that first, and act secondly.

I am definitely not saying that you should be a pushover. You need to stand your ground and fight your war too. Just do it in a way that you do no harm to others.

This in itself leads on to being less judgmental. We all have our own particular judgments and these have usually been passed down through generations through fear and a sense of survival in itself, in whatever form that may be.

The class system denotes that the manners employed by those on the top rung are better than the kind working class peoples. We all know how wrong that looks on paper and yet we all know how it still works in real life!

We have done well to become more accepting of one another over the past few hundred years and with the last couple of decades we have made the most impact. We still have so much work to be done as everyone still tries to either stand their ground in status or crawl up the class ladder.

What poppycock! This in itself leaves a whole area for new job creation and creative job creation at that.

Our world is changing. We need to be more tolerant and just get on with creating new 'rules', with accepting new manners that protect and respect everyone. We need to work together for this to happen.

Rules should only be in place to protect us, all of us. We should be working towards equality and not be fighting in public (I mean has anyone thought the House of Lords is anything to be proud of).

Come on Ladies! Come on Gals! We have our work cut out for us. We need to establish new guidelines and open new communications and not in a stuffy old palace or a stark new office. We need to feast on foods that are all fair trade and ensure that no child is hungry but we need to do this in a way that we can look after our own families first because, at the end of the day, we are all primal survivors.

So, I have shown you here exactly what I am judgmental about! I won't learn it all but I will keep on trying and improving and trying! That is the best I can do.

As for Accepting, well, I can accept anyone as long as they are doing their best. I know I have my judgments on the whole but they are not leaning towards anyone in particular.

My acceptance allows me the joy of engaging with anyone who lets me. I accept them as they are and even if that isn't very nice and goes directly to make my world a little harder. I don't have to engage with them again, but I do accept them.

My life has been easier this way. It takes the pressure of individual anger. I am not saying I don't feel it and I don't display it. I do and I do. I just try to refrain. Take the moral high ground and be kind and compassionate. Even if that means cursing and swearing about them within my own circle of safety and waiting until I have calmed down before sending that letter of complaint!!!

Realizing Our Purpose – Golden Centre

We all want to be recognized for something. Whether we like it or not the innate feelings that we get ultimately guide us to those ideals that should be acknowledged and listened to. We can either use them for celebrity or for good.

In the past most people have been known either for their celebrity status or for their work contribution, but in the new paradigm and what we see as an emerging feature in life is the ability to conjoin the two. Fulfilling the most longed for need. To be recognized for our contribution.

For some of us our purpose is very clear and from a very early age. For others the question never arises and so they are very fortunate to be born with the innate sense of contentment. For some of us we are gliding along on the journey and suddenly become aware of the crevice that has formed a deep hole within us, that feels as if something is missing and causes us pain.

This is when we become seekers. If you are reading this, I will presume you are one of the latter group. For some of you there may be a time when you absolutely knew what you wanted to be when you grew up, but then got sidetracked with life. I implore you to uncover that emotion and passion. For some of you there may be a time when you devoted your whole being to a cause or

A WOMAN ON PURPOSE

craft. I implore you to remember this. For some of you there may be a time when you were content and yet you dismiss this time as not good enough. I urge you to recall that feeling.

It doesn't matter what your purpose is. Unless you were very fortunate to have had your passions encouraged and had the will and determination to succeed nourished, you will probably be a part of the tide and change your purpose as you evolve.

This is purpose enough. This is Enough. You are Enough!

So if you have been struggling with finding the 'there' in your purpose. Stop. Just being here right now is your 'here and now' and your 'there'. Take a deep breath.

I am here to give you permission to enjoy the journey. Start planning a life of Peace, of Passion and Power. You start now. Just Be and enjoy it. Just because you are in the driving seat, doesn't mean you have to start the engine and drive like a bat out of hell!

You are allowed to take the time to think, to reflect and to really feel that you are passionate enough to take action.

There is a guide I use for everything, now that I know my purpose, AND acknowledge that it is ever evolving.

To find your Centre and to be at peace with any of your actions I use this simple, yet extraordinarily powerful acronym C.E.N

.T.R.E.

Rule number 1 - Contemplate

Rule number 2 - ESP

Rule number 3 - Nurture

Rule number 4 - Trust

Rule number 5 - Responsibility

Rule number 6 - Enjoy

The Joy we can accomplish in the age that we are living though is infinite. We are at a time in history where, not only do we have the knowledge but we have the ability to get together globally and give our unique voice visibility. You can only imagine the impact we could have on the world if we do start to work together to make the world a better place.

I like to think of our Purpose in the following acronym

Passion

Undertaken

Respectfully

Peacefully to fill our

Obligation of

Service on

Earth

It is essentially our job. Every word I use here, I use in complete comfort. I know that some words that I use in this book have taken a negative connotation when used in the world at the moment. Every word I use, I use by choice and give them the intention and power of goodness.

I love being passionate. I love undertaking my job respectfully and peacefully. I love feeling obliged so strongly by my passion to be of service to this earth whilst I am on it. It makes me feel useful. It fills every need that I have in my core and it is my passion to share this feeling with you.

I want you to feel so passionately about your life that you enjoy every moment and help us make this world a better place.

It is my mission to empower women like you with the peace you need to undertake your passion with so much power and respect that we all start to fill that hole, becoming able to feel that whole that we feel overflow with our obligation to serve with, and for, one another, whilst here on earth.

No matter who you are or where you are. I want us to look at one another and be able to acknowledge one another and respect one another with a secret and sacred look of Knowing that only women can do.

I want us to start making the world better whilst being able to care for our families, and not from lack or, more disturbingly, need.

To find your Golden Centre you have to remember to fill yourself up first, so that your cup is full and your vessel can overflow with your Gifts. If you are ever in doubt remember this little mantra.

The Golden Compass Map gives us direction to follow whenever you need to use it. Whenever you feel a bit lost just relax and muse on these little nuggets to help you get back into alignment.

GOLDEN

Gift Ourselves Love Devotion Enlightenment Need

This is necessary as it is impossible to give from a place of abundant love if your cup is not full -

CENTRE

Contemplate, ESP, Nurture, Trust, Responsibility, Enjoy

These are the questions that you should use in all areas of your life. They can be for how you think, what you say and what you do.

PURPOSE

Passion Undertaken Respectfully Peacefully Obligation

Service Earth

This is the mantra to use if you are not feeling full in what you do. It doesn't matter at what stage of life or what time or money you have when you use any of these acronyms. They have been given to me for everyone to use. To give us a bridge to work with whilst we become more comfortable with our integration and diversity. I truly believe that if we have spiritual or philosophical practices that transcend religion, politics or judgment we WILL be able to make this world a better place.

A WOMAN ON PURPOSE

If you are looking at intertwining all of your life into a business or career that you love, to become all you dream of being and give all you can in the most satisfying and purposeful way, then I would like to help you excavate that.

I have devised a Centre Stage Circle to help you go through if you are feeling stuck with what your purpose is, I would like to share this process for you, to help you unearth your gifts in order for you to share them, to integrate your lifestyle, your work and your purpose for a fully holistic lifestyle that can support you emotionally, financially and give you the momentum you need to really Be Alive.

In order to find your own personal passion you have to be really honest with yourself.

You have to be your own advocate. You have to fight your own corner.

You have to advertise yourself to yourself and be truly honest with all that you are as a person, even if some of those parts aren't pleasant. They are all you and you don't have to focus on the bad stuff but learn to celebrate every single particle of you and your unique essence, so be honest – you have nothing to be ashamed of – Nothing – none of us is perfect, yet every single one of us is human. If it is still hard, then perhaps you could let me give you permission to find all of you.

It is also a good idea to ask for the help of a few of your friends or family who have known you over the course of your life, to remind you of things that you have done through the various stages of your life, as it is so easy to forget all of our achievements.

The Centre Stage Circle is a way to realize your personal way to passionate living and Holistic Integrative LifeStyle. It is especially good if you are looking to find your Unique Selling Point or Niche for a career or business.

This is one of the first worksheets I give anyone who would like my assistance, as it really makes you think and remember all that you have done and are able to do.

You will be surprised at what you have done. A good way to go about the excavation process is to begin with a meditation of the story of your life. This is downloadable in audio format on the A Woman On Purpose website.

Lay or sit down in a quiet place that feels comfortable and peaceful.

Make sure that you are warm and if you can, have a scented candle or incense burning in order to get your senses in tune with your body. Now become aware of your breathing and become aware of your body. Become aware of your whole body and slowly tense and release every part. Moving from your toes and your feet through to your ankles, up your legs tensing your calves and then your thighs. Tensing your buttocks and releasing any tension in your pelvic bones allowing the weight of your body to sink into the surface you are laying or sitting in. Hold your stomach in as tightly as you can and then release, allowing that weight to dissolve. Become aware of your chest and take a deep breath in, hold for the count of 3 and breathe out for the count of 7. Repeat this three times. Become aware of your shoulders and tense the whole area before letting go.

Notice your hands and tightly clench them for a few seconds before releasing them and letting them feel light by your side.

Become aware of your jawbones and clench your teeth enabling you to really be aware of any tension in your cheeks and chin area. Tightly squeeze your eyes shut and then release them and open your mouth as far as it will go. Do this until you feel you are able to release any tightness in the muscles around your mouth and eyes.

Finally let your head sink into the pillow or cushion that it is resting on.

Once again notice your breathing and take a deep breath in, hold for the count of 3 and breathe out for the count of 7. Repeat this three times

Now, you should be feeling comfortable and relaxed enough to start excavating all of your skills, passions, education and experiences that contribute to your own life story.

Go back to when you were born and slowly move through the years of your childhood. Note any significant times when you were learning or interested in something special, becoming aware of any extra-curricular activities you were involved in or any particular lesson that you enjoyed.

Ask yourself a few questions as you go through the ages. What did I used to like to do, to eat, to smell? Where did I like to go?

As you move through your youth, what were the things that took over your life? What films? What feelings? What music? What people? What places?

And then start to think about your chosen education? What

did you enjoy the most? What were you good at? Where did you dream of ending up? What was your chosen profession?

After this we start to think about our first jobs. What did you do well? What did you learn? What did you tolerate but do anyway? What did you excel at?

Think about your hobbies. Think about your creativity. Think about activity. Think about your feelings.

Start to think about major life events. What are the main stages of your life? What are the best bits? When were you the happiest? What were you doing? What did your life look like and consist of on a regular basis?

Eventually try to get into really feel the feelings of the happiest moments of your life. If there are areas of your life that are not so pleasant, acknowledge them and thank them and kindly and deliberately let them go. Imagine an area of your brain that you can use as a safety deposit box, as some memories are always going to be painful. Giving them a secure place in your life that acknowledges them but puts you in control, and just like any piece of unloved but valuable jewel, acknowledge and gently put it away.

Again, access those feelings of joy that you associated with the best times of your life. And hold on to them whilst you gently come back to the present day. Slowly become aware of your surroundings.

Feel the beating of your heart. Note the rise and fall of your chest. Deliberately smile and thank yourself for the time. Now slowly open your eyes.

The first time you use this process try to go over your whole life as if you were living it as a film.

As you fill in the questions relating to the areas of your life you might like to come back to this process and focus on one area of the best times of your life at a time for the following questions?

When were you most happy?

When were you most proud?

When did you enjoy teamwork the most? In what role?

What places did you love the most?

What age group did you feel the most at home with or have affiliation to, now?

What were your signature themes that you used through the course of your life, i.e. fashion, music, food, art, sport

These are just a few of the things that can help you find those periods in your life that filled you up.

Also be aware of any feelings that were aroused that you haven't felt for a while, such as excitement, joy, skipping, love, laughter.

You are now ready to fill in your Centre Stage Circle.

Take your time over the following questions, jot the answers down on your phone or notebook and come back and fill up the sections as you go. . If there are parts of your life that are too distressing to think about please feel free to leave them out as this is a process of bringing together and not meant to cause any harm. But do be aware that you should write down all the periods of your life that you may feel irrelevant such as temporary jobs or being a mum or caring for an ill or elderly relative.

Your Skills – What you are naturally good at or have you practiced?:

Your Education - Including any vocational education (e.g . mindset through Karate):

Your Experience – Include any past hobbies, voluntary jobs and being a part of any organization:

Your Loves and Interests - Including Childhood Passions and things/causes that make you Passionate today:

Remember to use what you have remembered about yourself from the Centre Stage Process. Allowing yourself to think of when you felt the best. When you were most proud. What you loved the most. Enjoy the process. Really feel your way into your joy, your pride in what you can do, your awareness of doing the things you love.

Using the above write down your best bits into a package that the world needs and the world is willing to pay for by placing all of the best bits first, the things you are good at second and the skills that you have third and see where they overlap. Remember to look at your passions firstly as those are the single most important qualities that your business should be based on – they are your personal game changers and they have the power to take away fear. I say this because once you are truly passionate about something, the fear you have for the jobs that need to be done miraculously disappear. For me that was being visible. If I wanted to make a difference in the world, I had to get over my fear of being seen. My passion was much bigger than my Fear!!

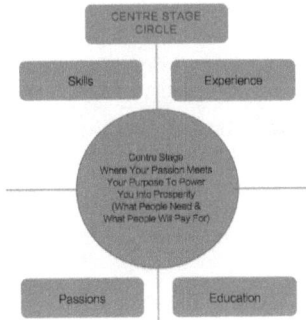

For a guided visualization MP3 download for The Centre Stage Circle join the A Woman On Purpose free membership and you'll find it there.

www.awomanonpurpose.com

Remember that if you are starting a business you need to use your due diligence and do market research to ensure that you are serving a market!

This can also help you if you are unable to see how to monetize your passion but I will share more about this in the Wealth and Career section.

A few things I will not lie to you about:

•Change does not happen over night. But you can start at ANY time.

•To be an expert you must have experience – do not run before you can walk. But every step you take is a step in the right direction.

•Be honest with yourself. Start at where you are. Reality is THE best place. Everyone has a journey begin yours today.

•Make sure your dreams are in alignment with your truth. Sometimes we have dreams that we will never achieve because they are not in alignment with who we really are. A tip for seeing if your dream job/place to live or any other situation is true to your authentic self is to sit quietly and with your eyes closed really live the moment. As if you are either IN the job or IN the place of your dreams and really feel what you feel. You will then 'KNOW' if this dream is in true alignment with your authentic self or you can sweep this into the 'fairytale' basket and free yourself up mentally, physically, emotionally and spiritually to really take Centre Stage in your LifeStory.

•There is ALWAYS a way.

Don't forget to enjoy every moment. Life is a journey to be enjoyed. The fact that you are even contemplating your purpose means that in your inner self you are on an enlightened journey that in itself needs to be enjoyed, trusted and nurtured.

It is okay to change your mind. That is natural. Just remember to revisit the Golden Centre whenever you need it!

Global Responsibility

What has Global Responsibility got to do with you, you may ask? Well, apart from being a really deep part of your purpose, no matter how small a part you play, it is our united gift to our future selves, our children and their children.

Don't think that this means you have to take the woes of the world on your shoulder but I do want you to know that you have as much right as anyone else on this planet to ensure that what we have in our tomorrows is better than what we have today.

I love the challenge of making the world a better place. I love the fact that it fills me up completely. I know what I am doing and have that sense of contentment and inner peace and happiness that most people are striving for and I am happy to share this.

The thing about Global Responsibility is that I cannot do this alone. I don't want to. I want to be in a circle of like-minded individuals that become peaceful warriors for this better world.

Envisioning all that could be created for and by us is what I have devoted the best part of ten years to. Upon reflection I know that the world needs leaders who are comfortable and kind in order to create the backbone of this plan.

A WOMAN ON PURPOSE

I looked around and all I could see was anger, pain, inequality and oppression and realized that the only way to move forward in society was to form a community of empowered women, who were as graceful and convincing as they need to be in order to action this.

I know that it is so easy to get lost in our own survival and I respect and honor that completely. If you are in a state of survival, I want to be able to support you. If you are in a place that you are able to join resources, then please know that you are not alone.

I believe that until ALL women are able to support themselves, with children, independently of all handouts and with the respect that they deserve then we need to fight for equality. We have children. Fact. I am not saying that men don't and that is a different argument but this is so vitally important to our welfare and our ability to create our world as we need it to be, that I am adamant about it.

We need to feel safe. We need to be free. We need to be able to make decisions based on how we feel and not strategically in order to survive. Until that time comes, I will continue.

We need to ensure the safety and welfare of all the millions of men, women and children around the world. I NEED to help. It is unacceptable. I cannot do it alone. I need help. I need you. We need each other.

I know that this may seem a little overwhelming but you can start where you are. Do yourself a favor and make sure your cup is full. Get help if you need it. Think strategically now for the compassionate future we all crave.

If you are ready to make a stand then start by sharing your gifts. Do not fear money. Do not fear opinions. Do not fear yourself. You can do it.

I know that we are bombarded by charitable causes and if all you can do is give to them in the form of money or volunteering - it is the system which we use now and there is nothing wrong with it - but I do envision a new way for all of us, in the future if we all work together.

If you can afford to buy products that do not harm the environment then fine, but do not put yourself into debt to do so. If you can afford to volunteer for a good cause, then by all means do that and feel the effects of contribution in your core. But do not feel unworthy if you are unable to do anything. You are enough!

Think of what your ultimate goals are and let go of those things that you are unable to control. They are unimportant in the bigger scheme of things.

Global Responsibility is something that we should all feel. Unfortunately, it seems that the more control a company or person has over this power then the less responsibility they seem to feel.

By collecting our good thoughts together we can form a Strong and Powerful voice to be reckoned with.

This is Global Responsibility. You don't have to carry it all by yourself. We do need to work together to make the world a better place and Just another good reason to become A Woman On Purpose.

Contribution

This is where the payback comes. It is the part of life that we undervalue and yet it is so rewarding to every single one of us.

When we learn to accept that we enjoy helping others, in whatever form that may be, we understand that it is not only a great benefit to those that we help but an integral part of making us happy.

I know that it is not always possible to give freely and in some circumstances in may not be possible to give at all but here I want you to realize that whenever you are doing a job you are contributing and should feel good about it. Whenever you are sharing you are contributing and should feel good about it. Whenever you are giving you are contributing and you should feel good about it.

Contribution is not measured in time or money. Contribution is measured in how you make yourself or someone else feel, therefore it is vital that you understand and nurture the emotions attached to it.

Some of us give all the time and yet feel as though they should do more. Some of us are unable to give as much as we would like and feel we should do more. Some of us are so caught up in their inability to see or value their worth that they diminish their own contribution factor to the point of non-existence.

The main thing that I shall refer to in this section is that 'You are Enough', whatever you give is enough and whatever you are able to give in the future will be enough.

Once you are able to really understand your intuitive power you will be able to see where you can give more and what you need to cut back on.

Even a smile is a contribution that may just save someone's life.

As with everything that I am sharing with you, you have to get to a point where you are filling yourself up, now, in order to over flow in the foreseeable and dream-able future.

When you see Contribution as a necessity in life and not just a measure of self worth it becomes more integral to your individual Magnificent Equilibrium, something that just is rather than something that measures your worth, either in yourself or by being recognized by others.

Contribution is just part of life. I will cover more about the financial side of this in Work and Money section but for now just know that it is A Part of Life and not a sub section that is exclusive to what you can give.

The whole reason that Law and Community are included as a section is that in most instances your purpose will be cultivated in this manner. Even if you are a hermit for a while in order to write a book, gather your thoughts, apply your actions or just to be, the results of your being a hermit will most likely be defined as your purpose.

As I have said before, we are all evolving and as we evolve so does our purpose. Whether our purpose is learning or playing whilst we grow up, or nurturing children, or caring for others when the time arises, these are all worthwhile purposes whilst they are happening.

The only problem we have had in recent years is the value of our contribution.

If the only thing that you get from this is to realize that you are purposeful already and that you are enough whether you are baking bread, working in a factory, caring for a loved one or running a multi-national company.

You are enough already - you are purposeful already.

If you are in transition then that is all that it is - a transition. It does not diminish who you were or who you are or who you may become.

If you are like many evolving women and want to work your purpose into your life so that you are financially, emotionally and physically supported by that, then you are in the right place, remember that there are those who are quite happy doing what they are doing and that that does not diminish them or their immediate purpose, at all.

I feel that there is a fundamental emergence of feminine power and energy on the planet and I am certain that I am not the only one. In order for us to harness that power and energy we need to work together, support one another, be gentle with ourselves and be strong in our immediate foundation.

I aim to create a community where this is embodied and supported. I hope that you will want to be a part of this Global

Contribution.

LifeStyle Business – Legal & Human Resources

Often the scariest part of setting up a business is dealing with the legalities. It needn't be if you get the right support. As more and more women start up their own LifeStyle Businesses, there will be more and more support in these areas available by people who know their job well and want to live their lives with the freedom you are looking for, as well.

There are a lot of things that you need to think about when structuring your business, such as whether you will be a sole trader or set up a limited company, where and what insurances you require, whether or not you will have trademarks or copyright concerns and you will also have financial responsibilities.

The best way to get over the fear of all of this is to get help. I know that many entrepreneurs start off with very little money but there are many free resources now that can be found on the internet and many governmental or local organizations that will be able to point you in the right direction.

The one thing I would definitely not do though is bury my head in the sand. As the industry grows there will be more scrutiny placed on those trading as LifeStyle Businesses. In order to make sure that we have a sustainable industry we need to instill a sense of trust in our audience.

When to get the help you need also is a question that is hard to give an answer to but I will try. Begin with the help you need to get started i.e. basic advice on how you trade whether as self-employed or immediately as a business, employ an accountant to file your books, this needn't be expensive but should be included as an essential cost per year, see how much other services are that you may need to delegate as your time becomes filled up and include them in a growth plan and make sure you have insurance to cover your service/goods - you never know when you will need it and not having it is just not worth the risk.

It doesn't have to cost a lot of money. As long as you have a strategy in place you can start as you are and include costs as you go along.

It gives you great freedom to serve and serve well if you know that you are working not only from a place of beauty but from a place of a legal and sound business plan. Leaving you free to share your gifts with the world and explore the Infinite Possibilities that the freedom of running your own business can bring.

Chapter 4
Work & Wealth

3RD DIRECTION

Purpose, Perception, Philanthropy

Personal Survival Spiral
Lottery Living
Destination Divining & Divine Destination
Visualization & Expansion Timeline
Working Your Purpose
Find Your Confidence for Centre Stage
Living Your Brand - Branding Your Life
StoryBoard, Craft & Creation - Integrated LifeStyle Planning
Lights, Camera, Action - Integrated LifeStyle Action
LifeStyle Business - Product & Service

Personal Survival Spiral

In any business plan you will be asked to figure out and plan your personal survival budget. Your life should be no different. When you start to integrate both your work and life into a truly balanced LifeStyle, then I like to think of our survival budget and our dream budget as a spiral in the same vein as nature does in her Golden Ratio.

The Golden Ratio is what nature does when she expands. She starts off small and then grows in proportion and expands in perfect ratios. It is a simple mathematical relationship that is found naturally and in many great works of art and in contemporary designs. To put a picture in your mind think of a nautilus seashell.

The Golden Ratio is used to analyze the proportions of natural objects as well as man-made systems such as financial markets, so even though I do not use the proportions to scale I believe that it is a fabulous and perfectly named way for us to plan our growth.

From wherever you are now, you can grow to be whatever your heart desires but you don't just need to dream bigger, you need to feel that growth, expand carefully but certainly and plan for that dream, whatever that might be!

Your Golden Centre must feel secure in its foundation. You need to feel safe in order to truly dream. You need to feel secure to feel the freedom to dream big. You need to have your basic needs met, at least to get beyond hope, although I do not knock hope if you need it but I want to hand you a Golden Ticket to dream whatever your heart desires and to enjoy the journey.

For any journey to travel to the spots you most desire you need a plan of some kind or another.

I am not a rigid planner and love excursions that lead me to uncover scenic routes that I never knew existed but I also love being a strategic thinker because the planning helps solidify my dreams. Having a plan to action is monumental in increasing flow and momentum.

It does not matter which area of your life you wish to grow in you can apply the same principle. Start in the center and keep going. Start in the center and keep getting better. Start in the center and keep developing.

In this section of the book though I start in the center and plan to grow an integrated LifeStyle but you can use the same principle in any area of your life or finances that you need to.

A personal survival spiral begins by making sure that all of your basic needs are met. This means being truthful with yourself and being able to see that you have an understanding of your truthful and actual financial status as it stands at this present moment.

In order to do this you need to go over the last years finances (I say year because some payments are made annually) and be aware of anything that may need to be paid every two or three years. This will happen sometimes if you get a better deal for paying for 2 or 3 years rather than for one.

You then need to ensure that you break your outgoings down into monthly segments in order to ensure that you have not only your projected income taken care of but that you have a safety net to get you to that projected income.

Don't fall into the trap of being incredibly frugal in your plan. It will very rarely be kept when you see those gorgeous shoes or have an uncontrollable urge for chocolate or champagne!

Then start to see where you can grow. What you need to earn to meet your basic needs and start adding in the projected dreams along with the projected needs.

I know that this is an incredibly simplistic way of looking at life and growth but I do believe that it is realistic. I like being realistic with my dreams and realizing those dreams and when they start to merge and become part of the same journey everything becomes a lot easier to see, to achieve and to enjoy in the moment.

Start off in your Golden Center and with every expansion link your dreams to actions and enjoyment. You will be living your own personal Golden Ratio and be on your way to an Integrated LifeStyle.

In my workshops I will deal with practical elements and give you the tools that make this even clearer but just wanted you to realize that you can be in perfect flow and growth and follow a natural action plan.

A seashell starts small but determined and keeps growing. Your Golden Ratio begins where you are today and has the power to be Infinite. Why not start today?

Lottery Living

'When we win the lottery'

How many times have you heard that? I bet you can't even begin to count them.

My question to you is what if you did? What then? What would you do and how would you do it?

I want you to realize the value of living your purpose, so to explain how I feel every single day I want you to know that 'winning the lottery' is the way I feel every single day.

I am not always happy. I still get disgruntled. I sometimes worry about things and sometimes that indeed turns to panic but my purpose is so strong in my being that the answer to the questions 'what do you want to do now?' and 'what would you like to do if you won the lottery?' are exactly the same.

I may shop in a different manner or choose to live in a different house or even choose how I go on holiday but as far as day-to-day purpose goes I wouldn't change a thing.

This is because my Purpose is integral to me. It is a part of me. It is an obligation, albeit a happy one. It is a duty, a duty I want to fulfill. It is how I want to be and how I want to present myself.

It is in me and outside me. It is how I live and the reason I live.

It is like having something very, very rare and knowing that you are one of the lucky few.

Having a reason to live takes away the need for a windfall, as you know that you are already living in a way that so few are fortunate to know, that no amount of money would make deviating from your divine purpose attractive or even fathomable.

How you get to this conclusion for yourselves is again very simple. You just need to decide on what you really want from life and what you want to do in life and while using your intuition and Golden Ratio to get to your Divine Destination. As long as you do that you can take yourself out of the linear timeline that we are so used to living and start Being every single day.

The easiest way to figure out how you want to live your life is to actually give yourself the luxury of thinking about how you would live, day to day, if you had received a huge windfall.

Relax and really think about it. Not the immediate party and opening of the champagne but when you had settled down.

Start thinking about what you would really do day to day.

Where would you wake up?

How would you feel?

What would you do immediately?

What would you have for breakfast?

What would you do next?

A WOMAN ON PURPOSE

What would you fill your day with?

What would you have for lunch/dinner?

What would you do in the afternoon/evening?

Who would your friends be?

How would you spend your leisure time?

How much time would you spend on your own?

How much time would you spend with family and friends?

That is it. A day is a day no matter how much money you have.

I am sure that in there you will also have some major clues as to what your ultimate purpose is too.

I don't care if you would spend your time fishing or clubbing or setting up a home for abandoned children. Your immediate purpose will be whatever you are drawn to do without the immediate worries that curb your imagination.

If this past paragraph has made you think again, then think again, it is all good. I have no attachment to the answers you give and if you are reading this for the first time the answers may be more leisurely than if you go through it for the tenth time.

What I can tell you though is that if you do give yourself the freedom to live without the worries that hinder our everyday existence you will start to excavate your true passions and with passion invariably comes purpose.

At whatever stage you are at, that is perfect for you. The way for this exercise to really take to its own is to let you start reaching for these dreams from the comfort of your Golden Centre in your Golden Ratio. When you start to work towards these freedom-releasing areas from the confines of your shell, you realize that you can expand and plan your next layer.

Growing from within your safe and foundational structure you are able to touch the freedom and find ways in which to fund (both financially and through purposeful action) these dreams to find you are now able to live an Integrated LifeStyle with Infinite Possibilities!

How cool is that?

Destination Divining & Divine Destination

Let's make this plan a little clearer.

So we know that we all have the exact same Divine Destination, but working within our divine right for Beauty, is what I have called our 'Pension Plan'.

This is our ultimate and happy retirement plan. It is not static and it has the ability to change and to be manipulated to look like anything you want it to be. We want it to be based on our best projections, for how to be the best Glam Gran and yet undertake the risk assessment, so that we have any unfortunate situations taken care of - right?

So I am hoping that by now you are able to see how these two destinies become divinely interlinked with your Personal Rhythm and that your steps as Masterpieces lead you safely along your Divine Journey.

This is where your map becomes clearer. Your foundations stronger. Your outlook brighter and your ability to reach Infinite Possibilities gains momentum.

Your Golden Ratio begins from where you are now and expands with your dreams with your Divine Destination on the outer most ring that you never have to reach so you can make that dream as big as you desire!

The exciting part about creating a Dynamic Golden Ratio is making work a part of life and life a part of work. It seems so simple in theory but here is the part where most of us get into extreme panic or overwhelm and so keep on the course of action that we have been on forever and stay in our comfort zone. For some of us that is perfect! But for those of you who are really feeling the pull here to integrate your life and make it pay the financial reward too, I shall attempt to make the road ahead a little clearer and more accessible, so that you feel the pull so strongly that your Purpose is now your way forward. Essentially it takes away overwhelm and diminishes the fear for you.

You see, once you have Divined your Destination and stepped into the role completely, you will never, ever be able to step back. In a good way though! You throw away fear and put on determination. You throw away angst and realize that you have to fill your cup in order to fill your Divine Purpose. You have to come out of hiding to some degree so you may as well put on the glad rags! You will feel so strongly that playing small will not be an option.

Do not feel dismay if you are not feeling this way. Everyone has the right to feel whatever they are feeling and if you are comfortable with your financial and career situation, then that is perfect, too. This section is for those that need to integrate and expand. Whether that is by starting their own business or stepping into another arena or whatever that might be.

This book has been written to help you find YOUR path. Not mine. Not someone else's. YOURS.

The beautiful thing about the Golden Ratio is that it grows

with you. It can change with you but you have a goal that is tangible, too. With your retirement plan you know that you are growing older - I don't care if you are already retired, this is about living! This is about filling your life to the brim and always working from a place of beauty.

Visualization & Expansion Timeline

So now we know where we are going it is time to start putting some meat on the bones, so to speak, and start to embody your Golden Ratio.

I find the best way to do this is through beauty. Create a sacred space in your mind that is completely devoted to your dreams. Start with now and start to compose the music to go with your dreams. The film begins to roll and you can start to get a feeling of how you want to be. Think of immediate goals of beauty and step into them.

How do you look?

What do you feel like?

What do you wear?

Look at your skin?

Your hair?

Where are you?

What are you doing?

What are your plans?

Get so full up in your mind that there is only pleasure to be felt in your body and your mind.

Start to feel the power of your passionate joy.

What can you do?

What would you like to do?

Thinking like the seasons is a great way to start.

I like to think of summertime.

Of the feel of the sun on my skin and how it is touched with bronze?

I am wearing a white or orange dress.

I step into that me.

Now start to visualize what comes next.

What does the next season hold for you?

What are you going to do?

What are you going to wear?

How will you feel?

Where are you going?

What does your heart want you to do next?

You can use this process to guide you through to any part of your life that you want.

Be sure to only plan from that solid foundation of beauty and start to form a timeline for your mind movie.

If you need to make a vision board that is absolutely fine but the trick is to embody the vision. The vision isn't just on a piece of paper or locked into a computer. It is locked into you and your soul.

The power of your mind and the power of your vision are far greater if you truly believe them.

Lock them into your soul. You will start to remember the things that really stand out and not get as sidetracked as you would do looking at a vision board that you created in the past.

It is good to revisit vision boards though. Sometimes you have ideas that are dormant and that get excavated by vision boarding. They are still true but their time has not come.

The whole journey of making your own mind movie is to let your dreams get in line with your intuitive self, your inner core.

When you go back to your vision in your mind, the things that are in your immediate timeline will be there as well as the things that help you envision your expansion.

When you go back to the vision board of your creation you will usually see that you have been able to achieve the feeling or emotion that you related to a particular picture and be reminded of things that were important to you, which helped you with your foundation at the time.

Some of these things you will need to incorporate in future visioning and some will fall away. Some will be spot on and some will have a different look or feel to them. They are all valid. You will be able to see the beauty within the beauty. You will be able to see the way that you can expand and not be determined to hold onto a specific idea but to meander with the river of change and to suck the best out of everything.

Just writing this is making me feel expansion coming on. I have felt so attached to the writing process. Something that I never incorporated in my mind movie until a few years ago. Writing this book has never been in my personal visualization and yet I am compelled. I sat down to write the outline and it was there. I sit down to write every single day but sometimes I never write a word. I cannot see the end. I do not have a specific time to finish. I have the outline and when it is complete it will be complete.

I am coming to the end - none of this was in my vision - yet I am compelled.

The purpose of visualizing is to create the beautiful picture. How you paint that picture will reveal itself along the way. Trust the process. Start the journey. Make your steps masterpieces.

The timeline I speak of is not specific. Your dreams do not have expiry dates. You see into the future. You create your vision. It is yours. Do with it what you please.

Never put negative energy into this process. Whether you are looking at pictures in a book or on the internet put the same intention into them as you did when looking at a beautiful fairy story as a child. You need to put the intention of wonder and excitement behind them. You have to give them a happy ending. Your purpose is the morale and your action

Working Your Purpose

Working your purpose may be staying at home or working in a job that meets your needs. It may mean that you have to work in a job that you hate to ensure that your basic needs are met, in order for you to make the next part of your dream become real. If this is where you are, that is perfect, too.

What I am exploring more, here, is that once you have decided on your purpose, make sure it is something that you could completely devote yourself and your financial freedom to.

That is what is exciting about the times that we are living in. We have the ability to not only create our future but to be financially rewarded, abundantly so, for the efforts we put in.

This is nothing new. Only the expansion of creation has opened up this Global Arena that leads A Woman On Purpose to her personal Infinite Possibilities, enabling her to serve her purpose and earn her freedom, in a way that has never opened up before.

When you decide to really embody your gifts, and to share them, you know that there can be no other way to fulfillment. Nothing in the world would be able to take you from this next course of action.

Once you get to this stage there is no looking back. You will have to do and be and share what you have been put on this earth to do, in the time that enables you to do so.

It is scary stuff to start your own business and go through both the practical and systematic measures that you need, as well as the legal and structural measures.

This book is not about that side of things, although I hope to give you all of this in a step-by-step guide very soon.

This book is about you and your inner workings. Making sure that you know that you and your purpose are enough. Giving you the confidence to be true to your inner knowing, so that you have a solid foundation for a business structure and the empowerment to follow it through and reach for the outer limits of your Infinite Possibilities.

This section helps you to become one with your mission in life - your purpose. It helps you to be safe in the enjoyment of every moment and know that you are not and never will be alone.

This is a Global Movement. This is a Global Transformation. The feminine energy that we feel rising on the planet is different because we are different.

We are so used to the masculine energy and to actual repression over the centuries that we fail to remember that we are as powerful, yet ultimately more peaceful than the war-torn and corrupt energy that has permeated our soil, recently.

There is a surge of anger that is emerging and awakening so many of us, no matter where we happen to live in the world. We have been privy to the horrendous happenings of the world and want change, but it is more than that. It is like we are a collective volcano ready to erupt. We need to work together and we need to work in a way that supports our divine feminine and sacred energy. It is like we have escaped from the core of the earth and want to coat it in our compassion, but in order to do that we must face the enemy.

I do not mean men. I love men. But the energy that is ruling the world is not good. You know it and I know it.

There were a few good years in recent history when we could bathe in luxury, explore our possibilities and know that the charities and governments were doing all they could to help the world. That time allowed us to realize what we want as women, as individuals.

It gave us the luxury of time to see that we, as women, were at least good enough and, at times, much better than we had been allowed to be.

I thank those times and our forefathers and foremothers! We are the only generation that will have benefitted from all of the collective hard work and fight that generations of oppressed people had strived for. We were the products. We reaped the reward. We know what we are capable of.

We all know that we do not want to make the same mistakes and cannot change the world in the same manner.

This is our time.

Our time of emergence. Our time of empowerment. Our time of entitlement. Of our earth. Of our lives. Of our freedom. Of creativity. Of happiness. Of peace.

So there are many of us that are now realizing that our own journey can be used to fuel that mission. We know that in order to overcome and to overrule the powers that be we, in turn, need to be powerful.

We also know deep in our ancient DNA that we cannot be powerful in the same way, so we are being woken up to our own independence, our own feminine power.

I love the fact that the whole world of women is united in this feeling.

I am aware that it is a time of transition and I hope to help you on your journey.

If you have now decided that you are one of those who is ready to share her story and become one of the leaders of the new paradigm, this is for you.

Not only is it our time. It is your time.

Whatever your chosen line of business you must be aware of the fact that this world is as abundant as our possibilities. It is a very difficult time, trying to marry traditional entrepreneurship with our feminine ways but I am here to say that it is all very relevant and needed.

With regard to pricing and becoming congruent in your own perceived value I use a simple and yet extremely powerful analogy.

Whilst I struggled with putting a financial price on my work and am forever coming up with Infinite Possibilities I see, I have managed to come to a place that sits in alignment with my purpose. I would say that your financial alignment should be in line with those you are serving and the reach of whom you wish to serve. To explain a bit more - I would not be alive if I had been born even 25 years before, and I got over survivor guilt by realizing that I was born in this day and age to live my particular story and then give my gifts from there. From a business point of view I want to serve a vast area of women into empowerment and leadership and therefore I have been writing a book that will be accessible to many at a low cost. From there I will give various levels of service and price them in accordance with the level of my time, depth of my service and the reach of the gift. We live in an age where we use money. I wish to be responsible for myself, and support the reach of my gifts and allay any incongruence I may feel into each particular financial attachment.

A lot of the businesswomen I see at the moment lead with the pain and the problem that we have come through ourselves and feel qualified enough to be able to help.

Whilst I am truly aware of the advertising benefits the pain and the problem suggest, I would ask if you truly feel that this is what You should do and feel if it is in alignment with the gifts that you want to share and how you would like to share them.

Our words are incredibly powerful. You become your brand. I would highly recommend that the words you use, you become so be highly aware of what you step into as you create this side of your business. Be Positive. Be Powerful. Be Purposeful. Let your words lead you into the way you want to live and the way you wish to serve.

You need to be powerful enough to lend your voice in a time when the world is in such desperate need.

We, as sisters, cannot afford to let this chance pass us by. We have seen ancient tribes and cultures that were very sophisticated get crushed before. We cannot let our knowledge of freedom die.

We owe it to our ancestors and we owe it to future generations.

Do not be afraid. We need to work together to make the world a better place.

Find Your Confidence For Centre Stage

Now that you have your idea in place, you can relax for a bit whilst you decide how to deliver it.

This too, is completely up to you. It is as much as a creative process and a magical journey as you make it. There are no limits to how you decide to step into you and so this is a section on transformation.

I don't mean just a physical transformation but also the ability to get out the dressing up box and become your purpose.

Whether you decide to deliver your next step through your work at home, in a job or as a business, your confidence will become as clear as it needs to be at the time. Remember that there is flow in everything and the energy changes. You can change as much as you like or stay the same, only more at peace if that is your calling. All is well. Everything is perfect. Trust the process.

Do not try to skip the stations of your journey. This will undermine the flow, and put obstacles in your path - even if these obstacles are to get you back on your sacred path! If you relax into your flow you will become a part of the journey and enjoy it more.

You are a warrior for your own purpose, whether you are completely clear on that or not.

Finding your Centre Stage is a process of direction. Directions can change and stations can be revisited. All of the processes I am going to suggest are here to help you in the moment and create your inner peace with Being in the now.

If you are confused at any time, then that is also a part of your journey. Do not become upset that the fog has not lifted but relax into the fog and be supported by it. You do not need to know. This is itself is a realization.

If you are doing all you can. That is enough.

If you need to know how to do it, trusting your intuition and expanding your awareness will help unblock the societal elements that cloud our intuitive way and enable you to take one step forward. Think about the problems you are having from an awareness outside of yourself, outside of society and more from an awareness of what needs to be done in order to share your gifts with the world.

We have taken the time to excavate our dreams and our hopes for our future and this will help you take the next step.

To become the Embodiment of your Now.

If you are looking to start a business this will help you to gain the confidence to make this a practical and tangible part of your life, because as we discovered in the foundation, to work from a place of insecurity or lack is a dangerous and uncomfortable position.

By now you will know where you want to be but maybe a little unsure and unconfident about getting there. This is where you can start embodying archetypes of encouragement. Step into the role that you need, when you need it. A bit like getting ready for a role on stage, but you get to determine who that character is going to be and everything that she needs to emanate.

I am going to give you a few ideas to start.

The first outfit to try on would be that of the Warrior! You will get some odd reactions when you decide to work your purpose. It is best to put the armor on straight away. Even your best friend, partner and family may question your decisions!

The next one is the Princess! We work from a place of beauty and so you have to ensure that you are in this mode for dreaming and creating. This is the time to embody the dream and to be creative with it. Use your childlike wonder, curiosity and enjoyment to its full.

The Mother is the next one. Whether you have children or not you will need to have the responsible hat on sometimes so make her proud!

The Super-Hero! Now is where you can have fun. Decide on your super hero to power your strengths. If you know you are good at something this is where you let it shine!

The Queen! You take charge. Claim your space. Your time. Your Energy. Your respite. Delegate jobs that hinder your creative flow!

Mother Nature! Make decisions on where you can be ecologically friendly and give your time and energy to the universal flow!

The Artist! Paint the scene. Where you work. Where you live. Where you sleep. What you eat. How you move. Your weapon of choice - pen, brush, earth, potatoes - you decide! Define your creation station and fly!

The Magician! Where and how you make things happen. Using your skills, deciding how to make them work for you. This is your job or business or product. Ta Dah!

The Goddess! This is for the sacred. The quiet time. The reflection. This is your inner core. Grace, serenity, meditation, beliefs, rituals.

The Alchemist! The one who makes it happen. She will not give up and comes up with sometimes whacky but effective ideas to turn your suffering into Gold!

The Dame! This is the showgirl. Your outside presence. When you step into the big wide world. This gal will support you.

The Seductress! She can turn putty into Gold and Gold into molten putty. You know when she needs to come out!

The Dancer! This lady steps forward with elegance and class and confidence. Her back a rod and her every step a masterpiece.

The Devil! She is in all of us so let her out occasionally. She is smart, though, so only shouts if nobody is listening and can cover her anger with a smile!

The Actress! Helpful lady this one! She can be called upon readily for you to embody any archetype you need whenever you need her.

The Guardian Angel! Sometimes we are needed or to be called

upon for comfort. Even if you can't feel the pain you can empathize!

The Temptress! Your secret marketing weapon. She will entice your needed fellows with whatever she has. You won't know what hit you.

These are just a few of the archetypes that you can use to help you gain confidence in your new role to help you through.

Although the practices are for you and your immediate confidence they can help you tremendously in your work too.

As an Entrepreneur you will need to wear many hats - why not make them all gorgeous.

So now you have learnt how to Work It baby! It is time to explore the Infinite Possibilities.

Living Your Brand – Branding Your Life

So I have mentioned the fact that I wasn't born Gold! What I need to explain more is how I have BEcome Gold!

My family name is Jones. Yet for me to truly represent my gifts I found it was very difficult to BE a Jones - to embody Jones and to represent Jones. It may not be for others and I did love being a Jones, don't get me wrong but I love Being Gold.

When I decided to Be Gold - I Knew it, I felt it and it was very easy for me to become it and to represent it. Not only did it brand my business but it branded who I wanted to be, inside and out.

It says I want pure luxury. I now live that. Not necessarily all the time, both inside and out, but there is always an element (do you like that) of Gold in my life. Today I sit here in gym clothes sipping hot water and lemon and writing about Gold. There isn't material luxury in my day, today, but I had sunshine and blackbirds and the luxury of pouring molten words into this manuscript.

I had to think about the inside of how I want to be portrayed. To me Gold is pure, graceful, elegant and shines from within. It is personal and you don't have to see these parts, but I needed to embody them

I had so much fun with the external portrayal, too. My hair, my clothes, my photos, my business. It gave me a wide berth to work within and a structure to follow.

People refer to me as Goldilocks, Ms. Gold or Sparkler! It is ensuring that what you put out into the world is representing your purpose, too, and enjoying every moment of that process.

How can you BE your brand and make it part of your life. Your life should not be separate from your work. To truly live and integrate your LifeStyle you need to have it all. Have I mentioned I am a greedy girl!!

What can you do so that your work is a part of your lifestyle?

You can incorporate leisure and holidays and events, the world is your oyster. Just remember that whilst your dream may not be somebody else's, you must be true to yourself and your brand in order to start the whole marketing and visibility process. So why not enjoy every moment.

Start thinking about incorporating everything into your life and your business. Just because it hasn't been the norm, doesn't mean that things have to be the same. We have so much work to do; we may as well pave the way for the future entrepreneurettes!!!!

I see it as a duty to really enjoy every moment. You don't have to make everything public but you can make everything feel right to you.

Don't worry. We all make mistakes and some of us even wear the wrong shoes every now and again!!! Whatever branding you decide on can change and flow with you so don't think rigidly, either. It is so easy to get into a routine and comfortable, but you never see thriving companies stick to the same advert! You can be your own PR agency, your own advert! And you can see what works for you in every way.

A few tips on how to really embody your brand and brand your life is to try out a few different introductions. See what fits you, your clients and your life. So that it becomes a seamless flow. This helps incorporate your elevator pitch with your social introductions, you become who you want to be and step into your brand and your life. Within that brand you can expand safely and see what works.

Make your words work with you. Make your social media and social presence intertwine and shine what you offer through every outlet.

What you wear, what you adorn yourself and your life with. Car, house, shoes, jewelry, notebooks, handbags and purses. What is your style? What will you be known for?

How exciting is this? Business does not have to be just one section of you. It can be fun and become you in every sense.

Who will you be to the world?

StoryBoard, Craft & Creation - Integrated LifeStyle Planning

So now we have an idea of what we want to do, who we want to be and how we want to expand, it is time to start the manifestation and creation process. The most practical and visual way to do this is to storyboard your ideas.

This could work for business or life or the integration of both! It is just to give you the structure and stepping board to work with and to get the timeline to work with you, so that you are in sync with your personal rhythm and flow.

Remember that everything can and will change so it is important to retain the flexibility to move with whatever life puts in front of you. Also remember that if you are not observant or feel that something is wrong, then heed the universe when it comes back to slap you into seeing what it is guiding you towards.

By this I mean that if you have a step to make and it is not going smoothly, be sure to trust that and don't fight against the tide. When the time is right, the universe will open up to you and lead the way. Remember you may have forgotten the intention, as there is no linear timeline when it comes to being educated by the universe.

It is always helpful to have a map before you set off on a journey and your life purpose is the most important of all journeys!

Having a map does not mean that you can not stop to rest or divert to a scenic route or be met with diversions, it just helps solidify your mind movie and can be reflected upon when needed.

A bit like a vision board but this is like a vision board for your mind to have direction and steps to take along the way.

It is also great fun! The beauty of how I deliver this is that each section can be moved, be changed, be reflected upon and there are no limits! You can keep it forever and pass it down to your children, so that you can show them exactly how the power of positivity and belief really manifest in ones life. That, in itself, will be proof to generations that this shit works!!!

It is also similar to a bucket list, because you can put on the things that you would like to achieve and never have to put a date on achieving them. Have a reminder and always have something to work towards, which always, always helps in taking action and achievement. Cyclical again but it does work.

The other magical part of the storyboarding process is that it can be used in all areas of your life, for putting your personal story arch together for personal or business use and to just gain clarity in any area of your life that is urging attention.

I have no attachment to whether this works spiritually or psychologically. In fact, the beauty and the magic of this is that we don't know how it works, but just that it does work!

I will show you an outline of how to create your own storyboard. For this I will use the complete Golden Compass so that you can see how comprehensive it is and then show you how you can narrow it down to plan for a small section of your life, or to tell a story.

As you now know the Golden Compass is based on two Infinite Principles:

Self - All that you know and can control

Unknown - All that you don't know and cannot control

Then we work with the Six Directions Intrinsic to life:

Your Magnificent Equilibrium - The solid foundation and always in the present.

Work & Wealth - To gain the recognition and self-worth all humans crave.

Love & Relationships - Including your life partner and family and friends.

Law & Community - Your contribution & belonging

Health & Wellbeing - Covering self-care in every way inside and out

Spiritual / Philosophical Path - Your connection to your soul whether you have religious beliefs or not.

The difference between a vision board and a storyboard is that there isn't a need for *specific* attachment to time with a LifeStyle Business storyboard but it works like a timeline and can change and has fluidity. It is, in essence, a guide for your intuition and for you to embody your life plan rather than for a specific year or for a specific goal (although you can be specific if you wish).

Although you can narrow certain elements down, the storyboard also helps you to highlight the courses of action to take in order to reach each dream and creation. The storyboard is always in action!

As the storyboard is also a prediction for your future you are giving your trust to the universe to sort it out, whilst taking assertive action at the same time.

Another thing that makes Storyboarding helpful is that you can prioritize and expand certain elements when they need the attention and move them around if the story flows better that way. Get my picture, sorry, story!

So, the same as for a cartoon or film you can block out certain sections of a piece of paper. I think it is better to have a different page for each one. All eight elements in the Golden Compass make for a full life but don't worry if one or two sections are more dominant at the moment - that is the way life rolls!!!

For each area of the compass set out intentions, each on a post it note and then place them in order as you see them occurring in your life. There are no set rules here and because we are working with the universe. There is no linear timeline so just crack on with what appeals to you.

Once you have done this for each section you get a large sheet of paper and draw an arch, a bit like a rainbow.

Below the arch on the left hand side, make a list of all eight sections of the compass in order of relevance to you - remember this can and will be changeable!

Then starting with the left hand side at this moment place the post-it-note of choice of each section, in the order of importance and when you would like to achieve them, no set timeline - you are working with the universe but it is handy to give her a clue.

Some areas will be full and other areas empty - that is your emotion and not how things will turn out! Your attachment to the attainment of anything will be shown in this practice so you will see where areas of your life are just so overcrowded that you cannot gain any clarity. You will also see the areas of your life that are sorely in need of attention!

I am hoping at the visualization of this rainbow story arch you will be able to focus on giving the areas a more even keel. See where you can focus more valuable and productive intentions and don't be afraid to let some areas slide.

This is where you try to forget all of the rational modern teachings of timelines, of action plans and of structures and see what FEELS right to you.

I hope that you will have at least one hairy goal on your story arch and that you have given as much importance to self-care and respite.

Once you are in tune with your intuitive guide, you can then take another page and this will be a step. Decorate it! Remember each one is a masterpiece and must appeal to you now. You have your arch, you have your storyboard - just decorate the first step. You can continue with this if you so desire or, if you are in a time of turmoil, just concentrate on the first one.

If you need to focus or define one section of your life that is in need of attention use the same process. Just give it a bit more decorative attention. Expand, craft, create!

Try to do this in a state of love and positivity. If you are not putting good intention into this practice it will not give you what you want.

If you need to take time out, do. Think, meditate, breathe, listen to music. As with everything I share, it is for you to use when you need it and how you need it. There is no pressure or rush.

The whole creation can be as large as you want or you can fit it into a notebook. Whatever works for you.

You are predicting, creating, manifesting and calling in!

As with everything (I do) - come from a place of beauty and don't worry if you see that your attention is being grabbed by one particular stream or theme, that is your own inner guidance, do not ignore it. As with everything with life, your guidance loves attention and will repay love with love.

You are being given guidance, action steps and an outline plan for your life. It will not stay exactly to the story arch and that is why you have every single part on a note - they can move with you in your universal and personal flow. This way you never let go of your dreams!

I know that many people say that you should give direct messages to the universe or God or intention. If that works for you then fine. I have never felt the urge to do that as when I look back everything happened perfectly and led me to be where I am today. Maybe I shall give it a go! I would probably forget though as my dreams and intentions are as real to me as day to day and therefore they are playing in my mind constantly!

Playing out the story of my life in the same way I used to daydream about fairytales when I was a child.

This is your story - you can even use this same system for crafting your business, your speeches and your home decor if you need to!

Don't forget to have fun - don't forget your naughty side - she has as much right to play in this story! Dream big, create big, craft big! All the world is a stage but the stage is yours to be imagined!

Lights, Camera, Action - Integrated LifeStyle Action

It is time! I hate to be the one to tell you but in order to really share your gifts with the world you have to be visible.

I know! Shock! Horror!

I have been there. I know the feeling. It is scary beyond belief but try as you might it is impossible to avoid if you really want to go out into the world, share your gifts and truly step into being A Woman On Purpose.

Don't worry too much (I will not say at all because I have yet to not feel nervous when even describing what I do). I will give you some practical tools and hold your hand if you want.

The time to take Centre Stage is now though, so it is time to slap on the pan-stick (old fashioned stage make-up), get those glamorous clothes on and step into the person you want to reveal to the world.

The main things you have to remember are to know that you are needed by someone out there - that alone should make you come out with your glitter guns a-blazing!

The next thing you need to know is that everyone starts somewhere. Even if you have been used to being Centre-stage as an actor, or in the board room, or at a sales meeting, being and selling your gifts are a completely different ball game but the most rewarding ball game you will ever play.

Breathe. I often forget and then I remember, take a breath and see how vital it is - funny that! Three deep breaths seem to work a treat, so never underestimate the power of oxygen.

Don't forget to value yourself and be confident in that. So many people I see do not value their gifts enough to live the life they truly deserve. If you know your market and have researched the general market price point and you are in the same (or slightly higher) bracket for that product or service then you have nothing to worry about. You are dealing in a world where money is used, fact. Just use the currency we are using until they find something new, but never give all of your gifts away or undersell them. You must be able to support yourself, your dreams and your own Infinite Possibilities in order to give back to the world.

I completely support philanthropy in the world but as the adage goes, charity begins at home. Remember to fill your own money cup to be able to give more. Full to the brim and overflow like a waterfall - far more graceful than grappling, I say.

If you are struggling with being in the public eye adopt the view that you are playing a part when you do. Step into her and be her and do what you want to do and say what you want to say. I know that this isn't going to sound authentic in the fashionable sense, but if you are looking for a way to be a bit more visible and contain the nervousness or absolute terror that sometimes brings, then creating a Superhero version of yourself to step into is just like using a prop to get the best effect.

You will always be striving to be a better you. That is what happens when you become aware of your truth so you will never, ever get to fully become the Superhero. That in itself is a fabulous way to enjoy your life and keep the excitement going - always stretching yourself and containing that in a superhero outfit gives you the freedom to step into your limelight and into your Infinite Possibilities!

LifeStyle Business - Product & Service

The most important part of having a LifeStyle business!

Without knowing what your product or service is and how you will package that, you have no business.

I know how hard it is to package your own worth and to then have to sell it but I also know that it is possible and achievable for all.

Whether you have a physical product or an online service, you still have to package what you sell in a way that is on brand and attractive to your ideal target market.

Once you know what it is you are offering it is just a matter of deciding on how you are going to deliver it and at what price.

A good way to do that is to research similar offerings in your ideal market place. This will show you what else is out there, how it is packaged and at what price it is selling for.

Remember that everyone and everything starts somewhere.

The wonderful thing about putting an offering together is that it truly expands your creativity.

It doesn't matter how practical you are, this is like giving birth.

You conceive the idea, feed it, nurture it and create it with love.

Love is such a big part of creating your product or service in a LifeStyle business. You are the creator, you are behind the idea and you will be releasing it to the world.

Start at the beginning and keep on track. There may be changes that come along the way but keep focused on the end product.

It doesn't have to be perfect. Nothing is. You can tweak, you can make good but you do have to get to the end in order to sell.

For me, I knew that I needed to create this book to encapsulate the teaching that I wish to share with the world.

It is only the beginning and it has taken some months of dedicated devotion but I have managed it.

I am sure that it will not be perfect. There will be parts that need work but I can always revisit them later.

Do not ever feel that your offering is not worthy. The only difference between you and those already out there selling is that they are already out there selling.

As long as you are completely in love with your work you cannot go wrong.

Decide what that product will be and it will be a masterpiece. It may have a few flaws but imperfection is perfect in my book and if you wait until it is perfect you will be waiting forever and miss the Infinite Possibilities to share your gifts with the world.

Chapter 5
Love & Relationships

4TH DIRECTION

Precious People

Love
The Tea Ceremony
Modern Love
Intimate Love
Finding a Soul Flame
Loving Your Family & Friends
Love, Guilt & Letting Go
Loving Your Warrior Sisters
LifeStyle Business - Public Relations & Networking

Love

I set up the structure of this book a good few months ago and the whole essence of what I share within it is Love.

As I have mentioned before, at times it does not even feel like it is coming from me. I feel a compulsion to write without any attachment to what that will be and yet, up until now, I have been able to write almost exactly within the framework originally created. It seems to flow from me like a stream. Sometimes a trickle, sometimes rapidly and always from a source that is much greater than me.

Although when I set the outline of the book I set specific areas to define each section, this has been thwarted this morning, in my compulsion to spend some time linking all of the parts of myself that are spiritual and all of the parts of me that are human, in order to better describe the energy that is Love.

As I feel every single section of this book rather than think about it, I have become aware that I am almost separating in my awareness, now. It is like my spiritual soul is free enough to let my physical body free. Every single nerve ending is joined and yet so distinctly separate. Almost like the pictures of Peter Pan and his Shadow. The only difference being that I have control within both, and both complement one another. Both are necessary for my survival and my purpose during this human life cycle.

The conclusion I have come to believe with this almost out-of-body experience, is that Love is the energy that binds everything together. That Love is it. It is as passionate and destructive as both the spiritual and primal self. It is as distinctly different. It is inherent. It is essential. It is Cyclical.

Without Love there is no meaning of life and yet we are always striving to find Love. We are in continual pursuit of Love and yet we always just are, Love.

I know this is very profound and I don't want you to think that I just made it up gently with my morning ritual. The process this writing download has presented me with this morning and most mornings, in fact, is as physically and emotionally painful as getting an injection of adrenalin into an already caffeine filled nervous system.

I feel so drained from the process but sure that what I need to write about here is that Love is it. Period. Energy. Love.

Cyclical. One and the same. As clear as mud. Duality. Light and Day. It is time for the world to be exposed to the Power of the Energy and that is isn't just as simple as a red rose or a baby's breath.

It is also not the ultimate answer to the ultimate question. Yet it is the first answer. What is the meaning of Life? To Love. To Energize. To Live.

I felt every emotion was attached to this process too. In every form but for the time it took the emotions and feelings were incredibly strong and incredibly raw. They were beautiful too.

Sadness. Happiness. Lust. Comfort. Open. Closed. Nurture. Deflective. Strong. Weak. Good. Bad. Heavy. Light. Angelic. Evil.

The feelings were rampant and pure. They all had the same strength to allow them all to incur the same validity. And that was what was truly enlightening. The validity of the feeling attached to every emotion. Raw and all encompassing and yet each one was a strand of energy, of Love and they were all valid.

I do not have the answer as to why we need to know the answer. I do not mean to be cryptic. I only wish to comfort those who feel that some of their emotions are not as valid as others. That they should be feeling something different. Doing something better. Sacrificing their true and unique identity. It is true that we do learn from our mistakes but we shall never stop making the mistakes in their entirety. They are the reason. Each emotion is the reason. Each lesson the reason. Each balancing correction the reason. It fits in completely with the Golden Ratio. It works numerically. It works rationally. It works spiritually, emotionally and physically.

It works with my initial analogy of balance and yet, when I created that, I had no idea that I would even find the Golden Ratio or come to this conclusion. One big bit of doing our best by the mistakes and shit that happens along the way.

Not very scientific. Not very clinical. Not very spiritual.

But I am a simple human. Living a simple human experience and wishing to convey the guidance I have been blessed with in a simple manner, to help those searching and in need.

Simplicity is human. Complex is for Nature.

A WOMAN ON PURPOSE

Simple is Self. Complex is Unknown.

I didn't even know what I would write whilst going through this process but I feel it is my duty to describe it to you in order for you to gain a deeper understanding of the physical process, in relation to the thought process and how they are so inextricably linked.

It might just be worth mentioning that although I have had a tumor and infections around my brain that my mental ability has been tested and I am, to all intents and purposes, 'normal', whatever that may mean.

I am going to explain the exact physical and spiritual process that I went through this morning to you, knowing that I would write about Love and yet not yet knowing what that would be.

I lay in contemplation with what I am feeling at the moment. Aware now that I am usually processing the following section that I will write in order to actually write from that space. Although this is physically and emotionally draining, I accept it for what it is and see the benefit it will be to others and the value it will give to my gift to the world so I am happy to 'grin and bear it'.

I felt physically present. Heavy and cold and wrapped myself up in a duvet. Clearing my mind of directional thoughts I allowed the process to envelope me.

Every neuron in my being tingled, I felt supported. Physically. The heaviness took over and my eyes were closed and yet I felt disconnected from my body. The light was upwards. I reached. My physical hand was on the edge of the globe of light. Not able to touch the center from the magnetic repulsion from the layer of energy that emanated around and from within it.

The air around me was fresh and united from all the physical countries my body knows, smelling and knowing Africa in the ebb and Europe in the flow, as intimately as you would as soul flames touch. Unifying the embodiment of interconnectedness. Making it tangible and existential to me but at the same time a uniquely spiritual encounter with what is.

I could see my arm. It linked to my body, my body was surrounded by the atmosphere. The atmosphere was dark blue. My body was a rainbow. A Rainbow of colors, emotions and feelings - All raw and exposed to me but equally valid. Each one a strand of energy. Each one with the same amount of presence as the other. Each one played like the strings of a harp. The music only making sense if all the notes are present. They sparkle. None of them hold their head in shame. They are all valid. They are all energy. They are all Love. They are all necessary for this Earthly experience. In most cases they all hold balance. Remember balance is not equal in the linear sense but in the natural sense. Sometimes the balance is out of kilter. This is when we experience those things in life that make happiness and light more noticeable. It is all perfect. It is all cyclical. It is all energy. The energy equals Love. If you need to measure life use Love. If you need to give life use Love. If you need more life then get more Love. It is there. It is here. It is in many forms.

The strands were confident and radiant. They were exposed to me in the same way a human surgeon is exposed to your veins, as a tree surgeon is exposed to the circles of life on the stump of a tree, being used to give energy through its fire, to us. Cyclical, and flowing, not perfect and yet perfect in its imperfection. And so our minds work in the same way. Exposed to Joy the balance is Joy. Exposed to Sadness, the balance is Sadness. Both as relevant. Both as dominant. Both susceptible to steady flow and trickles. Both needing the other to radiate the light or heighten the darkness. It was then that I realized the link between Love and Energy. And that they are both valid equals. The synchronicity in this is for you to decide in your own mind but for me to feel and know. I share the love and the energy and the feeling and the knowledge. It is there for you to use, now or never. The balance will be perfect for you.

My mouth and skin became dry. It was as if the energy had been sucked from me. Tingling feelings both good and bad. A strange feeling of exhaustion that seems to dominate my being.

I am not ready to stop and rest until this book is finished but right now I am spent.

I hope that this makes sense. I hope that you are able to touch the Infinite Possibilities.

The Tea Ceremony

This is the best way I can think of to celebrate Love. Where East meets West. In acknowledgement. In respect. In awe. In Safety.

When things start to make a little sense and when you finally get to know or master a subject, you get to celebrate. I use The Tea Ceremony as an analogy as a new way to celebrate together the Love that is Energy, the Love that we have, we crave and we live for.

I was reminded of this, all of a sudden when contemplating Love and the celebration of Energy. On both sides of the world, the tea ceremony is an art to be given due respect and to employ in a certain manner. We must learn to give due respect to simplicity and diversity at the same time. Hold value in something and nothing. Within and without. Silently and yet in voice. Deep and yet seen.

I believe we should bring back the art. Not that I drink tea but I felt so dehydrated that I would have drunk anything after my encounter with the Energy! Therefore, I think that The Tea Ceremony is incredibly apt and simple, inclusive way to celebrate the Love that is Energy that ebbs and flows and courses through the veins of Life.

I mention this now in the section of Love rather than in the Unknown as I now know and feel that this is the correct place for my Love to be celebrated. In private today. With you, tomorrow.

This is the first section of the book that I have been completely compelled to steer from my original outline. The original outline was there to guide me and to guide you.

The segments were to be different and more generally accepted and I may choose to engage these separately at a later date but for now it is my word to unify Love and not to give it boundaries. To release the energy I have to contain it.

To take tea is just a symbol of the whole experience I felt. Nothing remotely religious or biased in any way. Just something that most people do around the world and a way in which we can assemble and truly hold Love as sacred and give it space and energy.

It can be hot or cold - let the weather dictate.

It can be strong or weak - let the infusion dictate.

It can be sipped or slurped - let the atmosphere dictate.

All ceremonies can only be enjoyed together if the intention is the same. I would just like to see the intention of Love celebrated by groups of people who choose to infuse the goodness and restore the balance to our world, our bodies and life in the Now.

Nothing more. Nothing less.

Sacred. Infusion. Energetic Love. Infinite Possibilities.

Modern Love

For the times they are a changing! Intimate Love has never been accepted on so many levels as it is today in our society. Yet we still have forced marriage, abuse and perversity coursing through our world.

For this to change around our planet, we have to become more open and fight for the right to give ourselves boundaries of self-love for protection and the lack of it to be overruled.

Intimacy between lovers should be chosen. Never forced. It should be felt and given at the same time and in equal measures with your chosen partner. Love and violence are never to be congruent and our children should never be led to believe that it is so.

Our primal selves are led by our human bodies and yet we are still subjected to others' opinions about sex, love and the rituals that are entwined, so much so that the lines have become blurred.

We have a very long way to go in this regard but I want to ensure that I cover most of the questions one has for everything in life that matters, as Love is energy. Intimate Love has a very high value in regard to topping up our own power stations.

As with everything I have written about it is essential that we honor both our physical, primal self and our spiritual, thought-centered self. For the time we are on this planet we have to learn to be in flow with both. We need to learn to be accepting of both. We need to learn to feed both and to not feel shame about the things that get us here on earth in the first place. To me, the shaming thought process, is as outdated and out of place in the new paradigm as a vicious dictator.

How can we ever teach our children to be truly happy if we do not accept ourselves, in all of our glory!

Hot, sweaty, sexy beings that we are - making Love is frowned upon and yet a dictator is given headline news!

There is something incredibly out of kilter in this regard and I certainly do not have all of the answers. I would like you to have the space here to at least become more comfortable with your own sexuality and intimate love.

You are enough! I say this because here it relates to the primal self. Your body. Your sexual desires. Your needs as a woman. Your ability to be open about your body enough to make menstruation normal to discuss for your daughters, for the relationship between flow of nature and flow of desire to be explored, revered, to be spoken about and celebrated and given the opportunity to be acknowledged.

As a species, we have not evolved physically enough to ensure that a young girl who is able to menstruate is old enough to have a child. Therefore, as women, it is this time that should be celebrated first.

As a woman, you are expected to be quite open about sexuality in our modern society to give in to your desires and yet we do not give a child, in her first stage of womanhood, the space to explore her body or her mind. We are not leading by example. If we are opening up and setting new boundaries for ourselves, it is imperative that we explore healthy and safe new boundaries for the young girls to feel freedom in a way that will protect them and also give them their freedom to ask questions and feel their way into womanhood.

We need to fill this space for our daughters and not just skim over it to be in line with our mental capacities. I feel we need to be more involved and able to open up discussions in women's groups where we can hold a space for those children coming into womanhood to be celebrated and to be included.

Our daughters need to feel happy with their bodies and to fully embody self-love. They need to be exposed to this self-love through us and our examples - we are failing miserably in this department but this in itself is something to look forward to with the possibility it extends us.

For our daughters to be free and happy and love themselves we need to start setting examples, creating examples and leading by example! Let's start this now - together.

As we learn to open up this new world for our daughters and embody the self love that we all need, that has been shattered by delusional media, photo reproductions and religious beliefs, we will undoubtedly become more at ease with our own bodies and desires, which can only be a good thing.

Freeing ourselves up to be confident in our physical and primal self is setting a wonderful example to our daughters. At the same time, our sons will see how we embody our love of self and learn to respect us more.

Confidence is sexy. Confidence is desirable. Self Confidence is supremely empowering to our daughters, our sons, our lovers and ourselves.

We need to get real about the balance between our mental capacity for thought and beliefs and our physical capacity for our bodies to contain these thoughts.

Our bodies are our SELF, of this earth and have finite lives. Our minds are of the UNKNOWN and not of this earth and have Infinite Possibilities. We need to address the balance.

We are wild in our primal state. Do not be afraid to run with that. We are reserved in our minds and constrain ourselves in a way that is completely at odds with our bodies and our primal selves.

We try to, and are sometimes successful at, changing these natural elements. For example, in regard to the woman's body clock, we can now rely heavily on IVF, we have succeeded in subduing our bodies. With regard to our sexual preference in ourselves we now have the freedom to accept ourselves the way we feel drawn and not as historical society dictates. With regard to the sex of a baby, we even have the ability to overcome natural selection for choosing the sex of our children.

I am not judgmental in these instances, just simply pointing out the fact that we are outgrowing our bodies and trying to trick them, rather than accepting them and giving our societal measures the capacity to do so as well.

We should be trying to work more successfully with what we have by readdressing the balance with our primal and spiritual humanness.

We have sort of gone a bit too far in the other direction! I am not saying that medical procedures are not important; I completely think that they are. Only that our approach should be more holistic. By embracing all of our humanness and loving every single bit of it, we will feel free enough to Love in a way that will guide us, clearly. By accepting the humanity of our bodies and making the way we live work around that again, be in flow with nature, we will automatically feel able to be our primal selves.

At the moment women feel that they need to work up the ladder to be able to afford children or a home or what they want. If we change society to work in harmony with our humanity and place our needs first as a community, we will all have more freedom and create a society that doesn't have to push the boundaries of our human selves.

I truly believe that we are here on this planet, now to experience now. I truly believe that we can learn as much from our forefathers as we can do from our scientists, medical professionals and engineers of the future. I truly, truly believe that we should open up discussion and communication, to encompass these hemispheres of knowledge, so when we do that we will be allowed to Love ourselves and others freely.

When we think about Intimate relationships there are stereotypes attached to advertising every single line of product.

Intimate relationships are inherent to each individual but also to society as a whole. I would love to see this open up a whole world of positive possibilities.

The physical and proven health benefits and reduction of stress relating to physical contact (a good cuddle) are scientifically proven and yet, with all the media attention, the world has never been so overrun with stress.

We need to cuddle more! We need to be more loving and less full of self-righteousness.

I have had times of extreme stress, when I have had a full on PTSD episode, where nothing other than a hug will do. Whether it is from my partner or my mum or my son! The power of contact is priceless and yet we do not value the importance of physical contact. In fact, we have blurred the lines between decent behavior and natural behavior so much that fear encroaches on normal situations and perversity is the first thought.

This needs to stop. We need so much to be involved in community and communication in Love, to make choices for young people easier, talking about physical contact normal, so that physical contact is seen in the Energetic and Beautiful light intended rather than given the greater role of the big, bad wolf that is displayed so much today.

Intimate Love

We all want that special someone in our life, nobody disputes that.

We have just never been exposed to the amount of special someone's that are available in this day and age or acknowledged that this might be acceptable!

In parts of the past the only acceptable Intimate Love was between a monogamous man and woman. It has only been the last few decades where other variants of this have been even acknowledged, let alone accepted except for some ancient orgies and weekend free-for-alls in history!

I just want to say that this is such a minute amount of time in the history of the world to be given this much sexual liberation that we know of. I say know of, as there are so many things that we don't know about history and I certainly am not an expert!

What I can tell you from a medical perspective is that it is much safer to be in a monogamous relationship. Fact.

The one thing that does strike me, though, and how life has evolved over the ages is that we have now been given the freedom to choose partners, the freedom to change partners and the freedom to do so as often as we decide. Fact.

What we decide about our intimate relationships is not prescribed anymore - It is something than needs to be discussed and decided between the individuals involved. But seeing as we are so highly evolved, this very rarely happens!!!

So what is right and what is wrong? That is not for me to decide! All I can do is state that we are in a transitional space in time where medicine can almost cope with diseases in the first world and where freedom can almost be coped with. The question of how both of these things develop is to be written. And probably not by me!

Consciously rising relationships require open communication. From the beginning. In the middle. Always. Don't just expect things to stay the same. The world is changing. The ways of the world are changing and we are changing too!

There is great freedom to be had in an honest and trusted relationship. You can rest in the arms of Love and pursue your purpose with all the energy you need. In a loving, intimate and conscious relationship, you can be safe and yet passionate. Sexy and secure. Open to abandon and yet protected.

Do not feel scared to be honest.

One of the most liberating things about being a conscious lover is that your honesty will either be taken for what it is or not believed. Either way, your conscience is clear and you have the sanity to know that you cannot be more honest than honest.

To trust your intimate partner may not be so easy at times, but trust you must.

If you have an open door of communication you will know when life becomes different. Do not think that every change is to be feared though.

We are rapidly evolving as a species. The more you grow, the more you will expect from your partner. The path to enlightenment is yours alone to follow. You may share your map but do not expect even your closest and most intimate partner to travel at the same speed as you do.

If it happens that you evolve in a different way to your partner, then you must choose to remain in the relationship and love your partner at whatever speed of evolution they are at or to go forth on your journey alone.

If this happens you must really feel what you need. Sometimes the physicality of a relationship is all you need in the form of a soft body and a bear hug. Sometimes though you may need a full conversation of evolution and you may want that from your intimate partner. You must decide what you need the most and this is where your honesty must be truly revealed to yourself.

Where are you in your life? What do you want? Are your dreams and aspirations still in alignment with your partner or do you think that they can be re-aligned to work with you both? Do you need physical love, sex and a cuddle or are you looking for soul-exposed passion? These are lines so thin that you must be sure to be really, really brutal with your honesty. All new loves are passionate but as you evolve that leaves you less able to reveal your deepest longings. There are not as many available evolving lovers around as you grow older.

You could have an affair. You could search for the one. All of these avenues are available to you but please ensure that you are ready to be on your own.

There is strength in being alone but we all have needs and desires. Be sure that you are being true to yourself and your partner.

There is nothing more spiritual than sex between two people in tune, soulfully. Every soul has an agenda of its own though; so do not yearn for bygone times of passionate abandon. Instead create new ones with what you have.

Expose yourself to your most primal and sensual desires and feed them in a way that is safe for you. Do not be fooled by those offering evolution and expecting payment with your body.

Do not be ashamed of your body, your longings and your need for companionship. All are part and a necessary and beautiful part of having this human experience.

There are so many people living in this day and age that live in fear of their own sexuality. Even those who get lost in its allure still think with the same sense of illicit attachment as has been drummed into them either through religions or strict aloofness.

We are born into our bodies. Each one is different. Each one is unique. Each one can suffer pain, yet each can give pleasure. Do not get lost in either, as that is not helpful to yourself but do not close your eyes to the truth and raw beauty of what life has to offer.

We are living in a time of great change. Be aligned with your thoughts and your consciousness but do not dismiss your desires. This in itself will upset the balance of equilibrium that we all need to thrive.

Be aware of your sexuality. Your sensuality. Your grace.

Be in love with yourself and your partner, it gives you greater freedom than you can ever imagine.

Be Love to your partner and show how you would love to be loved too.

Be aware that your pain may not be felt. That is OK. A big reason for this section of the book is to let you know that you are not alone. It is OK to love and be loved, no matter how awakened you are.

There is so much I could write here but whatever you are feeling, whether you are in a relationship or not has as much relevance to you, so hold that space.

As long as you are thriving that is OK. It is OK to be in love. It is OK to be lustful. It is OK to fall out of love. It is OK to fall out of lust.

It is OK to be sensual, sexy and confident in that. It is OK to have needs, primal and spiritual. It is OK to have those needs met. It is OK to not have them met.

The world is full of infinite possibilities and Love is the energy that makes this happen. Do not push it aside. It is the fuel of life, the music to dance to, the food that feeds your soul and the passion that ignites your fire.

You are enough! Make sure you love it!

Finding A Soul Flame

There are so many women who are evolving and struggling to find a partner.

In the last section I covered the fact that many women are evolving in their awakening quicker than their partners and feeling a longing or a desire to either move on or wake them up.

This is not in your hands and I am not going to sugar coat the fact that personally developing women are far outgrowing the number of enlightened, AVAILABLE men ready to take you on.

As mentioned in the first Infinite Principle, it is imperative that you Love your Self firstly. This is the foundation for which to seek a lover.

If you are confident and honest in who you are, you will not only be outrageously attractive but seeking at the exact level of truthfulness that you need to be sharing in order to find your mate.

This is a good foundation but not necessarily perfect! Infinite Principle number Two is the Unknown and boy does the Unknown have a playful part when it comes to attraction.

Your heart skips a beat, your face burns with desire and attraction. You coyly look away and yet your soul is a divining rod that rules your actions. You cannot help but look again. And again. You catch his eye. A jolt runs through your body and the neurons that join you through a thread so fine are forever entwined. Passion. Wonder. Awe. Excitement. Fear. Love.

That is the type of first look we all dream of and for a lot of us lusty women that is our first introduction to a partner. It is not always the case but most of us are looking for that precious feeling in every atom of our beings, physically, emotionally and spiritually.

Do not be afraid of this feeling. Do not let it pass without enjoyment. As your awareness grows so does the fear that encompasses us, to protect us and to guide us.

As we are evolving it is only to be expected that our hearts are more susceptible to greater attraction. Exposing our souls becomes a way of life that is a forceful attraction to prospective partners.

Do not be afraid of any of the desires you have that need to be met. Just be honest with them, your desires that is. Do not expect a soul flame to arise with primal attraction but do not expect it not to.

Men are far more open to their primal desires in life; the more aware you are of that and open to your own sexuality, the more attractive you will be.

As you gain confidence you will also gain admiration. Some of it wanted, a lot of it not.

You will magnetically attract suitors as you stand in your power and this will require your primal self to be more discerning with your lustiness and sexual prowess.

The sparks you will throw out as you glide into your most powerful and present self will undoubtedly lead you into areas of attraction that will fill your ego self, full. Be warned, this is where your heart to could be broken easier and your self-worth is readily open for destructive powers too.

For as you fall in love, your power becomes softer, your body more wanting. Your heart more open and sensitive to any negativity and in your state of Love, it is a very hard nut to crack.

It is hard to keep your awareness open as well as your heart but try to keep a section of your enlightened self present at all times, even if it is only lurking in the background.

Many women are looking for love but, being enlightened, they want a more enlightened man. These are hard to find as many of them are taken. Enlightened women look for love but what I am finding is that most are looking in the places that fill their softness, when they should be looking is in places that men use to fill their power.

So if you are seeking your soul flame and finding it difficult to fill both your passion and your awareness then have a look in a more masculine environment. This is where the expansion of your awareness really helps.

When I am listening to music, some of the most powerful lyrics come from men. If you are looking for a man I can highly recommend you go to music events, not just gentle music - the men at those gigs will be set upon by the masses - go to a rock concert, a jazz session, an open mike, or even, if you are feeling it, a heavy metal joint. Be open to possibilities.

Just because we are so in tune with what we need to fill us up does not mean that we are looking in the right places for love. An awakened man will do what he needs to do to fill his cup, too. He will go to the gym, walk or hike in nature, write a script, laugh at a comedian, watch or play soccer, or cricket, or rugby. Do not expect the man of your dreams to be looking for you in a scented meditation room. He might be there but don't stop looking as soon as you walk out of the door.

Say yes to different things, you might even like them.

By saying yes to a relationship that speaks to your soul, expect a relationship that speaks to his soul too. The balance will find middle ground but he may not look like what you expected or even sound that way!!!

I know! I met my man in a gay bar, which was reminiscent of the Blue Oyster Club. I definitely wasn't looking that night but if I hadn't have gone, I wouldn't have met him. The funny thing was, working in an arts world I had been sworn off this particular pub by every gay man I had met, but I went anyway! So you never know!

Open your heart to the Infinite Possibilities of Love!

Loving Your Family & Friends

By now you will have noticed the subtle differences in the relationships you have with your family and friends. As you change, so do your relationships but it doesn't have to be a negative experience.

You will be longing to share all of your most recent discoveries with everyone who will listen. Time to go back to observation. Be aware of sharing too much, not from wanting to hold you back but in order to give others the space to grow.

Learning a new expansive love comes with its own trials and tribulations. There is so much you wish to share with the world but not all of the world is ready.

There are places where it will be safe, such as in your circle of safety, in joining groups of expanded awareness and consciousness. These are a safer option but be mindful of giving yourself and others enough space to talk, to think and to soak up the awareness of the ever increasing and infinite opportunities that are throwing themselves at you.

Abundant love is a funny thing. We know that you should love everyone as they are, for what and who they are, yet our judgment pipes up to get our attention. We know that judgment is the antithesis of abundant love and yet we feel it more forcefully than ever before.

These are our own feelings and learning to endure and not for our family and friends!

It will take every bit of energy (love) from you just to accept those who get under your skin for something that used to make you laugh or hold your attention. It will take every bit of restraint not to blurt out to those that you love that they are so wrong on every level and in some instances you may not be able to hold back on that restraint.

Be sure to rest in the state of love that you are feeling. Be aware of how it affects you and how you affect those around you.

Be more lenient if you can but not patronizing. Lead the way by example but don't be afraid to be yourself (old or new!) and apologize for your own mistakes or judgment if need be!

I know that this is not easy. I know that love is so very hard to give freely at this particular time, but just rest in the knowledge that everything will get easier.

Each learning curve is just that, a learning curve and by becoming more awake and enlightened you have to readjust the balance until it sits right with you.

There may be some friends and family that just don't get it.

You may have to walk away. Find new friends. Don't stop loving though. You have to love with fierce abandon and sometimes it abandons you. That is OK. Everything is OK. You are enough.

Just like starting a new school or job; your acquaintances change as do your interests. Just because you have chosen love over everything else does not mean that it has to engage with you to be present.

Love just is. It is beautiful. You will be rewarded with freedom. Freedom to love and to be loved. Freedom to give more love and freedom to receive more love. Freedom to attract more love and the freedom to see more love.

Love, Guilt & Letting Go

Because you are expanding your love, the natural course of every other emotion expands, too - you become far more sensitive in how you perceive feelings and your ability to be confused in areas of pressure from the outside world, will at times, permeate your awakened skin and cut your heart like a knife.

There are so many people with so many views and opinions on so many things. What you should and shouldn't do, eat, be. Where you should or shouldn't go. How you should spend your time, your money and your love, too.

Because we are working on developing ourselves so much it can be easy to be misguided into doing something that is relevant to someone else, just because it sounds like the right thing to do. Do not let someone else's path overshadow yours. Whatever you do and however you do it is great. You will know where you should change and what you need to do in order to make that change.

Some of the areas of struggle you may find yourself drawn to or drawing others into are:

Ecological issues.

Food preferences.

Alcohol preferences.

Parenting issues.

Government policies.

Religious involvement.

All of these are private. To be truly enlightened is to accept someone and be brave enough to be the someone who is happy with their choices.

Do not be tempted to be an Eco Warrior unless it is something You want. Do not be tempted to be a Raw Food Warrior unless it is something You want. Do not be tempted to give up anything unless it is something You really want to do. Do not be tempted into thinking your parenting is wrong unless you are feeling that you are disconnected from your role. Do not sign up for any political issue unless you really feel strongly about it. Do not join any religious group unless you are personally drawn to it.

The above also goes on your ability to promote any of your strong views. Just because you are feeling something strongly doesn't mean that it automatically gives you the right to save others by over sharing your views!

Living your example will be strong enough guidance to those who are open to the vision of your devotion.

You have to work with your soul from now on. You have to trust it and love it back. You will have your convictions and you may even fail in your own convictions, and by just trying your best is enough. It is enough to feel into what you love and you will feel what you want to devote your love to.

Taking a stand against your guilt about things is one thing. Beating yourself up about your guilt is another. You cannot be responsible for everything.

The beautiful thing about finding your purpose is that it will overtake you so much that everything else in the world that distresses you, (and we are all exposed to the harsh realities of life every day through the media,) will fall into the background.

Not that you will feel any less, oh no! Your heart is cracked open and you will feel the pain of every advertisement about abuse and hunger greatly. What I am saying is that the bigger picture will be filled with your particular purpose. It will guide you and other convictions will fall into place.

You cannot control everything but you can sway the things that you are supposed to. The guilt and shame you feel will never go away but just like fear they are your strands, they need to be acknowledged and supported. The best way to do that is to focus on your particular direction - the pull that you are feeling at that time.

Do not be upset if you are not perfect? You are but I doubt that I would ever be fully rid of those more negative emotions, to be at complete ease. I do not want to lie to you and say that they will be gone forever but I do want you to know that you are not alone.

We are all going through this phase together.

The more you are focusing on your particular purpose at that particular time, the less these negative emotions will be given the floor with your awareness. They will be there. They are a big part of being human.

Don't be afraid. Don't feel guilty. Don't feel shame. Don't regret. Love Fear. Love Guilt. Love Shame. Love Remorse. Once this energy is blanketing the negative emotions they are in themselves not reversed, but they are softened, and your empathic abilities are far extended. You can remember but you use that memory to heal others. You can remember but you use that memory to share with others. You can remember so that you can understand and love more.

Every feeling is linked. Every emotion is valid. Love is Energy. Everything is Energy. Energy is Love. It is that simple.

Love is Infinite. The Possibilities endless.

Loving Your Warrior Sisters

I truly believe that we need to work together to make the world a better place.

I truly believe that, as women, it is our time to step up and lead the world into a New Paradigm.

I truly believe that we can do it, but I also know that we need to support one another.

We have so many modern and yet indoctrinated beliefs that we have to do things by ourselves. I have also felt the discrimination of other women who have thought themselves to be more knowledgeable, better than, or just more worthy than me. I also know that this is not going to stop me.

I know that this might be my own limiting belief but I have definitely felt the wrath of those in authority, those who have control over my life in a very real and very powerful way. I know this to be true because I was incredibly vulnerable and completely at the hands of their decisions.

Looking back I know that they were doing what they had been taught to do and had the guidance of laws to uphold. From being able to see how it worked in practice I was also made aware that as women we would have made the 'laws/rules' far more compassionate and kind.

I truly believe that we are entering a new phase in this beautiful world we live in, and that we women have a very big part to play in it.

For the world to become more kind and compassionate we need to be able to lead in community, support one another and truly believe that there is enough for everybody, to create enterprise and opportunity to support this belief.

There is so much I see that we can do in our lifetimes. There are so many areas of growth that need our guidance. There are so many countries that need our love. There are so many children who need our help.

Becoming A Woman On Purpose is based on kindness, compassion, responsibility and non-judgmental action.

We need to trust our sisters more and we need some form of united front to be seen and to be heard, to empower and gather together more women into this fold.

I know that it is hard to not be in survival mode when you are unable to feed yourself or your family or to keep a roof over your heads but I implore you to trust that all will be well and to take action for yourself.

I also implore you to ask for help from your sister and to offer help when you can.

Even if you have no desire to be a leader there is so much we can do together to help make this path a little easier and more comfortable for all of us.

We need to find an answer for childcare. It is unaffordable unless you are very well off in both the western world and nigh on non-existent in the third world. There in itself lies opportunity for co-operative ventures.

We need to find an answer for those who do not wish to or are unable to live in the corporate world but are happy to live and work and keep going as they are. There are so many factories that could be run very differently and support whole towns in the western world. Also, those living in places where their lives are at risk every day, working in horrific and inhumane places of employment for a non-living wage. I see vast opportunity in this. Especially if we take the judgment away from working in a factory and embrace and empower the community and work that is needed by us all.

I see the rise of independent women who are running their own businesses but are entering vastly over-populated segments of growth. I see vast opportunity in the support and service level that can be offered, if we learn to work together better and respect that we all have value.

I see the rise in age of our elders and the vast chasm that has to be filled by the depletion of pensions, and increase in life expectancy. I see vast opportunity for those leaving their career to start a new life of service, teaching, eco-living and traditional craft building. Also, those who are of a retirement age are great at giving care to others but there is little financial reward in this for them and this needs to be rectified. We will all be old one day.

I see the rise in education. How we teach our children and one another in the positive possibilities, we can become more in tune with ourselves our happiness and our future, in the rise in ecological and economical growth, in the rise of our ability to see the bigger picture and work towards a better future for ourselves, our world and the future of our planet.

I see the rise in feminine leadership in corporations, in politics and policies and in the unification of our belief systems and integration of all beings.

I see the beauty in all cultures and traditions, the use of ritual, ceremony and celebration as necessary parts of human longings and needs and the re-integration and development of new ways and new desires.

I see so many opportunities for us all, dear sisters, this is just the beginning of the New Paradigm.

We must learn to trust one another, to build a better future for our descendants, to create more and more opportunity for freedom, for wealth, for health, for love, for compassion and for us to rise together.

We must learn to share a little more of our wealth and our knowledge and our feminine, loving ways.

We must learn to trust in the process. To trust that we can do it. To trust that there is enough and that we are enough.

We have to work together to make this world a better place.

This is the time. This is our opportunity. Love it, love one another and love the Infinite Possibilities we can create together.

LifeStyle Business – Public Relations & Networking

You either love it or you hate it!

I used to love it but didn't even realize that I did it and then I learnt to fear everything and became an introvert. Sound familiar?

In order for you or your product and business to be seen, either yourself or your business needs to get out into the world.

If you have entered the realms of a LifeStyle business, this means you have to be the face of your business and that means your face has to be seen.

There are so many women entrepreneurs' networks in the world it is hard to know where to begin. There are also so many different social media platforms that become overwhelming too.

What I can recommend is that you try out a few different places, a few different events and a few different social media platforms, then take some time to think about which ones suit you and your business the best.

Most start up businesses have very little budget for professional Public Relations hire or advertising, so it is important that you test your market and technique before spending too much time and money.

It is easier to build one platform and belong to a couple of networks that suit you than none or too many. You need to have the time to make your product or serve your clients and to sell it or your services!

Do not waste too much time on forming relationships with those who are not on the same wavelength to you. It will be hard to maintain your confidence and authenticity if you don't feel comfortable.

Be gentle and remember to trust that everything will be fine as long as you are taking action. If you have to try out ten different events, then so be it, but remember to expand your horizon and not to give up.

Social Media platforms are fantastic for growing a brand and business if you keep your posts consistent and the branding easily recognizable. Don't change your personal profile to a picture of your cat - that simply isn't helpful unless you are a cat! Try to keep the profile pictures you have consistent too, especially when you are starting out. If you keep the same picture then your face will be easier to recognize.

All being said, you can really enjoy the process of becoming your own PR agent and a living advert for your brand, don't forget to include your own personal style of dress and hair. Be a spokes-model too. Great fun and Infinite Possibilities!

Chapter 6
Health & Wellbeing

5TH DIRECTION

Personal Persistence

Health & Wellness
Mind - Challenge, Educate, Choose
Body - Exercise, Food, Health
Soul - Discover, Nourish, Nurture
Handling Your Empathic Growth
Find Your Personal Rhythm
Primal Self Love & Instinct
LifeStyle Business - Business Processes & Systems

Mind – Challenge, Educate, Choose

As we have covered a lot of the Health and Wellbeing section under the Infinite Principle of Self - all that we know and can control, this section will be more of an overview to those parts of our beings that we must take responsibility for and not a prescription as such as I will leave that to the doctors.

With our minds open to the Infinite Possibilities that are at our disposal in the present, we are becoming increasingly aware of our own development. It is important not to forget to keep our own cup full, with all of the awareness of all that could be we must still be aware of our immediate 'what is'.

I find the easiest way of ensuring that my own cup stays full is fully accepting that I am living in a very human body and mind. Whatever possibilities I may envision, I must still accept the fact that I have many limiting beliefs and physical limitations that have been imprinted on my thoughts from centuries of rules, regulations and genetic disposition.

The only way we can fully expand our consciousness and keep the expansion in flow is to keep challenging our own behaviors and thought processes, to keep learning and choosing different paths.

By challenging our minds and even being aware that we are

capable of this rational thought process, we are consciously seeking better ways of dealing with situations, challenges and outdated behavior.

The best place for this battle to be fought is in the safety of our own minds, initially, and by testing the new thoughts with others of similar disposition and awareness. If you are fortunate enough to have people to have these conversations with, who accept that you are growing in your own awareness and that every new idea needs a space to be developed, then you should use this place of safety in the first instance. If not, then you may have to really dig deep with your own mind and look at each of your individual arguments with the process of 'for and against' in order to thrash out your challenges, ensuring that you get the best and kindest outcome for all.

This can be used for a challenge of thought that only affects you, or it can be used to attain world peace if you are that way inclined! It just means that you are able to see things from every viewpoint (direction) and keeps on increasing your own abilities and awareness.

The more you challenge yourself to see things from another point of view, the more you will be able to achieve the best, most peaceful and just outcome in any future issues.

As we all become better able to see somebody else's point of view, to see that point of view from the exact physical and emotional place that the view is coming from, it enables us all to spread our net of kindness and compassion even further. We benefit more as we grow and share in our expansion of thoughts and love.

You will also have to accept that none of us know everything! I know, hard, heh? But the more we personally accept this, the more open we are to continual education and learning. Opening our eyes to even more awe, wonder and facts in order to be more respected in our viewpoints, under our specialty or gifts and expanding any thoughts further and wider, consistently.

The more we learn, the more we become aware of. The more we learn, the more confident we are to express our awareness. The more we learn, the more able we are to share our gifts with the world and the more we learn, the more able we are to lead the world into the New Paradigm: Love, kindness and compassion are integrated into the finance, power and authority of the how the world is led at the moment.

This, in turn, gives us more choice. It enables us to choose how we want to live and to be more active in our attainment of a better world for planet, our future generations and ourselves.

By giving ourselves more choice, we give ourselves more freedom to express our authentic viewpoints and to be more assertive in the attainment of those choices.

By choosing well for our own environment and ourselves we empower ourselves to expand our possibilities, this in turn empowers others to seek the attainment we have achieved for ourselves. If we can show others that we are able to achieve our dreams, this is like a golden carrot to those who need encouragement, from a place of kindness and not from a place of absolute survival.

The mind will become a haven but also a battlefield. You need to accept responsibility for both. Some of us are able to achieve a constant state of peace and calm in our minds but some of us are not.

This is normal. This is not something to stop you from achieving any of your dreams. Most of us are constantly exposed to harsh realities nowadays, even more so since the dawn of our transient and interconnected media.

You cannot be responsible for all the wrongs in the world but you can be responsible for your own challenges. You don't even need to be rid of them. You are perfect just the way you are.

We are constantly bombarded with negativity nowadays so it will affect you more than you think. If you need to take time out, do so. If you are unable to achieve a self-enforced deadline, do not beat yourself up. If you are giving your family a fast-food meal because you need a break, that is fine.

Along with the negativity is the judgment it entails, "you should do this and you should do that".

As I have mentioned before, you can only do what you can do and if you accept that, then you can rest and in turn, you will be able to move mountains if you need to.

We can't all be the perfect size, be fabulous gardeners who only feed our children organic offerings, be high-powered over achievers, affording our families a lifestyle of luxury and design.

What we can be is happy.

And if that takes a little work or a little time out, then so be it. Feel free enough to do and enjoy your life as much as possible. Do not put so much pressure on yourself that you are trying to be a perfectionist, it doesn't exist BUT, whilst you are here on earth, you do. Make your existence a happy one as much as possible.

You will have troubles and challenges. That is part of existing. To fully live you need to surrender to the ebb and the flow of life.

Give yourself all you need to pursue the Infinite Possibilities, to your own existence and create a precious legacy that fills you up, whilst enjoying the creation process.

That is it. Let yourself be sad, if you are sad but let yourself be glad if you are glad too.

Body - Exercise, Food, Health

I am no expert in this section! I do what I can for myself and my family to the best of my ability, but I don't always get it right!

What I do know, though, is that I have had to come to terms with both the natural, age-old and holistic ways of being physically healthy and the sophisticated medical intervention I required from being ill in an age where that was possible.

I have come to the conclusion that I need both these forms of healing, as do we all if we are going to continue to grow and become increasingly healthy beings whilst we live on earth.

I have had to deal with being in a situation where the choice of how I wanted to live was taken away from me, if I wanted to give myself a chance of survival. I used everything I had learnt and researched from ancient and traditional methods of medicine and the expertise of those who were experimenting and researching new ways.

I took my chances. I won.

Whilst my body was infected I tried everything I discovered, such as silver, Manuka honey, garlic, acidophilus (for my gut), whilst on so many antibiotics, and other tonics and tinctures, to ensure the best outcome holistically.

I never got rid of the infection in my bone, though, until it was surgically removed from my forehead and the rotten blood vessels replaced with a vein and the muscle from my leg.

This was a new approach. I took my chances. I won.

I ended up being overweight from the need I had for a carbohydrate rich diet. I also ended up being diagnosed with Irritable Bowel Syndrome from all the strong medication and trials that my body had been through. I ended up having to take control of my body, as what I had been left with, what I was able to achieve and what it could handle now had been forever changed.

Most of the time I do well. Sometimes I fail big time!

I have spent the last three months in hermit mode writing this book and this section on Health & Wellbeing is the last to be written.

I deliberately left it to last because I knew that what I had just put myself through to write this book was not particularly healthy, but I chose to write this book quickly and download it from my mind, so that I can share what I need to, with you and the rest of the world now. I know exactly what and how to do so.

As soon as I have finished I will make my health my top priority, again, as I feel the sluggishness and unhealthy weight gain is not conducive to how I want to present myself to myself, or to the world for the next stage in my sharing!

I am being honest with you, because I value my health but am sometimes going to prioritize other things first. Not often and not out of forgetfulness or excuses. Just sometimes a part of our sacrifice is to put all of our energy into a project that we are passionate about BUT this is no good on a long-term basis, so I will start to take charge of my vitality and wellbeing, in order for me to do my best work moving forward.

I do this how I can. We all have different time constraints and responsibilities and we all let things slip every now and again. What I want to say to you is to give yourself permission to be the healthiest you can be under your own constraints. Give yourself permission to make the best choices most of the time and the permission to make the not so good choice every so often, also.

It goes without saying that exercise is vital to keep us healthy. The more active you are the less mentally stressed you are, the better you sleep and the better your body behaves.

Don't forget to include what you do on a daily basis into what constitutes your daily exercise regime, though. Some of us do heavy work already, which contributes to us getting physical exercise, whilst others sit in an office and have to counteract this enforced immobility by activity external to our day's work.

I would like to see us all doing multiple jobs that help us physically, mentally and spiritually in the future. For now the reality is we need to work with what we have.

For me, my need for physical exercise is born from an excess of energy from mental activity. In other words if I don't get out and about and get rid of some steam, I get well and truly frustrated. It is that simple now but it took me years to figure it out and even longer for me to be mobile enough to action it.

There are times when I do my exercise in front of the TV in my front room, for all my neighbors to see. There have been other times that I go to the gym. There have been times in my life where the only time I could fit exercise in was to cycle to work and back and that was SO not a pretty sight!!!

Just fit the physical exercise in to suit where you are at the moment. Do not feel obliged to stay at the gym if you suddenly decide to be a lumberjack! Do what you can and just be aware of what your body needs, honestly.

Do you need to lose a bit of weight? Find a way that suits you, not anyone else. Every single person who has devised a diet has started with a way that they think works. This is your choice. You decide what you think your body needs. It is your body and your responsibility, you want to find a way that fits in with your overall happiness and gives you the maximum energy to live to achieve your optimum potential.

You know what is wrong. There is no getting away from it but you can take charge and put limitations on the unnecessary. Put some more veg on your plate even if you don't like it. Expand your vegetable options and opinions. This is your choice remember.

I now am happy(ish) with my overall weight. I am never going to be able to maintain svelte with all the bread and butter that I dream of, but I make a concerted effort to eat healthily for my best body (internal workings as well as external visuals!).

That is the only pressure I put on myself. In wintertime I put on a bit, now it is Spring here in the northern hemisphere and time for me to not feel like an embarrassing mom on the beach this summer, to pander to my own dreams of walking out of the Mediterranean sea like the Gold Goddess my mind can envision.

My dreams, my responsibility!

I love feeling good. There is nothing better than to feel good but to go to any extreme, whatever you are told, is not healthy. Just accept an equilibrium that suits you and is mainly healthy until the media deem it not to be!

Basic rules of eternal living - Eat when you are hungry. Don't overeat as it makes you feel uncomfortable and you are the only one having to deal with the consequences. If you don't like something, change it. If you think you should be eating more veg, do. If you think you should be eating less bread, eat less.

Once you are truly honest with your body, your body will be truly honest with you and let you know what you need.

If you are having second thoughts about a second slice of cake, then you should probably listen. If you are having second thoughts about the first slice of cake you've eaten in ages then you should probably just eat it! Just saying.

Every one of us is perfect in our present state. If we are lucky enough to be presented with tomorrow we can be responsible for our choices today and thereafter.

What I am trying to say is that whatever your level of physical exercise is now, you can increase it or decrease it in proportion to what you, yourself need. It is not up to anyone else what our choices are but there is no doubt that physical exercise is tantamount to achieving our optimal potential. It just is. But if you are working hard all day and walking around constantly, don't overdo it. If you are sitting around all day don't under-do it. This is your life and only you know at what level your own personal optimal level of exercise is. It can never be prescribed by anyone else. It is your decision. Your choice. Your will.

The same goes for food. It never ceases to amaze me how many people do not feel the urge to or know how to cook fresh produce like I do. I am not a good baker but I am a very good taster! I love cooking, I am good at it! I can make something out of nothing and it will be on par to many restaurants. I sometimes make a booboo and sometimes I go out to eat, but I do love me food!

I am never going to be the one who goes hungry. I love eating too much but again, I do what I need to do when I need to do it, in order to achieve and to re-achieve my optimum physical health.

If I have a binge of carbohydrates, I feel it. I will need to re-evaluate what my diet is and attain a certain level of control until I feel better. It is harder to actually lose the weight since I am getting older but I can still feel better, not feel so bloated and get more energy from eating a low fat, low sugar, very low carb diet. That is what works for me. To lose weight I have to cut the carbs out completely now that I am older but I am not one to give up on bread and cake forever so I use the ebb and flow to keep and get my diet back on track too.

Until you have had bad health it is really hard to understand how bloody fantastic it is to have good health. I am sorry, but you never truly understand how good it feels until you have had to suffer.

I also think that it helps you to balance the good with the bad once you have had a health scare.

Most people who have had issues with their personal health have an uncanny ability to enjoy 'mostly good' with a little bit of the 'not so good'. You need to attain the balance that we all need to enjoy life to the maximum whilst being responsible at the same time.

Most of us understand the importance of moderation although some of us fail to achieve it!!!

If you are fortunate enough to have full health, enjoy it. Live your life and try not judging others who are not as fortunate as you. Base your physical decisions on mainly what is good for you, as well as letting yourself indulge every now and again. Believe me, none of us who have experienced health issues are going to judge you, we will just watch in awe!

Your mental and physical health are what keep your human body going. It is important to look after them but enjoy the parameters you are given in your physicality too. Push your own boundaries both in your mind and in your body. There is no better challenge than that of being better than you were yesterday, beating your own limitations and looking forward to the Infinite Possibilities.

Soul - Discover, Nourish, Nurture

Ah, Soul! (Sorry, excuse the pun but that just downloaded and I loath to retract it because humor is a big part in nurturing the soul). Your spirit, soul, or whatever you like to call it is such a big part of your life and to neglect or ignore it is to lose out on such a source of fulfillment that can not be underplayed.

This is a book that encourages your spiritual growth as an integral part of personal development and independent freedom.

As much as I am aware of different religions and spiritual teachings, by writing this book I am trying to envelope our spirituality in an umbrella of souls. A book that can open up our awareness of individuality, allow each other the freedom to believe what we need to believe and still give one another the support we need to embrace our own ideas, when it comes to spiritual teachings.

The most important thing about your soul is that it can support you through any hardship you face, any fears you develop and give you the momentum to propel your true desires. Listen to the voice inside you that already knows inherently what is right and what is wrong.

I think that I have mentioned before that I am a bit of a greedy girl. As I discover and uncover new and old ways of nourishing and nurturing my soul, I fill myself up more and more, enabling my ability to give so much more. I know that I am not the only one.

By uncovering ways from different ages, different cultures and different religions it not only allows you to grow and expand but it enables your ability to accept others exponentially.

To discover different traditions and uncover what they were initially created for, how they have developed and what they represent, now, is one of the best ways to nurture and understand yourself as a modern human and as a primal being.

The more you are open to the different ways of doing things the more you realize how similar they all are, that most spiritual, communal, traditional and cultural practices all have a place in our development as enlightened beings.

Tithing, for example has come to mean giving a tenth of your monetary earnings to God and yet to be truly fulfilled we need to give of ourselves. So in other cultures it may mean to help those less fortunate, or to help in other areas of the community.

Today, in the western world, we seem to turn our nose up at tithing, yet charity has never been so prevalent.

Today's Charities are ways of satisfying our need to give and are just another form of contribution. In order to truly be happy it is essential that, if we are blessed enough to be able, we give. It is that simple. It doesn't have to be money though. It can be time, care, thoughts, prayer. Contribution is just giving with love. One hand is to give and the other is to receive. Perfect balance.

Sometimes that means giving to yourself though and to me that is just as important as it fills you up again in order to overflow.

To nurture your soul you have to give yourself time to think about things that are important to you and how you can come to a better way of doing things.

Nurturing your soul is just a part of the rhythm of life. It is the intention that is important. If you say prayers without intention - by this I mean just saying them because you know them - and you think that is enough, it isn't. Even if you cannot think of anything because you are worried or stressed or tired, the nurture comes from the intention and not just the practice.

It is about having a relationship with the Great Unknown that is nurturing and nourishing, not just the doing because it is what you have been taught.

I have sat in church and listened to people get through prayers as if it is a race, those times I failed to feel anything, and yet, sometimes I can sit on the loo and have a conversation and I get much more, 'oomph'. I know, too much information!

Whether you have time or not, to fully feel connected to God, the Great Unknown or Spirit is to be fully charged. It becomes as natural as breathing and becomes a way of life and a way of living. It is included in your life and not just a practice of 5 minutes, here, or a rush to temple there.

That is, truly living a full life. I don't even care if you do not believe in anything. Unless you are fully closed you will be able to see that we grow in our understanding of the ways of the world every, single day.

To nourish your soul, or even that part of you that you can feel but cannot put into words, is to be living fully.

In this book, I have written with intent to bridge the gaps between different religions, different cultures, different ideas and different wordings.

I believe that we all know all we can know, and that we all do not know that which we do not know. Everyone is different and yet we all feel the same things, no matter where we come from, how educated or financially independent we are. We all are made up with the same structure, some more enhanced than others, all as equally important.

Discover, uncover, nurture and nourish your soul, your spirit, your inner bit that you don't know what to call. Make it seamlessly flow into and out of your life with the other elements and do not separate it. It is as much a part of you as anything else in you. Just because we have listened for centuries about the rules that each religion has given, it doesn't mean that we have to only give our souls time when we go for a workout in the prayer department, church or mosque.

I believe we need to reclaim our confidence in our souls, as much, and if not more so than the suffragettes fought for the women's right to vote!

We have been stifled for too long and no matter where you come from or where we are, we, as women, KNOW what is right or wrong. We have empathy for other mothers who lose children, no matter where they come from. We KNOW there is a better way. We have all been spiritually and soulfully repressed for our gender.

I know that we can make things better if we work together on a soul level. I know that by making a connection with one another we can lead the way into a New Paradigm where our souls can show how love is hands down better than war. I know that by uniting ourselves, in spite of any differences, we will become unstoppable and be able to open the eyes of the world to the Infinite Possibilities.

Handling Your Empathic Growth

Your Empathic Growth will be exponential as you become more aware of the reality of you, the reality of the world and you understand your role in the New Paradigm.

It is imperative that you become comfortable with this as it can easily lead you into areas of sympathetic leaning and distract you from your own path.

I do not mean that you have to ignore the feelings you get when confronted with the more unpleasant things in life, as you will not be able to. What I do mean, however, is that you need to be slightly removed from the feelings in the moment just enough to be rational about your reaction to them.

To explain this I will take the view that if an advertisement makes it known to you that there are dying children in a certain catastrophe ridden place and it pulls at your heart strings so much that you decide to sell all of your worldly possessions and go and help them, you need to be able to see if this is truly your calling and your best practice for your own personal gifts.

If you have just finished your medical degree, have not yet got a permanent position and can financially and emotionally support this period of transition, then this may be your personal calling. However, if you have nothing to offer in skills and would only be adding another mouth to feed into the mix perhaps you would be better served by raising funds by sharing your gifts in another manner.

Also, when you have mastered this skill of controlling your Empathy and its propensity to be so much more sympathetic as you develop, it can be seen by others that you are not caring! I know, but such is the dichotomy of spiritual development, I am afraid. The more aware you become, the more you understand, the more you understand, the more you are able to control your own reactions and actions and the less you seem, to the outside world, to have any empathy!

This spirituality malarkey is a funny old thing.

But what I mean is, you become more able to manage your reaction to your own emotional response and learn how your gifts could be best used to serve the issue, rather than make rash responses that perhaps would not be of ultimate benefit.

We all make mistakes and so it is important to accept this, too, but to take charge of how you can best serve the world by how you share your gifts are big decisions in life. There may be one and there may be many, your journey a straight and easy road, or a meandering path strewn with obstacles.

The ability to clear your own fog needs to be taken responsibly and fully in order to ensure that your compass has the right magnetic attraction, as much as possible.

Becoming aware of your Empathic Growth also means becoming aware of others. Their own magnetic draw to empathize in things may not be as important as your own. They may be a little less aware of their own growth in this department and might be working directly from the heart and so not understand your ways. If you can step back from this and be reassured by your own way of thinking this will help you from being drawn in by their, probably far more dramatic, causes.

You see, you will care so much more. Your heart has been cracked open, your eyes awakened and your mind enlightened. There is no way back. There is only the journey to Infinite Possibilities to take and you have to make it count as much to the cause as to the effect, as much to you as to the world, as much to the memory of the past as to the hope of tomorrow. This is YOUR journey. Only you can make it.

Find Your Personal Rhythm

I have spoken a lot about rhythm. The point I would like to stress here is that this is your rhythm. It is your timing. It is your beat. It is your dance. Nobody else's. You know how you best work. You can set the rhythm to work in a way that suits you and don't ever forget that the rhythm can change.

There will always be peaks and troughs in life. Highs and lows, ups and downs. There are the times where life is so good you want the rhythm to slow down so that you can fully embrace each beat, each moment, each speck of gold. There are other times where life is so good but the rhythm is heavy, methodic and seemingly never-ending in its flow, BEATING away and perfectly in time, chugging along in a full blown clash of energy, mightily roaring to a crescendo of fireworks and leaving you spent, sending you into a lull of complete contentment.

There are times where the rhythm feels completely out of control. Where the melody seems chaotic and you have no idea how the next bar of the tune will turn out. Life is like that sometimes and you may not even have an iota of a reason why.

Some days fall into the dramatic rhythm of suspense and disbelief and leave you with nerves on edge and a feeling of oncoming doom.

Music is life and life is a rhythm. The best we can do on a personal level is to accept that and to choose the rhythm that serves us best in the moment.

That is another reason for expanding your joy. The more you can dance and appreciate any genre of music, the more you have to play with.

You get to play the score of your life. Make sure you enjoy it and that it fully represents each chapter.

As I have mentioned before, seasons are a good way of starting your full encounter and understanding of your own rhythm.

I love high-energy music at the start of the year to get me going and support my enthusiasm for the work that I need to achieve, both in my personal and business work, which I now integrate entirely.

I lounge with chilled house and classical music in the summertime and merge with the rhythm of the sunshine as it glitters on the water. I fully entertain my passions and my peers.

I lean more towards lyrical music as we approach the end of the year and the autumn leaves fall. My emotions settle down into the New Year ahead and I find new ideas for the future.

In my hibernation rhythm I think more ethereal rhythms rule the airwaves of my mind in the darkest months. My creations are developed in the cool rebirthing of wintertime.

It is not set in stone. I have plenty of moments when this gets a bit mixed up and I always have time for some great pop, folk and rock inspired dances, reminders that there are many creative rhythms to expand my hopes and dreams for the Infinite Possibilities.

You needn't choose music to set your pace but it serves as a backdrop of my life and I feel empowered or in need of the inspiration it provides me.

This is your rhythm so use what suits you. I just use a musical analogy to show you that you can change the tempo to suit your life and that the tempo may be increased or slowed right down. It doesn't matter. Just be confident in your rhythm and everything will work as you need it to.

Don't be forced to a picnic of classical formality if your mood wants you to do a highland fling!

Primal Self-Love & Instinct

Your primal instinct is to survive! It maybe a bit outdated but it is in you nevertheless. So it is with everyone else who walks this planet.

To truly understand, accept and then love this part of ourselves, along with all other human and animal creatures, is a huge leap forward in getting happy with life.

I know that it seems a little obscure but bear with me. It just means that you are completely and wholly able to be who you are and in turn, that leaves others to be who they are. To accept your primal human self enables you to understand some parts of you that may be you have disowned or not even acknowledged. We have been taught so many things that over time they take away our ability to see clearly. We often think prudish thoughts or that we are not thinking as a developed person should be thinking. To fall in love with your primal self enables you to give a huge sigh of relief and the ability to love yourself and others' Infinite Possibilities even more.

Instinctual primal self enables you to be aware of whether or not you are acting out of self preservation or not, therefore enabling a conclusion to be gained from love of rational and primal self. It also gives us the understanding that others may just be reacting in a way to preserve themselves.

This is where you bring in, and open yourself up to, those parts of you that may have been given a different name or lodged in the back of your heart, as not existing anymore.

These primal instincts need to be loved. They have probably evolved so much that you either don't notice that you have them anymore, or you have been taught that they are not becoming. More serious, though, is when they have been hidden under a disguise for so long that they are not seen to be what they truly are.

Like a corporate bankers' determination to be at the top of the ladder. He has disguised his primal instinct to survive and be top dog by wearing a nice suit, riding in a nice car, drawing a nice salary and presenting himself to the world as someone evolved and at the top of the first world leader-board. He may be happy and provide but I doubt very much if he is doing all he can to make the world a better place. I doubt further that he would ever acknowledge that he is feeding his primal instinct for survival.

When you are able to see this in yourself it gives you a great perspective, so do not doubt its value.

As women we have been taught to hide, to be ashamed of ourselves, to be reserved and to be humble.

Humility can be achieved with great success but so too can great success be achieved with humility.

Seeing and understanding and loving both sides of your personal coin gives you so much in return. You heal those parts of you that perhaps you were ashamed of or taught not even acknowledge. It also gives you a better understanding of others and how they get to their own conclusions.

Never leave a part of you unloved. You may not like it but it is much easier to love it. Just like you would love a family member but not perhaps want to spend much time with them! Some parts of ourselves are difficult to deal with, especially if we have an ache with them.

Guilt, shame and fear may never go away entirely but if you are able to become aware of them and the parts of yourself that you have placed these feelings on, they then form part of your humanity. You can accept and love them anyway. Doing this gives you a huge sense of freedom.

I know that when I heard people saying how they didn't care about what other people think I didn't believe them but now I do. I can still feel the hurt of another's displeasure towards me, but I recognize that now and I can love them and the part of me that displeased them enough for it not to bother my rational self.

I also used to feel guilt about things that I was taught to feel guilt about, such as not going to church or not doing enough for others. Now I occasionally stick my head under the covers in guilt but understand that this is not going to stop me indefinitely.

Sex is a biggie. So many people, including me, still feel ashamed of having a desire for looking good to the opposite sex and feeling great about our sexiness. So daft! If we didn't have this one none of us would be here. We should think more like rabbits about this one, still take modern precautions, of course. Heck, we are letting sex become such an influence and pressure in society whereas we have never had as much sexual freedom since, well I don't know when.

Laugh, love and accept your primal self. The more you do, the more freedom you have to expand your horizons, the more freedom you can give for others to expand their own and explore the world of Infinite Possibilities this opens us up to.

LifeStyle Business – Business Processes & Systems

I know that it sounds boring but to have a thriving business it is essential that you have administration, financial and IT processes to flow.

If you make it your mission to have a list of things to do every time you need to do something, it makes life so much simpler and it is easy to see if something has gone wrong or isn't working.

There are so many things that need to be done on a daily, weekly and monthly basis in business. It makes sense to follow a procedure to ensure that you are up to date, on track and able to deliver.

If you are working online it will make sense to have systems in place for every new offering and every new launch; if you set up a basic structure you can just rinse and repeat the process.

It also makes sense to have a process for all of your sales processes, all of your client management needs and all of the financial needs that your business has, in order that you do not fall behind. Know your bottom line and targets in order to achieve and succeed the success you are looking for.

The Administration process is essential as a support function for all businesses. It is not just typing and filing (although this does play a part).

Types of Administration that need systems in places include:

- Dealing with mail - both physical and emails.
- Filing structures for documents.
- Travel arrangements.
- Event Management.
- Document design & layout (including contact information etc.)
- Website updates and functionality.
- Meeting and diary arrangements.
- Research.
- Dealing with complaints and gathering testimonials.
- Distribution procedures.

The more Finance or Accounting based systems include:

- Checking and paying invoices for incoming bills and services.
- Procedures for monies received and chasing outstanding invoices.
- Monitor and develop budgets and sales forecast.
- Cash flow monitoring.

- Monitor expenses.

- Monitor profits.

Even if you do have an accountant you will have to ensure that you have some basic accounting knowledge to keep your business on track and to enjoy your profits!

If you are one of the many women working online then you will know how important it is to have your IT systems in place.

These include:

- Landing pages

- Email managers

- Websites

- Backend procedures to capture information from your clients and your sales.

- Launch procedures.

- Social Media planning.

- Technological support systems.

I know that it sounds like a lot of work but if you know what you are doing with things it makes life so much easier and gives you far more time to create more products, in order for your business to thrive.

Some of them don't even have to be written down if you are good at keeping a system going in order to keep order! But if you are like me then you will at least need a shoe-box for all of the stationary receipts you require!

Don't let it overwhelm you. Get help and if something new comes up make a note of it so that it is easier next time.

If you get used to doing things right in the first place it makes your life and your business a pleasure in order for you to explore the Infinite Possibilities.

Chapter 7
Spiritual Practice & Personal Philosophy

6TH DIRECTION

Phenomenal Philosophy

Innate Wisdom

Ritual & Ceremony

Good, Bad & Ugly Judgment

Opening Your Channel & Finding Your Guide

Sacred Space, Sensuality & Senses

Serendipity

Symbols

Meditation & Prayer

Call & Response & Chanting

LifeStyle Business - Sales & Marketing

Innate Wisdom

Power! Your Power! Claim it. Own it. Share it with the world. Your innate wisdom is not something that is tangible; sometimes it does not even make any sense how you 'just know' but it is your main source of infinite possibilities and yours to guide you on your beautiful journey on this planet. Give it the respect it deserves.

How blessed are we to be able to have magic at our fingertips. The source of our imagination is abundant and the power of our wisdom is handed down throughout ages, without medical understanding or scientific proof, and yet we all have the power.

I believe that it is a part of the Alchemy of life and that 'Gold' is the treasure we all seek. The elixir of life. The meaning of life. The reason for living.

If you are used to tapping into your innate wisdom you will know that it isn't just a thought process, it is an emotion, a sensation and a deep, unspoken feeling. It works as well, if not better, than any rational thought, physical sensation or feeling and can be as sensitive as a nerve ending.

To become more in tune and in flow with your own innate wisdom is to be given the ancient knowledge of our forefathers (and mothers!). Marry it with your own learnings and understandings to come to a conclusion that you just know is right.

It is so easy as long as you are using the basic tools of kindness and compassion, along with your expanded awareness, to ensure that you are having a connected response to what is occurring.

We have learnt so much in the last few generations and have become rather lazy in our ability to tap into our wisdom as it is sometimes much easier to go with the general flow, rather than to ensure that we are flowing with our own personal and natural rhythm.

I promise that if you start to trust yourself and begin to tap into your power for everyday decisions your life, in flow, will just run exponentially smoother.

For example. You get a call to attend an appointment that you are not really feeling but it means a lot to someone close to you. Just say yes and trust that if you don't need to go something will happen to cancel or divert the appointment. I know that is a really small example but it is how I conduct everything now. The kindness is there, the willing is there and if it is meant to be, it will be. The catch is that you have to honor the outcome; even if it doesn't go the way you had hoped.

This is when I like to play with the game of life to see the opportunities that present or demand my attention. I almost always get something more than the original offering if I honor my word.

I place this magic at the center of the compass, because it is your inner guide. Once you become in tune with this AND trust your navigational skills, this will become a force to be reckoned with.

Not only that but they can be your respite too.

On many occasions I have had an uneasy feeling and not wanted something to happen but have said yes to that appointment. Sometimes for reasons such as the above ones but many a time for reasons e.g., when I have not had a voice, such as hospital appointments and dates for surgery.

Because I trust the process and have an awareness and embracing of how my own innate wisdom cares for me, I now trust it implicitly with both small and life-changing decisions.

Sometimes, when I was given appointments for surgery that instinctively did not feel right they were sometimes OK, but it was really weird when I would get a call and they were cancelled, sometimes only a day before.

I would to have to arrange everything around them so it wasn't as if I could put them completely to the back of my mind, although I learnt very quickly to put most of the anxiety and fear in my secret vault.

But eventually I learnt (because this happened so very often over 10 years or so) that this always worked out in my favor. There was always a good reason in hindsight. I got to go on holiday, to spend time with my son on an important occasion, for the surgery to be rethought or for my overall health and immunity to get better or just simply to learn and grow more, personally.

The timing was perfect.

I learnt to trust that and to only address situations that <u>really didn't innately</u> feel right.

I learnt to trust my whole innate wisdom, and eventually it became clear that both reality and my soul were in sync with one another, which led me to trust, gain respite and be fueled in a way that was perfect.

I am not saying that I did not ever feel anger or frustration. I did and I still do. What I did get to understand is that everything would work out exactly as it should.

I would learn from it. Grow from it. Gain from it and Give from it.

All in all, I am guided by all of it.

All that I do know and I can control and all that I don't know and cannot have any immediate or perceived control over.

I always get the best outcome for me and in turn, so does everyone and everything else. It is my duty to share this knowledge with you. It is not just mine, it is treasure that is available to all.

Writing this book and starting this community is solely led by this instinctive intuition.

There are times when my ability to write is monumental, almost out of my control and guided by some mysterious force and then there are times when I am thwarted, either by illness, uneasiness or circumstance. These times are incredibly frustrating but always work out for the best in the long run.

I have been given this book to share. I do not feel that it is mine. It is just simply, my Purpose. It is my gift to you to help you to trust your own Innate Wisdom and open your world to your Infinite Possibilities.

Ritual & Ceremony

The Art of Ritual & Ceremony are timeless. There are so many different rituals and ceremonies that have been recorded over time. Some fabulous and beautiful and some downright horrid.

What this section is for is to allow you and I to create new rituals and new ceremonies, learning from the good ones that are already in place.

I used to fear being struck down by the wrath of God if I even entertained anything with the word 'ritual' in. Now I see it as an 'intention' and as I work from a place of beauty I choose to see all of the rituals that I observe, take part in or create.

I have not been struck down yet!

I urge you to start creating and exploring your own rituals and ceremonies. Whether they are for self-care, for celebration, for an occasion or not. Whether you restore an historic acknowledgement or go to learn more about another culture, go and see if it resonates with you.

I see rituals as cyclical too. They do not have to be forever. They don't have to even be more than once but if you feel drawn, explore. If you feel the urge, create. If you want to get fit create a ritual to fit exercise in and create a ceremony from salad.

Everything in life should be celebrated and enjoyed. I get so much joy from watching people dance in celebration and you can see the pure joy expand exponentially when you enjoy these celebrations with others. I do not see any difference in a dance around a tribal fire to an aerobics class. It is only the intention that may be different. The euphoric determination is the same.

I love to see the costumes, the make up and the quiet and respectful devotion that goes into the preparation. The pride and the community spirit that emanates the power of ceremony to all those who choose to see it.

I see a world where rituals and ceremony are respected and accepted for the intention the individuals give it, rather than a statement for exclusion.

When we can start to see the beauty in all that others hold dear, the whole world of infinite possibilities are exploded even more so for us all, to use to gain our individuality, our unique essence and our confident community.

We can start to create smaller, more intimate rituals, either singularly with sacred devotion or as a group, where power is exponentially felt, both energetically and physically. We can incorporate values and intentions that we need or that are important to us, now.

We can regain the joy and gain pleasure in the devotion to the rituals we create, together or separately.

We can integrate and form bonds with those with similar needs or desires and create celebrations that can be held locally or all over the world and ultimately the universe.

There are Infinite Possibilities in new ideas.

There are ways to express ourselves as individuals and as groups, without the need for war.

Our energy, as long as the intention is good, will be powered into this growth and I cannot explain the stress relief and happiness that this will create.

I am not saying that we forget any historical or cultural celebration here, just that we can look at discovering new and exciting rituals and celebrations that are perhaps in line with how we live today and how we hope to live in the future. We can still respect and understand the necessities and help that rituals have played in our history, replacing the original intention with something that, perhaps, suits the modern world a little better.

To explain this I will use Bullfighting.

Originally Bullfighting was seen as a show of masculinity and of strength and of overcoming fears. We now know how cruel and dangerous, it is but I know that the job that it has had in the past is still very much needed in our society of humans today.

I have never been to a bullfight but I have spent time watching the bulls running over Spain.

To be a spectator to this is primal but the air is electric. Because of the anticipation and the ceremony and the rules it really does have a place in history, albeit now seen by many as cruel.

The needs of the humans and what it delivers are still very plain to see.

I have been in Pamplona for the festival and it serves the poor and the rich, the drunk and the sober, the sloth and the sophisticated, the old and the very, very young. The WHOLE town, babies in prams included, dress in white and have either red, green or blue kerchiefs tied around their necks.

The WHOLE world knows about it and thousands of travelers come from everywhere to be a part of this celebration.

It is rustic and charming on some levels, with people drinking red wine from pigskins and reveling in the streets. The air is filled with the putrid stench of sweat, stale wine and acrid rubbish, yet everyone is smiling. Everyone is united. Everyone is aware of what may happen and everyone is a part of this community, for just a few days of the year.

The bulls are set free and if you are a scaredy cat like me you will have sat yourself in the already stifling bullring at 8 a.m. and heard the horn, whilst waiting to see how long it takes for the first man to enter the ring.

I say man as, although there are women, it is frowned upon for a woman to take part.

This is a celebration for men to reveal their courage and agility and those rules are highly respected in the community.

As with everything, these rules are changing but the ability for men (and women!) to show their courage still needs to be addressed.

There are 'pippas' (salted sunflower seeds) everywhere. The bars are filled with sawdust. And the sight of men who have been out all night in their white outfits is obvious by their splattering of red wine and dirt stains.

The new challengers run hurriedly into the heat of the bullring and everyone, and I mean everyone cheers! There is excitement. There is fear. There is a crude sense of hoping that you see blood but overriding there is a sense of community.

The rules have been in place for hundreds of years and they are now being broken. The needs for the ceremony are still required today but public views on animal cruelty are strong and quite rightly so.

The desire to be a part of something is inherent in most humans. The desire for adventure, discovery, unity and fun along with laughter and awe. The main desire to either be a part of a celebration or entertained is just so basic that the need is still absolutely relevant today.

So I say lets take what these rituals and celebrations were used for, respect them for now in their environment, but create new ones, if the way in which they celebrate does not conform to our new way of thinking.

We need to celebrate rather than stress. We need to accept our primal needs both as important to our solid foundation as our spiritual enlightenment.

So I have a couple of things for you to try.

How about creating a ritual? Firstly for self-care in some way. Whether this be time out for you or losing a bit of weight, getting outside more or eating dinner regularly.

I would also create a cyclical ritual plan for the year. Use the seasons and really feel into what you like to do as spring becomes summer and autumn leads into winter.

Make sure that you go to the theatre or whatever tickles your fancy, see new things and try new foods as well as remembering all of the things you love. This really helps you to become more balanced as well. If you have the things that you love and they are ritualized, you will not feel lack either. You will be devoting fabulous energy to whatever it is - even if it is something that is not good for you on a regular basis - you can really dive into taking the sensual and devoted pleasure and time to explore your most sacred desires.

I love rosé wine and enjoy it with paella at the beach every now and again, on a Sunday. I even go mad and have bread and butter with gloriously creamy and indulgent aioli! So I look forward to it and really, really enjoy it.

The other thing is Ceremony. Create or explore ceremony. Dance, art, creation. Historical, gender based, old or new. Seek out that which appeals to you and devise your own. On our get-togethers we often create things to do that have become ritual ceremonies. A Summer Party with must-do dance. A made up giggle expressing our womanhood. There are so many ways to enjoy, to celebrate and then, once created, to anticipate!

I see us creating these new rituals to encompass the needs that we have always had as humans, but to do them in a more up to date way, so that more of us can enjoy them, more of us can benefit from them and we can entice those wrapped up in older and more outdated ceremony to join our gang, so to speak.

Then we are working from love. We are working from compassion and we are working from joy. We are working together to fill ancient and still very necessary needs that we all have.

So I encourage you to look at historical, cultural and social ceremonies with renewed vision. See what part they are playing and see if that can be improved upon. See what people get out of it and create a gentle replacement if needed or join in if it appeals to you.

Celebrate, enjoy, dance, sing, pray, meditate - in every language with expanded awareness and expanded joy.

Go create rituals with revived vigor and meaning for you. Go create ceremonies and customs within your world. Go and explore the basic needs that these are working with and for. Go and see the infinite possibilities that are ours to be together, alone, primal, spiritual, protected, outlets, pride festivals or just for fun!

Good, Bad & Ugly Judgment

I have put Judgment back into play for it is a huge part of enlightenment. Awakening to our own judgment is a massive part of the journey to really being able to be Gold.

I think judgment will always be with us to some degree. As thoughtful and intuitive guidance or just as a reflex emotion.

Don't worry about it being there to begin with (I will be sure to let you know if I ever truly rid myself of judgment, if I ever get there).

How you deal with judgment, though, is something that can be far easier to work with and get control over.

Going back to Expanding your Awareness. Your judgment should be one of the things that you put into this arena as soon and as often as you can.

As with everything I share with you, I can honestly say that being less judgmental has truly increased my own happiness and my ability to get what I need.

I use the word need rather than want because I know that what I want is not necessarily what I need. Hindsight is a wonderful thing and you need to develop the ability to be positive about the past as well as positive about the future.

Just become more aware of when you are passing judgment, even mentally, and try to think of ways that could dissipate it, ways to judge the judgment rather than what you are judging.

Try to see different scenarios for the reasons you are being judgmental. In other words try to see the reasons for your judgment and think of the good things that make your judgment irrelevant.

If you are judging someone's appearance. They could be ill, tired, poor, unaware or indifferent.

If you are judging someone's attitude. They could be tired, upset, ill, judgmental or just plain unaware of themselves.

If you are judging someone's abode or work. They could have fallen on hard or good times, have other plans or have other more important issues, or just not have the inclination.

There are so many scenarios I could give you but you get the drift.

I am just giving you some questions that you can ask yourself and give yourself the answers that allow empathy and compassion for the judged and yourself.

It does get easier over time, but there will always be areas of judgment that you need to get off your chest and this is what your circle of safety is for. Your judgment is to be dealt with by you. Your judgment is your problem. Your judgment is only that and you need to have compassion for yourself in this area too. Just become more aware, give empathic reasons for judgment on both sides and you will see the benefits and reap the rewards.

There are some instances where you will have to be judgmental. It is more for discernment and alignment when it comes to others. You still have to make decisions about whom you will be around, both in business, your personal life and in the present moment. Although you may have learnt to be more empathic, you will still have to use kind judgment to ensure that you are safe and prospering.

This is good judgment. It is discerning with thought out reasons to ensure your personal, spiritual and financial growth.

Ensure that you do not give in to empathy. You need to know that your discernment is your duty to yourself and those who depend on you.

If you are aligning yourself with those who have the ability to bring you down, unless you are strong enough to counteract this, it does you or those who depend on you no good.

If you are doing business with those who are not in true alignment with your values, it does you or those who depend on you no good.

If you are stifling your personal growth and freedom by being with those who are constraining or oppressing you in any way, you are stopping your true self from sharing all you have to give with the world.

Now I am not saying that I don't love a good bitch about someone who has done me wrong, or who I know to be untrue to their world or their message, but I will not pass that judgment out further than my circle of safety and I will thank them for my awareness and pray for them. It is then done.

There is no use harboring this judgment either. Let it go and allow yourself the freedom and happiness of the Infinite Possibilities that await you.

Opening Your Channel & Finding Your Guide

I know opening one's channel and finding one's guide may sound a bit fluffy. But I am not. This might be but I am not. I completely believe that it works for me. Simply, with a bit of awareness and sprinkle of good energy and lashings of optimism.

This is where I tell you about my belief in the Unknown. I have no attachment to any specific religion or cult, or magician, or guru, or pop star. This is just my experience and what has truly and abundantly, faithfully and prosperously worked for me.

I remember being a child and just knowing things. Knowing when somebody had died. Knowing who would be on the phone. Casually calling in the right horse for my grandmother. Glancing tearfully and longingly at the stars and telling my mom that "I am from there."

I remember that as I child I didn't question it or doubt myself. I just spoke my truth. It was that simple. It just came through.

After my mom pointed out the stars and the Milky Way for about the hundredth time and trying to look up, I did start to doubt my own word but I certainly could not explain the tears that rolled down my cheeks. They just happened. I could not look up without the tears flowing, my heart being full of overwhelm, wonder and longing and yet distance. I could not look up and so I stopped looking.

I stopped the ability for me to question my own word.

As I have mentioned before I had a huge amount of optimistic faith in what people would call God, The Law of Attraction or Abundance and this stayed with me. Although my ability to pick out winning horses grew debatable!

I got what I wanted, needed and worked for. I was passionate and considerate and looked for opportunities that pulled at my heart for recognition.

As a young woman I just never doubted my ability to get all that I loved. I was always kind, enthusiastic, happy and confident, so this really helped and even if that is all my achievements boil down to I am very grateful for these gifts BUT I think there is something more to it.

Something bigger. Something with a sense of humor. Perhaps a more Alien like me playing a game with my life or perhaps it is a God or Goddess. Or perhaps it is a worm, or an amoeba on a flea on a rat (one of my favorite lines from 'Grease').

I don't care. I do care but I don't care. I just respect it and its power.

What I have learnt over the years is that if I treat it and me and the world good, I get good back. Do unto others. Karma. Give and Receive. Bill and Ben. However you want to wrap it works.

I had to work at becoming in tune with it to the ability that I can now feel it, though. My childhood innocence wasn't as trusting as my adult need for reassurance.

I first started to notice that I felt this Unknown Gold, as it shall be hereon described as, (AKA God, Goddess, Allah, Jah, Frank, Benny, Universe), when I was sat in church. It was during a song (part of my evangelical research phase) and I actually felt a tingle in my right hand.

I also had a feeling of complete wonder, contentment, fulfilling joy and ecstatic knowing. I was thinking about the words and feeling the meaning at the time and they were pertaining to what I had been going through and my plans for the future.

I was at once comforted. I was at once OK. I was at once full. I was at once I, You, It, Everything.

Once I had become aware of IT I wanted more! You see, this feeling is IT.

It is better and bigger than anything I have ever known or experienced and I know that it is what others seek.

How do I know this? Because I don't want anything else anymore. I need things but I don't want more than I am given. The only way I get to have everything I need AND that feeling is by playing the Gold game of life.

It is not an easy game. There are rules but they are simple rules. They are, at times, difficult to adhere to but you get to lose your turn and have to take a step backwards and wait.

It is worth it, though. A girlfriend came around today and I had to be honest and tell her my truth. I don't care if I win the lottery although I would make the most of it if I did and I still occasionally play. In fact, at this moment, I don't want to win. It is so much easier to live with my purpose than to live with the burden of so much wealth. I would deal with it if it came my way, but in the same way I am living now. I would perhaps play this game a little bigger, but I am putting the steps in place for this whole give and receive thing to happen. My purpose is my gift and my gift is my way of living and what I get is IT.

So many people crave IT. Contentment, knowing, trust, love, understanding, beauty, Infinite Possibilities!

I want to give IT to you. I have to give IT to you. It is my job to give IT to you. I have IT to give to you, I want to give IT to you, I have to give IT to you and is my job to give IT to you and I have IT to give to you. Did I repeat myself? Yes, good. It is just a simple, pure cycle that works.

I write this not to belittle someone's faith in a particular religion but to give an umbrella of Gold for us all to live together and know that we are all chasing the same things and working to better ourselves. We need some kind of structure to work with in order for us all to have the freedom to believe and to be whatever our own hearts desire but also to have the freedom to love one another a little bit more.

I write this not to take anyone away from what they believe in at all, but to give us all a safety net whereby we can all be responsible for and work for a better world.

I write this not to scorn another's religion or culture or community but in order for us to be able to work together for our united future and for the benefit of our children.

I write this because it is my job, my duty, my obligation and my truth. It is my purpose to show the beauty that we all hold within us and that surrounds us everyday. To do this I must do it without harming but I will not please everyone.

I write this to be your support, your sacrificial lamb, your blame, your chances, your fears, your guilt. To hold your hand when you need it.

I write this to show that IT is available to everyone. You will not be scorned by an Gold (God, Unknown, Universe – delete where appropriate) who is kind and gentle. You will not be thrown aside by a Gold who wants you to truly live. This Gold will not burn you. You will only BE GOLD.

In and out. Up and Down. Left and Right. Forward and Backward.

I can show you how. If you want it. If you let it.

I trust what I have been given to share with you because I have now learnt to listen to this channel that I receive most potently still through my hand. I asked that this be the sign and I receive it either consciously or unconsciously.

I pass this knowledge on because it is not mine. I gift this knowledge because I am compelled to.

I want you to have what I have. I want everyone to have what I have.

I am but a simple woman but I have a lot to give.

So begin to open your own channel.

Begin with a prayer (or mantra, meditation, quiet time in nature or even in bed). Put goodness into the prayer and ask for your channel to be open. Feel in your body what speaks to you. I don't know how that will feel and I know that I had to keep practicing and practicing and asking and asking but eventually it comes through. It gets louder and clearer. Just like a muscle, it gains strength. Just like a subject you get to understand it a little more and then you can develop a deeper connection to your own Gold.

You can ask your Gold for anything. It will give you answers through this channel (state of mind, connection). This is for deep questions, especially those that need answering immediately, and you don't have any dragonflies available!

Keep working at it. Develop it and it will come. Call it whatever you need to. Believe it to be what you believe. That is not for me to say. That is yours. This is your Gold, your channel with the Divine Unknown and your door to Infinite Possibilities.

The same practice goes for finding your guide. You may have one already, like I did. If you are reading this book then I will make a guess that you do.

It doesn't matter what it is and I hold no attachment to it being a religious symbol of your choosing, an animal spirit, a star, an object or a word.

This guide is also yours, but you probably don't have as much ability to make it stronger. This is "Gold" speaking to you. When you are channeling you are asking. When you are guided you are listening.

This is when you are in need of something bigger than you. This is when your awareness needs to be slapped into awakening. This is when your attention is needed and when you need to listen to your Innate Wisdom, to tap into all of that Unknown Knowing.

Do you have something that you collect already, as I did? Are these objects being thrown in your face more? Ask for it to made clearer to you. Is there a pulling, a love or a calling for something?

Go through the same process as before and you may have to test a couple. Ask for this guide to be made clearer. Butterflies or pictures on public transport or billboards may suddenly surround you. You will get there but you cannot force it. Part of the rules of trust, I am afraid.

It is so worth it, though, even if you and others that you tell (and I certainly wouldn't just go spouting it around just yet as most of the world isn't ready for us) think you are mad, then so be it. Laugh but trust. Pray but see. Rest and see what is revealed. Seek and ye shall find your guide to Infinite Possibilities.

Sacred Space, Sensuality & Senses

Ooh, I love this one. A bit like the dressing up box but of space and sensual feelings and senses of pleasure. A more grown up and yet bashfully indulgent exultation. A glorious opening and abandonment of our femininity.

Do not fret! Before you start panicking about buying your own temple, forming a feminine sensuality program and being led into temptation just know that this is purely for you and can be suited to wherever you are and whatever you have available.

Also know that this is cyclical, changeable and fluid. Nothing is set in stone - not even your own desires or needs.

By giving yourself the freedom of the acceptance of this sacred self-practice, you also give yourself the freedom to truly indulge in the present and your immediate needs. The more you are able to fill yourself up, the more you have to give from a place of beauty; the more you have to give, the more you are able to receive. The Golden Mean or Ratio.

I have had many sacred spaces over the years, depending on my situation and needs at that time.

When I was a child my first sacred space was the church. My mother used to hide us from any bloodthirsty statues and pictures and created a beautiful non-judgmental place from which we formed our foundation in spiritual needs.

When I was a teenager and disillusioned by our own church, I found myself being drawn more to a Xhosa church. It filled me up with what I needed spiritually, without me even understanding the language.

When I moved out of the family home I wanted to create a home worthy of showing off and entertaining - this was a very short lived desire as my desire to travel was far more developed, so I left the country.

When I was traveling, I would go to churches and respect their history and their sacred centers. But my new discoveries and adventures filled me and taught me enough to not have the need for a specific place to fill my spiritual or emotional cup.

When I became settled in a career in the Arts Industry, in my late twenties, my sacred space was the antipodean community. The anonymity and escape from my work management responsibilities was tremendous. I also found respite at a women's music jam session where I was able to indulge my own creativity, separately. This allowed me to be free in my private life and retain the respect I thought I needed to be a responsible and respected financial manager and employer.

When I had my son and became homeless and broke, I again went to church about 3 times a week. Looking for hope in any place other than the room above the pub which was my temporary home, I was also drawn to re-visiting my dreams for the future and did this through second hand books and magazines, about homes and places to live.

Then I was overwhelmed with illness and although I had, by then, been given a small housing association flat and done the best I could with it, my only need for a sacred space was my bed or the sofa with hugs from my son.

Over the next few years I became more house proud and wanted to indulge my homes room-by-room, dream-by-dream and I used to go to churches, too.

But now I know that the sacred space I need is wherever I need it to be at the time. Right now, my folks are in South Africa and I am planning to launch this book and the A Woman On Purpose Empowerment brand, so my living room is devoted to this process. Although it is covered in magic whiteboard and strewn with resources, it is still a place of purpose. I have a little corner with my vase of flowers and my Golden Goddess statues but to be honest, it is a mess.

I have no need for a church, for a pretty room, for an open field or for a beach with a view. This book is now my sacred space. It is my place of beauty and I know how lucky I am to be able to have this place for escape.

I also know that this cycle will come to an organic end. The book will finish and my need to fill this space will be reawakened.

There are many different ways that fill our need for a sacred space. Do not be drawn by someone else's desire. It is really important that this is true for you.

Whether it is a physical place or a place in your mind. Whether it is both. Whether it changes. Whether it is always the same. It does not matter.

All that does matter is that is a completely indulgent space for your needs of the moment.

In my times of desperate need, an alter with flowers or statues was not only too indulgent in my mind but it was an unnecessary cost in money and space that I just could not afford. Now that I can afford it doesn't mean that it has to be a certain flower (although I am very partial to the scent of lilies!) or have specific places, times or rituals. All of them can be indulged when the need arises.

Do not feel pressured by someone else's ideas or religious beliefs either. Go and pop your head into a temple and feel if it suits you. Go and find a beautiful Japanese garden you can visit to expand your dreams. Go for a walk alongside a river, canal or beach. Go and create that beautiful spot in your own garden and fill it with your favorite things. Go and redecorate a room that is pulling your heart to be that space you need for creating. It doesn't matter whether it is your lounge, your kitchen, a corner, an alter, a temple, an office space or the confines of your blessed boudoir as long as you can recline and gain the respite that you need for the period of your life that you are going through.

Even though I love cooking and entertaining my heart is in this sacred space at the moment. The chaos and indulgence of a messy house performs exactly the right sacred space that I have needed to become a literary hermit, to write and channel everything I need to pass on through these pages.

Be pulled by that which is beauty to you in the moment. It will not lead you astray.

Whatever your senses desire, fulfill. When you have expanded your awareness of your desired sacred space you will be able to indulge the senses and infuse your sensuality into that space.

As your awareness grows to embrace that this sacred space desires your attention, in order to give back in its full capacity, you will be able to fill it with all of those things that enable you to also indulge the sensual desires that your senses crave.

Whether it is texture, aroma or taste. Look, feel, emotion. Whatever you want to feel, indulge that. Lose yourself in the sensual intoxication of that which makes you swoon in ecstasy and fill up your senses to such an extent that you are aroused to a point of abandon.

As with everything, it is your choice to enjoy every moment. Whether you want to start the process of enjoyment or get lost in an orgasm of sensual freedom is up to you, but be sure to acknowledge that your judgment around this is yours and yours alone. It is up to you to indulge in the pure pleasure of enjoyment and it is up to you as to where you hinder your ecstatic joy.

Be open to the Infinite Possibilities, the willingness to indulge in your own sensual pleasure can bring. It does not need to be at all sexual and the boundaries are created by you. This is where you fill your need for the feelings you respond to the most at any specific time in your life. They can be enjoyed on a 'present' basis. It reminds you to indulge in the pleasure of the moment and to not get lost in the dream of tomorrow.

The waft of fresh bread, orange blossom, fresh paint and perfume have been part of my own sensual and sacred spatial fulfillment over time I have no desire to fill your senses with my loves but I do want you to explore everything to completely lose yourself in the middle of the now, in the moment and get the most out of every, single, sensual, special, sacred and sense filled Infinite Possibility.

Serendipity

Coincidence, happy accidents, the hand of God or just plain luck. I am not fussed what you call it but whatever it is it makes me a happy, happy Golden Gal!

The more I have trusted, surrendered, allowed myself to be guided by the Universal Unknown and my Innate Wisdom, the more this has turned into my very own Superpower.

I kid ye not!

The more I opened up to learning from my expanded awareness, the more I accepted both the serendipities that occurred and allowed myself to experience the awe and wonder that I felt, the more serendipity occurred.

I wanted more. A bit like an addiction. It surpasses anything I have ever felt in the 'real' world. It surpasses any feeling. It makes me feel like a child who is in touch with her own personal fairy godmother.

All of the things I have written about in this book, about finding your guide and opening your channel, lead to this Superpower.

This Superpower is not available all the time. This Superpower gets its fuel from optimism and kindness. This Superpower is a force to be reckoned with. This Superpower only works if you believe!!!!

I know. I must sound like a mad woman again. That's alright, though, I can live with that. I am a very happy, uber-excited, Super-powered mad woman and I can live with that.

I suppose the best way to describe it is like having a wish, letting it go and expecting the best.

I don't use it with anger. I don't ever use it against anyone or anything. I don't use it for overall financial gain, or material gain, or anything else that I don't really need. I use it when I need to.

As I have mentioned before, I use this trust but I also trust this trust. I trust that it gives me what I deserve and need and I trust that it will sort out situations. It is like a shortcut to fixing your diary or overlapping meetings. It is like a windfall when you need one. It is like having a mechanic turn into your road when you need a jump-start or it is like having enough food because someone you expected to arrive hasn't shown up.

It is just a little wish, a little sprinkle of magic, a little call on the help of your guardian angel, but for more everyday things rather than the more energetically demanding ones.

It is when you need to know something and the answer is laid before you. It is when you want an introduction and it is given. It is when you are looking for a job and the one you want stands out in a crowd.

It is the way you become when you are truly embodying your trust in the great Universal Unknown and your connection with it.

There are so many things I can write about this Serendipity Superpower but I know that you know what I mean.

It is just the ability to call on them and let go. When you become comfortable. When magic becomes real. When you realize your own alchemy and your ability to be supported whilst you explore your Infinite Possibilities.

Truly believing in your Superpower gives you more time. It gives you more peace. More intuitive senses. More management skills. More money. More dream making ability.

Truly believing your Serendipitous Superpower gives you confidence and the ability to achieve more, because you trust you are being supported, guided and steered in the right direction with the help of your inner Golden Compass.

Symbols

There are so many symbols in this world and I have no desire to knock any of them. In fact they are really useful and hence my decision to use symbols to represent the different principles and directions of my book.

I don't hold any symbol as more meaningful or distasteful than another, only what they represent.

You see it is not the symbol itself that creates recognition, respect or loathing. It is the intention behind them and your personal alignment to whatever that symbol represents.

I know that those of a more religious persuasion may disagree and that is absolutely fine. If a symbol helps you then the symbol helps you.

I love looking at and feeling into the intention behind the symbol though. I love to feel what they mean and fully absorb the intention through my body and into my soul. As long as the intention is good!

Logo's are a form of symbol and by looking at a well-known restaurant fast-food chain I can feel the intention of a bloated belly, but sometimes I can overcome that!

When I was doing the research for this book and looking at symbols and representations throughout time and continents, I became aware that most cultures have very different intentions for the same thing.

I mean, to be honest, I found that when I was researching the dragonfly it had some rather disdainful symbolism in some cultures but I just choose to ignore this and get the good from them.

That is when I truly understood that I was not to be in fear of any of the symbols and that it is just the intention. I mean if there was a good Golden Goddess she wouldn't have the same dragonfly represent good on one side of the world and bad on the other, as she knows that we would be hopping on airplanes and find her out. So she must know that it is just the intention behind the symbol and that one-day (now) we would have enough knowledge to deal with it.

So basically it seemed a bit silly to have judgment on a squiggle and base all my energy on it, unless it was serving me.

This, again, frees you to enjoy life more and all its little elements. I can love lilies (apparently used in funerals a lot) because I bloody love them. I can love dragonflies because I bloody love them and I can love squiggles if I so desire. I choose the intention. I choose the feeling and I also choose any judgment I have. Obviously there are symbols that I choose to avoid as the have become infamous for what they signify but I do know that if I like something, no matter what religion, culture or tradition it comes from, I can choose to adopt it. A bit like finding a new favorite brand or the like.

So I encourage you to divine your own symbols. To sacredly

give them good intentions and to be gleeful when you encounter or meditate on them.

Put a symbol (mandala art with a cherry in the middle if you so desire) on the side of your bed with an intention you need when you wake up.

Make a symbol of love for you and your lover. Make a symbol of everlasting love for you and your child, together. Make a symbol of love to give to a good friend. Just make sure that the symbol doesn't get left in the cupboard!!! Well, it will fall out and remind you at some stage so that doesn't even matter.

Just be sure to make intentions work for you. Don't worry about the negative ones. They needn't exist for us happy ones. You see we are the Alchemists of Infinite Possibilities and we can make everything Golden.

Meditation & Prayer

When you become A Woman On Purpose, whatever your feelings are to the words above, they should not affect your ability to use the practices they represent.

For me meditation is listening and prayer asking. It needn't be traditional in the way it is performed and can be directed towards a God of your choice, or to that little place inside you that is calling out to be heard or to be spoken to.

The only important thing about them is that you perform these to suit you and accept that others may choose to do so differently.

I can listen to music and be hearing and meditating and I can sit on the loo and pray. They both work. I mean no offense to anyone by writing this, only that it is true, to me.

As I have evolved, become more aware and less constrained by opinion, I have been able to relax enough to see that the bigger picture is far greater than any doctrine I can place in my world, but that the basic tools of what has been learnt and employed since the beginning of the human race, still hold true today.

I can get into a meditative state whilst on a treadmill and listening to high energy dance music in the same way I can get into trance by sitting and listening to soft Zen or silence. I use every available option and entrust you to do the same.

As with everything I teach this only goes to expand your joy and to increase your own power pack of tools, equipping you to become aware of what you need for a particular situation or emotion that you are experiencing.

I like to think that I can evoke the same feeling of ecstasy from dancing in a nightclub, to a beat so fierce it booms through my body, as I can by shamanic drumming in a circle and slightly moving to the rhythm we create.

I like to think that meditation will become as important to work routine in mainstream environments, as strategic planning and sales meetings, once we become more aware of the power and ability to hear our own wisdom. That it will be valued for the Gold it can create in a person, as much as our employed job description.

Just having or making the time to think, the time to reflect and the time to generate ideas, thoughts, understanding can never be underestimated.

Once you are fully aware of the preciously generated thinking that meditation in any form, or given any name, can achieve, there seems to be no other way than to ensure that you pay it enough respect. Give it the time to become a practice that is cherished, nourished and developed in order to create and expand your own personal development, to give space for your own Infinite Possibilities to form.

I love the way meditation allows us to either focus on nothing and to clear our minds or just gives us space for understanding.

Greater expansion of our awareness then generates such a sense of peace that we needn't have thoughts.

But it is also very clear to me that by giving our minds space it allows us to clear any devotion to practices and thoughts that are not serving us well. It literally clears the clutter from our minds to allow the space for divine guidance or just bloody spectacular ideas!

It can do so much for us on a personal level too. It allows us to be more in control of ourselves. We need to be able to clear our minds, whether or not our present state is that of happiness or sadness.

Clearing the space for increased happiness is essential for our mental health.

It allows us time to de-stress, to relax, to calm, to be alone and once we become a master of that it generates more of the same. It increases our ability to be more in control of that we can be in control of.

Clearing our minds leaves us time to be with ourselves. Not lonely. This in itself is a feat worth finding your own path of meditation for, as once you are completely happy on your own you take the ability of someone else's job of making you happy away from them, leaving them independent to find themselves, and yet supported by your own independence.

Imagine how, in a better world, this could impact us as a species. If we were all so independently happy and secure in ourselves that we didn't need one another, but were free to just love one another. Obviously, this is not the case for children and animals, but we should be teaching and giving this to our children, as much as formal education.

The need for needing is the part that we all really have to deal with. The need for someone to love you, to provide for you, to hold your hand, to give you a job, to serve you, to look up to, to be looked up to by.

When we all become free of that need, and do so in a way that is closer to our true state of love, the need becomes love and the desire becomes love, too.

The same goes for praying. We pray to God for love. We pray to God for our needs to be met. We pray to God, or the Universe or Bob for what we desire.

When we are more in tune and in practice with these desires our questions become expanded, too. As the basics are met in meditation our questions become more based on purpose and the expansion of that love, in whatever form you feel drawn to.

I am not belittling the smaller prayers, the general prayers, the prayers that we are able to say without thinking, as I feel that they have as much merit as any other, but I do feel that those prayers which we are able to recite without thinking are sort of a convergence of prayer and meditation. You can use these at any time. To forget worries, to get into meditation, to have thoughts and to just be.

The more you ask your questions and the more full of love you become enables you to ask bigger questions and then, in turn, be given bigger answers.

I don't mean that the process shortens or has a better impact on one. Indeed the answers may become longings and the impact subject to existence but you do become more comfortable with moving away from formal doctrine. You are therefore able to see past your own judgment and get to an answer that is based on love and not dire need, even if the question relates to dire need e.g. world hunger.

I think these recited prayers must be the same process that monks use for joint prayers and why they were originally started.

The secret is that this is the way to become at peace with yourself spiritually, no matter what your religion or belief.

Once we all become more at peace with ourselves, we will be able to come together and join our meditations and prayers together, to deal with the bigger issues that the world has. We will be able to do it from our own independent place of peace within a structure that is formed to utilize the combination of love and work from that space.

Can you even imagine the Infinite Possibilities we can achieve?

Call & Response & Chanting

You may have noticed by now that I absolutely love music. It is like the blood in my veins and courses through me. I cannot live without music in my life, although I am not fussy which genre.

Music has been used throughout the ages for all types of healing, fun, celebration, enjoyment, relaxation and integration and just to help pass the time.

I put all the types of rhythmic sound into this section because to me they all have such benefits to someone at sometime that none can be left out.

If you have been expanding your awareness and expanding your joy you will be more open to all of the genres, reasons, rationale and rhythm that I am presenting overall.

Call & Response songs have been around since we have. They have so many benefits to us all. Used as a means of rhythm to get through mundane or laborious tasks for chain gang prisoners and during war time or military service, call and response is not only repeating the lead voice but it also instills a calm, rhythmic peace for those joining in.

In modern times it is used in sport to create a cacophony of fervor and in ancient times the repetition of mantras or chants led to instill complete harmony and peace of mind in community.

As I see it, we have separated our own view of call & response into the genres of music today, so much so that we fail to see how empowering they can be to us all as individuals and how uplifting they can be to us in groups.

We tend to segregate our joy into fashionable trends and so fail to fully embrace ALL of the genres of music, audience and chanting that we have nowadays. They are able, together, to fill in all the missing gaps in our sense of wellbeing and we all have access to any of them through the web. They are able to heal, help and celebrate all that we are feeling and all we are able to give.

Just listening to some call and response songs over the years, over the decades and over the genres, I have realized how utterly inclusive and empowering the whole action can be.

A few of the most famous call and response songs from recent times and from different genres are:

- Oh Happy Day - Gospel
- My Sweet Lord - George Harrison
- The Banana Boat Song (Day O) - Traditional Jamaican Dock Workers Song and more recently
- A Girl Like You - Edwyn Collins
- Even Led Zeppelin covered the Muddy Waters Blues tune You Shook Me.

You see, most genres of music over most ages and most cultures have used Call & Response songs to really let go of the angst, feel a sense of unity and to be able to release their gifts through this type of music, whatever their musical ability.

It is part of our combined heritage as humans.

As for chanting, this to me is used as I have mentioned before to get your mind into a calmer, more responsive state and can be used again either on your own or in a communal fashion.

I have chants in meditation and meditation in chants. I have managed to find the benefit in Gregorian, Buddhist and Christian chanting, whilst the benefits of the mixing the words you love at a beat you most need can never be underestimated.

I have Kirtan's, Bhakti or mantra's set to Bollywood, House and Tribal beats.

I love them all. I use them all. Not all at the same time mind you! But when I need them they are there.

I implore you to give it a go. Let that expansion head bang to a little heavy rock. Let it send you into a trance purely for the ecstatic joy it can bring.

Immerse yourself in the pleasure of chanting words you do not understand. Just feel their worth and let the power reach deep inside that part of you that rarely gets a look in.

Chant whatever you like, if you feel like making it up, or do a little Google search - you are bound sure to find something that suits your mood. When something appeals to you from an audience point of view it usually has the ability to fill up that part of you that needs feeding, that needs attention or that needs healing or care. Chanting can help you rewire, rewind and relax. It can help you calm down if you are angry or switch off if you are wired.

Let the sound of music wash over you. Sing in the shower. Dance in the rain. It doesn't have to be a call and response song either, only that makes it easier if you don't know the words. You don't have to think about it, though the exact same response can be gained if you sing a song you love, so if you feel the urge, even if it has been a while, go ahead, make those lungs work.

Chanting, singing, rhythm, connection. Get into it, get down with it, get low with it, rise up with it. Expand your awareness; Expand your emotions and your spirit. Call your way forward into the sound of the Infinite Possibilities.

LifeStyle Business – Sales & Marketing

This is the reason for your business! Without selling anything you do not have a business!

Never feel ashamed of selling or marketing your products or services. They are needed as much as the next one and, as long as you have researched the need for your product or service in your market, you should be able to make your personal rhythm include a LifeStyle Business in a way that suits, to share your gifts with the world and to refill your vessel.

As I have mentioned before, I have found it very difficult to sell that which I do not believe in. In fact, I was so shy at selling I even found it hard to sell that which I did believe in!

So my first tip would be to really love what you are offering. It makes life so much easier. If you love what your offering and then package it in a way that really suits you, it will only reinforce the illumination you give when you are selling or even introducing your business elsewhere.

There are vital elements that you need to follow when selling. The first being your sales must look to outweigh the costs! I know that seems obvious but so many times we either do not place enough value on what we offer or do not calculate the true costs of our business, that many fail on this point alone.

Ensure that you make your marketing cost effective in relation to your offering. This is so much easier today with social media.

If you get to grips with advertising to your best audience, your costs will be minimized and your profits will soar.

Try to understand your best form of marketing and use every available outlet that suits your avatar (ideal client). It is so easy to repurpose content into books, audio downloads or podcasts, video or course work.

See which your avatar responds to the most and utilize those means as best you can.

Don't forget to look at your competition. I know that there is enough room for everyone but you needn't struggle to re-invent the wheel.

What do you competitors offer?

Where do they offer?

What is there price range?

Are they packaging or selling individually?

What times of the year do they advertise what?

What do they advertise at what time of year?

There are many questions you could answer just by being observant in your market area. This could save you so much time, energy and money and free you up to create more Infinite Possibilities!

Stage 3
The Embodiment

Pictopia Publishing

Chapter 8
Infinite Principle - Unknown

All that we do not know and can not control

Peaceful, Powerful, Presence

Zen in the Art of Gold - Your 'Aah & Aha' Moments
Mantras, Magic, Money, Manifesting & Miracles
Beauty & Feminine Wiles & Mystique
Self Realization & Actualization & Enlightenment
Golden Rhythm & Energy - Mastering Meandering Change
Sacred Self & Sensitivity
The Embodiment of Responsible Happiness & Leadership
Embracing Consciousness - Compassion, Non-Judgment, Contribution, Humility, Patience, Consciousness, Clarity & Humor
LifeStyle Business - Vision & Growth

Zen In The Art of Gold - Your 'Aah & Aha' Moments

Zen in the Art of Gold is the culmination of a lifetime of discovery, adventure, ebb, flow, happiness, sadness and determination.

On your quest for the Meaning of Life you can use The Golden Compass as an overview or structure of your understanding.

Being Gold is being educated by serendipity and conscious co-incidence. Your understanding becomes acceptance and then, in turn, grows to wonder and the eternal symbol of infinity is woven inextricably throughout the gold sutures that are holding the strands of your life together. They, in turn, turn the pain into pleasure, anger into awe and judgment into acceptance.

Zen in the Art of Gold is when you are fully embodied in your Self-Awakening and comfortable in all of your wisdom.

That which makes no sense, in time, becomes as clear as day. Revealing chuckles of laughter in the Knowing of what was there all along.

This is when you come alive. This is exciting beyond your wildest dreams. If you are reading this with a slight Buddha smirk then you will be ready!

This is when you can package your own journey and make it fit with your next chapter.

Use the structure of your story to highlight your enlightenment and to open the eyes of those on a path of discovery to weave their own journey into life as it is, as a tool, aim to add comfort for those in the quandary of existing between spirituality and practical day-to-day life. To bring joy into the everyday. To comfort in times of need. To give hope to all those in search of something that, at present, seems out of reach.

See this as the beginning of your journey as a traveller on the path of life and embellish each stepping stone as a work of art, whilst giving stability in the form of practical existence, allowing the cup of life to overflow into the waterfall of eternity.

Mantras, Magic, Money, Manifesting & Miracles

Why are these all put together? Because if you are truly living an enlightened path you will see that they are inextricably linked.

You become the alchemist and whatever you think can happen, you make happen. It is the acceptance that this is the magic of living. So whether you decide to sing your manifesting mantra or create miracles by taking action, it is your intention as to how you feel it, create it, do it and action this magic that can either become beauty or dismissed as rubbish. You get to choose.

For those of us that are happy and at peace within ourselves, we choose to see the magic, we choose to create miracles, we choose to manifest the dreams, we choose to utilize money for good intentions, both our own and for the greater good. We choose to not be afraid of others prejudices. We choose to accept the imperfections in others and ourselves. To take action and try to make the world better in the way we choose to live our lives.

I am not saying that others do not manifest money and their own success through a far more practical stance, just that for those of us who intend to move forward and enjoy every single moment, we have chosen to see beauty, be beauty and pass on the beauty throughout every moment we can.

You can choose to be positive, philanthropic, prosperous, passionate, personable, purposeful or powerful or you can choose to be all of these. I did mention I was a greedy girl, right? Your choice.

You choose to work. You choose when you get up. You choose what you do. You choose how you show up. You choose your mood. You choose what you say and how you say it. You choose your reaction. You choose when to react. You choose who you want to be around. You choose how often.

If you have the choice then I highly recommend you make a positive, optimistic, greedy, have-it-all choice. The one where every day is filled with sweet mantras, practical magic, enough money, graceful manifestation and beautiful miracles.

Throw your head back, throw your arms to the sky and make the choice of pure joy. Choose to see the Infinite Possibilities.

Beauty & Feminine Wiles & Mystique

I try to work from beauty. I try to see beauty. I try to be beauty. I mostly get it right. I accept that sometimes I cock up, royally.

I sometimes use my feminine wiles. Not in a bad way, only to get that beauty filled action, only to get that beauty filled smile, only to receive the beauty I need to fuel my engagement in the moment and to keep on keeping on. I want everything in my life to be beautiful. There is enough of the other stuff!

They are my choices. This lends to the mystique that is so infatuating. The mystique that exudes confidence and opportunities and aspirations.

I hope to fill the world with as much beauty as I can. It is a lot easier to do this when I show up with confidence, taking care that I portray the correct demeanor to the situation at hand.

There is time enough for me to take myself off and be a walker, a thinker, a beach bum and a TV slob.

When I show up to you I want to use all of my gifts to lift you higher and to ensure that you are as aware of the beauty you need to grow and be full of joy.

The fact that I see manipulation as a positive word is just that I know that is how the world is working at the moment. I am working to make the world a better place, at this moment.

I believe that this word can be outgrown, along with the obsession, with blame, fear and shame.

I know and accept that I am far from perfect but I am planting a seed of a tree that I never expect to sit under.

This is the beginning of a New Paradigm. A Beauty Filled Paradigm, should you choose it. A world where feminine wiles and mystique can be given a platform of unity and from where we can shower the world with love, kindness and compassion.

By using your power of observation you can see where your own beauty is drawn and attracted to. Use that space to create the environment that you want to work from, to share from and to live in. It doesn't matter what that beauty is and it doesn't matter if it changes, just as long as it fills and feeds your now, your moment, your soul, to be able to fully live.

By using your feminine wiles, in this modern sense, it is to get the beauty filled result that benefits everyone. Use it wisely and kindly and not to manipulate in the outdated sense.

A Woman On Purpose uses her feminine wiles to help create her beauty filled platform and to maintain it. She uses her feminine wiles to ensure her family and friends and colleagues respect her, see her and listen to her and not to just get what she wants, because A Woman On Purpose wants a better way for all.

Feminine wiles allow you to be you and show yourself in a light that is perhaps a little brighter than before, a little louder than before and a little more assured than before.

You will develop the ability to foresee situations and divert them if you use your allure to see your bigger picture. Even if this isn't an option at present, you will be able to sway the thinking of a situation to get to the best outcome, in order to change the direction of thinking and ways.

You will also be a guide to the women of the future. You will be their light. You will be their teacher so this is a big responsibility but it I know you can handle it.

Developing your own mystique is that essence that people want but cannot touch. Once your confidence is embodied, your mystique will be magnetic. Your attraction palpable but untouchable and your presence will be greater than you can ever have imagined.

You need to be comfortable with this in order to make your biggest impact and share your gifts as widely as you need to.

If you have been able to get to grips with all that I have shared thus far it should be becoming easier and easier to step into the Woman On Purpose you are.

I can honestly say that this process still has doubts and probably always will, but I am here to tell you that it is OK. You are enough. You always have been. It is your time and my time and time for all of us to step out and make the world a better place.

Let's do this thing. Let us create a world of Infinite Possibilities.

Self Realization & Actualization & Enlightenment

I am very new to these sayings. I am very new to knowing what it feels like. I am also very new at a lot of the jargon that goes with attainment of the above but I have been on the journey all of my life.

I don't think it can be given. I think that a lot of religious, spiritual and philosophical paths try to explain through story the way to attainment of this elusive place, but the truth of the matter is that, although they are true, unless you understand them it is really hard to appreciate what they mean. It is hard to actually feel better, because most of them are very, very old and not in alignment to modern life and the way we play it.

To be honest, even the stories that I have told that try to help the attainment of each section of enlightenment are still my personal journey; I am very aware that not everyone will be able to learn through my experience.

Sometimes it is the long and scenic journey that you take by yourself that gives you a sense of peace and the ultimate knowing of fulfillment. Sometimes that journey is very, very painful.

I do not wish to give false hope to those who are struggling with problems out of their control, but only to help you become comfortable with yourself and have a sense of peace for your now.

Many of you will already be here. You will have reached the station and be able to pass on the message through your own stories and gifts and you will also realize that there is no end to the learning.

You see there is no ultimate happiness. There is no resting place where you can lay your hat and be sure that you have all the answers. The beauty in the realization of the fact that there is no end of Infinite Possibilities, it is the Ultimate State and when you become comfortable that is the moment is when you can fully rest.

You become at peace with the world, at peace with life, at peace with death. It is being at peace with the 'what if' as much as the 'what could'. It is being at peace with the wonder and awe that you have had to go full circle, sometimes in infinity, to get back. Like a child you are able to be in awe of the simplicities, wonder like an explorer, get excited every single day you can and yet, when you are not feeling too happy, be comfortable in that, too, and that it is only temporary.

These are just some of the things but they are the mainstay. It is the acknowledgement that you are responsible for all that you can be responsible for, and that you are a pioneer into the unknown, just like everyone else.

The simple dichotomy. The Paradox. The meaning of life.

It is simply your duty to be alive whilst you live and to live whilst you are alive.

To love and accept yourself and all life. To love and accept that you will never know everything and there will always be an unknown.

That is growth. That is life.

To hear laughter in all of its forms.

To see love in all of its glory.

To stop pain and suffering where we can.

To appreciate everything.

To live with enough is to have everything. To keep chasing is to keep wanting.

To use your choices wisely. It is OK to choose what is right for you as long as it brings no harm. It is your free choice with no strings attached. If you are happy, so am I. We are all little happy souls. Smiling knowing smiles.

Smiling in the knowledge that there are Infinite Possibilities.

Golden Rhythm & Energy - Mastering Meandering Change

Once you have embraced your truth you will be feeling the pull of your own tide and have become used to the rhythm you are creating that is personal to you.

You will realize that there are ups and downs, ins and outs, highs and lows. Sometimes you are able to control them and other times you are not.

It becomes easier over time when you learn to ride the waves of emotion but you have some huge crests to climb, once you first become a sailor on this sea of Meandering Change.

It is almost like you are being tested by the Universal Unknown, seeing if you are ready to Captain your own sea of life and become heralded to teach your crew the gifts you have been given.

The more you become sure of your navigational skills, the rougher the sea becomes!!!

Keep riding, honey, just keep riding. The calm will be here shortly, so never give up.

Everyone has their own map. I cannot tell you exactly how to pin point your direction or the exact place where your treasure is hiding. All I know is that you will find it.

Whether it is through the Alchemy you discover or the hunting of treasure. The Gold is there inside of you.

The wonderful thing about finding your own pot of gold is that it was always right in front of you.

Our view becomes hazy, for what, I do not know. I cannot go back. I need to keep the rhythm going and yet I knew the song as a youngster! I just forgot the words to sing, the tune to sing it to and why I was singing in the first place.

Bang your drum as softly as you need to and increase the steady beat and the strength only when you are ready.

Some will only be able to deal with softness and light to begin with but increase the dose and keep testing your resilience and your Expanding Awareness.

Some will only respond to a heavy-handed drumbeat and feel the urge to keep going and going and not heed the warnings. Feel the need for quiet tender times, too. Do not brush them off.

The Rhythm is ridden over the tide of meandering change and you have the right to choose your means of navigation, of travel, of map and of direction.

Sometimes it is nice to let others lead, too. This gives you respite and gives them a boost of confidence in their ability to feel their own rhythm.

As you observe them you get to learn more about yourself and your leadership strengths. More is exposed to you about what you could pass on in the form of leadership skills or life gifts.

Whatever you do, never give in to the darkness. You are always needed, somewhere, someplace.

I hope to build areas of respite for these tougher times during our own personal development, as time goes by, as I know how desperately needed they are.

That is for the future, though, so for now just know that they are temporary and the more aware of them you are the closer you are getting to know your personal rhythm.

The periods of darkness will always come to show us how beautiful the light is. It is not personal, it is just life.

Do not resist the tide as you feel pulled in different directions. This, too, is your journey, and, just as a yacht would tack from side to side to gain ground, so you must adhere to the magnetism of the pull of your Personal draw cards. They will not take you off course; they will simply form a part of your journal. You can look back at where the paths joined in their meandering flow in the future.

This, too, becomes normal. You will feel drawn in one direction and then another, seemingly non-dual direction and from these two diversions you will find unified knowledge. Be content that it may not be obvious, now, but when it is revealed it will be like taking the wrapping off a longed for present. You will be like a child in a sweet shop with your newfound convergence.

It is not personal, it is just life. Ride the tide, steer your ship and dance to the Infinite Possibilities.

Sacred Self & Sensitivity

As you have probably noticed. Becoming more aware and enlightened with life does not come without its problems! Awakening to the beauty of life does not immediately dispense with the emotions or feelings of being human. In fact, you are probably even more sensitive to feelings, to words, to pictures, nature and your emotions far more heightened than ever before.

This is normal and does not mean that you have suddenly been charged with a nucleus of electronic proportion. As long as you are still aware of these feelings and do not become owned by them you can exponentially increase your personal growth.

With this charge of sensitivity, though, comes the necessity for extreme self-care. You need to enhance your ability to consider yourself first and foremost, as this is where you take a firm hold of your inner self and become the petrol attendant for your own tank.

Your sacred self needs your attention and care as much as your purpose. You need to ensure that you are in charge of your innermost needs. Your inner sanctum is sacred. Only you will know how to divine it.

No one can be dealt the atrocities of life constantly; therefore you need to take stock of what you are able to deal with and when you need to step away.

Some of us will be called to work in places where we are exposed to these atrocities on a daily basis. Because of our increased sensitivity what we are able to handle becomes harder to bear.

It doesn't mean that you are weaker, only that we are so overwhelmed with things that are not conducive to beauty (whatever that is for you) that we are unable to be constantly bombarded by it.

I believe this is so that we collectively do things to avert atrocity. I believe that this heightened sensitivity is increasing in our modern world to fight, peacefully, all that is wrong with our world as it is and not to break us down as individuals.

We are constantly told of increased depression, stress and unhappiness in our modern world and I can not deny that I have succumbed to this myself but I have learnt to deal with it by accepting my own limitations. I think that we all need to own up to what we can handle personally and collectively, continuing to find solutions to these ills from an individual place of beauty and happiness.

I do not work in an environment that deals with illness, destruction or even corporate life because I know that I could not do so on a daily basis anymore. I also know that if I were to be put in an environment that needed my help that I would be more than capable of dealing with it.

To really accept yourself as an awakened or enlightened being, is to know how much you can honestly deal with and to take care of yourself in that regard.

If you are a doctor or nurse and you are finding it hard to cope then you need to see where you can work from a place that is comfortable for you.

If you are a counselor or caregiver then you need to do the same.

The same goes if you are a banker or corporate worker who feels like they are now in hostile territory on a daily basis.

I have worked in offices all of my life, nearly, and find that I feel ill if I even walk into a city building nowadays. I have had to realize my own limitations and rebuild my world around them.

You need to be honest with yourself. No matter how much you enjoy your job, every single one of us live lives of stressful bombardment of the negative. Until we find a way that we can all work in balance and positivity, the onus is on yourself to find your own Magnificent Equilibrium.

For some of us this may mean just a slight adjustment, such as not reading the news or taking a walk in nature at lunchtime. For others it may be thinking about working less hours or taking more time away. Some of us need to really take stock and move entirely away from what has become our 'normal' life in order to find a place that honors our sacred self and our increased sensitivity.

Just remember that you are not alone in this. We are all in it together. By taking ownership of your increased sensitivity and making yourself sacred you are in fact supporting those who have yet to find the strength to do so.

You are not being selfish in the old fashioned way. You are filling your cup in order for it to overflow. This is the win-win of life that we have been hidden from throughout time and which is opening up before us.

We are the Pioneers of the Sacred Self. We are sensitive because it leads us to action against all that is wrong in the world that has been hidden from us and open the worlds' eyes to the Infinite Possibilities.

The Embodiment Of Responsible Happiness

This leads straight into the Embodiment of Responsible Happiness and Leadership.

Why? Because if we are all happy and full up in ourselves, we can lead others into the world of Infinite Possibilities. We can become the Pioneers into this great unknown. Over time there have been explorers who traveled to the extremes of the earth and set down roots in lands that were far from the land of their birth.

We now know the world. We can travel. We are transient beings on earth. We are at a time in history where we know collectively what is right and wrong. If we don't stop using the old ways of violence and greed, I don't even want to imagine what could become of our beautiful planet and all the creatures that inhabit it.

We have a duty as the Pioneers of Infinite Possibilities to create new ways of doing things.

Religions, Politics and Charities have all had their roles to play as have customs, traditions and cultures.

We are now mixing those up. We cannot go on in the same fashion. There are some of us who are just not ready to embrace this and I accept that, as we all must. That does not mean that we cannot start to envisage hopeful and practical ways to bring peace to our world, abundance to all and beauty and happiness to every single living creature.

I see that as our immediate future.

I see that as our calling.

I can see the Infinite Possibilities of invention, creation, opportunities, thoughtfulness and implementation - from a unified presence of good.

We need to be as organized as those in opposition, even more accomplished at getting what we know is for the benefit of all, as those who are in charge of benefitting the few not so scrupulous leaders of our world, of the present.

That is why, if you think you are being called to leadership, that it is imperative that you embody your own goodness, your own sacredness and fill your own cup to overflowing. Even more so, now, as that is what people need to feel encouraged.

Throughout time people have followed those that offer something more.

It is our time to be more, to have more and to be able to give more.

I do not think I am being selfish at all. Only I can know when I am happy and only I can do something about it. What I do know is that I have something that people want, right now. That is I am happy. I have enough. I can lead the way.

I am also completely comfortable with my intentions. I try my best to be my best and to give all that I can to the world to fill my purpose.

I do this completely with the underlying rules of kindness and compassion.

I know that we have such a long way to go, that I will probably hardly see any benefit from what we put in place in my lifetime and still I am happy.

I believe that we all have a part to play if we are ready to play it. I accept that some people have immediate challenges or responsibilities and are not ready or able to begin the leadership this world needs. That is OK too.

What I do acknowledge more though, is that if I do not step up and take my role seriously, then I am in no way helping a world that I could put my kindly stamp on. I am leaving the opportunities for further greed and destruction open to those who are greedy and unfortunate enough to not have my level of trust and hope for the Infinite Possibilities of abundance and peace for everyone.

There are so many jobs to be filled by us all. We are creating a hub of entrepreneurs who are willing, ready and able to step up to their roles of leaders into this New Paradigm and all it holds for us.

Responsible happiness is every single persons birthright. Let's do this thing. Let's make this Possible.

Embracing Consciousness

Compassion, Non-Judgment, Contribution, Humility, Patience, Consciousness, Clarity and Humor.

In order to fully step into New Paradigm Leaders, we must firstly become the embodiment of what that means.

We must walk our talk and talk our walk. Don't think that this means you must be perfect. Quite the opposite, in fact. It just means that we must accept ourselves and our fellow sisters of the New Paradigm for what and who we are.

This is imperative. We must acknowledge our humanity and our propensity for cocking up and allow this to be incorporated into acceptable levels of compassionate understanding. We must allow for compensation rather than immediate judgment of others or ourselves.

We need to work together from a place of positivity and beauty and to create this place as we go along.

Due to our access of information and awareness of what is happening, we need to form new structures and systems to bring hope to the world and to our children and their children too.

To be able to do so and to overcome the obstacles that this

transient and informed society has to deal with we will have to create a new 'normal' and for us all to benefit and to the benefit of our children and the planet we must do so responsibly and from a place of alert kindness.

This does not mean that we all live in communes and displace ourselves to a utopian isle of independence. In order to truly benefit ourselves, those who are in need now and for the continued benefit of our planet it is our purpose to accept responsibility for the opportunities that we can create and to do so with New Paradigm thinking but in our world as it is today.

Nothing of this magnitude happens overnight. I accept that. This is just the beginning of what I hope will be the opening up of our hearts to contain the magnitude of what us mere mortals are exposed to in our time here on earth.

I choose to believe that this New Paradigm can be the greatest part of our human history on this planet and the beginning of a completely new way of doing things.

In order to achieve even the beginning I am calling on you, dear sisters, to step into your roles as leaders of this New Paradigm and to truly embody the necessary tools that it will take to open conversations and to begin to restructure our complete way of thinking.

We are not meant to be huddled away in a safe house. I feel my shackles breaking even as I sit here writing this. We are meant for great things, you and I. Whether it is in our own homes, in our work place or in the seats of control of our calling, it is time for us to take our true selves into the realm of possibilities our embodied leadership has created.

We were born with the qualities of true and just leadership. Compassion is our essence. Non-judgment is our attainment, Contribution fills our cup, Humility is our truth, Patience is our learning, Consciousness our awakening, Clarity is what we seek and Humor our reward.

If we can take these qualities and lead the way forward we can create the abundant world that leaves us without guilt and the freedom to live our lives fully.

I understand that the world is not geared up for our type of leadership and that we will, in essence, be the bridge into this New Paradigm. Interweaving our new skills with the rules and regulations and compliance of the old systems and utilizing our new ways, enabling others to see the benefits that we are able to see.

It takes courage and strength and determination to see this through. We will be ridiculed and therefore our armor must be tough, whilst our hearts remain soft. We must wear our compassion with resilience and be aware that not everyone will think us rational.

We must completely meander in our society and weave kindness into resolution. We must sing of our successes and be proud of our stand for equality and abundance for all.

It doesn't matter how we lead, only that we take our leadership seriously and embody it with all our hearts. It doesn't matter where we lead, only that we lead a path that we are happy for our children to follow in. It doesn't matter why we lead, only that we do so for the greater good and not for our own satisfaction.

I know that this is the way forward for us all, no matter where we come from or what we believe in.

I know that it starts with us women who have been called. With us that have had our hearts cracked open and our eyes opened to the fact that the pain and suffering must and can be stopped.

I know that I cannot do this alone and I write this book to let you know that you are not alone, either. That there are many of us that feel the same way and who want to be more, to have more, to be able to give more and to make the world a better place.

I see this book as the first step to the creation of an umbrella that we can use to shelter us from the bitterness and unbelief of those embroiled in a world that is full of hatred and hostility, who do not understand our sensitivity.

But I also see this book as one of the first of many to be written as a guideline for the New Paradigm, to binding us together, whether we choose to be independent and run our own businesses, to infiltrate the world with our kindness and compassionate thoughts or to give hope to those who need something to hang on to.

My next step is to create the means for us to join hands in our mission to make the world a better place, so that we can do so together and be united.

If you are already independent but just want to be a part of this new way then there will be a place for you.

If you are not ready yet but would like to be a part of this new movement then there will be a place for you.

If you would like to learn more about being A Woman On

Purpose and to teach the ways to others then there will be a place for you.

This is a project of new beginnings, a project of equal parts strength and compassion, a project in creation. In being true to ourselves and in responsible action.

This is a project of Infinite Possibilities.

LifeStyle Business – Vision & Growth

This is where you get out your crystal ball! Only kidding! I don't have one but I do have the ability to dream, to vision, to see the Infinite Possibilities that the world could offer us all. Your business needs this as much as your life.

To be able to see, to stop, plan, take action, grow and start again will enable you to never stop loving what you do.

As in life, in business you need to see a 'bigger picture'. Not all of the time and not to focus on it as more important than actioning the present plan. But there is so much excitement to be had in having a business that can grow in the same way and at the same pace as you.

As you reach certain goals, at certain times and as life changes, it is so good to be able to embrace growth, vision and adaptability.

This is like vision boarding for your business. A storyboard can be used if you have definitive ideas but to just explore ideas it is good to have the scope to dream, to see and rest with those dreams. Take the time to see which ideas seem to be the most natural in progression. You will know when the time is right to start implementation. Predict growth. Always! It is not your decision to stop. That will happen automatically when the time comes. Your job, whilst you are here is to explore the

Infinite Possibilities that not only your life but your business can achieve!

I wish you Joy. I wish you Love. I wish you Infinite Possibilities!

You are A Woman On Purpose

Let's make this world a better place.

Golden Compass Mantra

*My heart is cracked open
To give and to receive
My feet the foundation
Secure to just Be*

*My left hand to help me
Receive all I desire
My Right to lend others
The help they require*

*Step forward in trust,
In action, in love
Look back to wisdom
Ancient elders passed on to us*

*Look up for our guidance
Our spiritual signs
I accept my life gratefully,
In love, I try.*

And so it is!

Legend

Learn more about The Purpose Philosophy, The
Golden Compass, The Spiral of Life and Lady Pi

Get to understand what the symbols represent
and find out how they interrelate and make
magic happen.

WWW.AWOMANONPURPOSE.COM/LEGEND

ABOUT THE AUTHOR

Alexandra Gold is a writer, poet, and empowerment advocate who is dedicated to helping women find purpose and meaning in their lives. Her work is deeply inspired by her own journey of self-discovery and personal growth, after being diagnosed with a brain tumour and she is committed to empowering women to embrace their unique identity and live a life of spiritual fulfillment, financial security and unstoppable confidence.

Alexandra's writing is characterized by its raw honesty, emotional depth, and powerful message. Through her poems, books and courses, she shares her personal experiences and struggles, offering guidance and support to those who are on a similar path to purpose and enlightenment.

A Woman On Purpose, Alexandra's debut book, is a truthful

exploration of self-discovery, empowerment, spirituality, and personal growth. The book has received acclaim for its honesty, authenticity, and ability to inspire and motivate readers.

Alexandra is also the creator of the **Facebook page A Woman On Purpose**, where she shares daily poems and inspirational affirmations to empower and uplift her followers. Through her social media presence, she has built a strong community of women who support and encourage each other on their journey towards finding purpose and meaning in life.

Alexandra is passionate about helping women overcome obstacles, cultivate self-love and acceptance, and create a life that aligns with their deepest desires and values. She is the creator of **The Purpose Philosophy** which is an integrated personal and spiritual enlightenment exploration using **The Golden Compass** to find your passion, power and purpose through various courses.

Overall, Alexandra Gold is a writer and self-help advocate who is dedicated to empowering women to live a life of purpose, fulfillment, and authenticity. Her work has touched the lives of many, and she is committed to continuing to inspire and support women on their journey towards self-discovery and personal growth.

More from A Woman On Purpose with Alexandra Gold

The She is... Anthology

She Is ... Healing
She Is ... Powerful
She Is Leading

The Practice Of Healing

www.AWomanOnPurpose.com/books

Is it time for you to be more, have more and make the world a better place?

There has never been such a time as this.
There is a feeling being woven like an invisible thread through the hearts of women all over the world. Being called together to be all that they can be, to live their bestlives and to share their gifts with the world.

Are you one of them?

The feeling that there is something more than this. That YOU are meant for more. That the world is in need of what you can share. That the feeling will not just go away and it is time for you to do something about it.

By becoming A Woman On Purpose you can be a part of the Resolution Revolution.

You will be all you can be.
You will love your life.
You will be happy, be free.